POWER AND RESTRAINT IN CHINA'S RISE

CONTEMPORARY ASIA IN THE WORLD

David C. Kang and Victor D. Cha, Editors

This series aims to address a gap in the public-policy and scholarly discussion of Asia. It seeks to promote books and studies that are on the cutting edge of their disciplines or promote multidisciplinary or interdisciplinary research but are also accessible to a wider readership. The editors seek to showcase the best scholarly and public-policy arguments on Asia from any field, including politics, history, economics, and cultural studies.

For a complete list of books in the series, see page 217.

Power and Restraint in China's Rise

Chin-Hao Huang

Columbia University Press
New York

Columbia University Press
Publishers Since 1893
New York   Chichester, West Sussex
cup.columbia.edu
Copyright © 2022 Columbia University Press
All rights reserved

Library of Congress Cataloging-in-Publication Data
Names: Huang, Chin-Hao, author.
Title: Power and restraint in China's rise / Chin-Hao Huang.
Description: New York : Columbia University Press, 2021. | Series: Contemporary Asia
in the world | Includes bibliographical references and index.
Identifiers: LCCN 2021038655 (print) | LCCN 2021038656 (ebook) | ISBN 9780231204644
(hardback) | ISBN 9780231204651 (trade paperback) | ISBN 9780231555623 (ebook)
Subjects: LCSH: China—Foreign relations—21st century. | China—Foreign relations—
Decision making. | Security, International—Government policy—China. |
Civil-military relations—China. | China—Military policy.
Classification: LCC JZ1734 .H835 2021 (print) | LCC JZ1734 (ebook) | DDC 327.51—dc23
LC record available at https://lccn.loc.gov/2021038655
LC ebook record available at https://lccn.loc.gov/2021038656

Cover design: Noah Arlow
Cover image: Shutterstock

For Vanessa

CONTENTS

CONTENTS

FIGURES AND TABLES

FIGURES

TABLES

PREFACE AND ACKNOWLEDGMENTS

The premise of this book parallels a statement Ambassador Chas W. Freeman, Jr., made at a public event on U.S.–China relations a few years ago. In his usual coherent and articulate manner, he explained: "We have a copious literature of coercion. We have almost no literature of persuasion, and yet in ordinary life, when we have a problem with our neighbor, if we're wise, we don't pull the gun and say submit or else." No doubt this point of view draws from his decades of experience in U.S. foreign policy circles, but there is evidence for it in the theory and praxis of international relations. How do we explain the complex interactions between large powers and their smaller peers? Is it always the case that "might makes right"? Do small states retain any voice or agency in their dealings with more formidable neighbors? All these questions have been percolating in my head for a number of years. I wanted to take a stab at answering them and in so doing develop an explanation that is logically consistent, empirically valid, and, most important, cogent and relatable to all those interested in the rise of China as a political phenomenon. As will become clear in the pages to follow, I wanted to focus on how small states can work together to induce change in a large power's behavior—not least in relation to the efficacy of the use of force—and thus make a positive theoretical advance forward with a probative argument about the causes for strong-state restraint. It is my hope that the findings in this book will offer a refreshing perspective on what is arguably one of the most consequential developments in Asian security and international politics.

It takes a village to produce a manuscript, and this project is no exception. It would not have been possible without numerous sources of support, inspiration, and advice. I am indebted to Don Emmerson, Tom Fingar, Bates Gill, Evelyn Goh, Iain Henry, Dave Kang, Andrew Kennedy, Amy King, Gi-wook Shin, and Nina Silove for their thoughtful comments on earlier drafts. In particular, Dave's insights have made this a much better book than it would otherwise have been. Likewise, I am grateful to Caelyn Cobb at Columbia University Press for her editorial stewardship throughout this project, and to the anonymous reviewers who went above and beyond in providing detailed and constructive feedback amid an ongoing pandemic that has caused much disruption and uncertainty worldwide.

A version of the manuscript was presented at Stanford University's Freeman Spogli Institute for International Studies in summer 2018 and at the Australian National University's Strategic and Defense Studies Center in fall 2017. I am also tremendously grateful for the research institutes, archival centers, libraries, scholar-practitioners, and research interviewees in Addis Ababa, Bandar Seri Begawan, Beijing, Canberra, Hanoi, Hong Kong, Honolulu, Jakarta, Kinshasa, Kuala Lumpur, Manila, Monrovia, Palo Alto, New York, Singapore, Taipei, and Washington, D.C., that provided a rich array of research materials to help me complete the manuscript.

At Yale-NUS College, the collegiality, friendship, and good counsel of Charles Bailyn, Scott Cook, Eugene Choo, Trisha Craig, John Driffill, Andreas Heinecke, Jeannette Ickovics, Jane Jacobs, Nomi Lazar, Pericles Lewis, Michael Maniates, Brian McAdoo, Steve Monroe, Rohan Mukherjee, Terry Nardin, Paul O'Keefe, Steve Oliver, Anju Paul, Joanne Roberts, Kate Sanger, Naoko Shimazu, Tan Tai Yong, Risa Toha, and Brandon Yoder are instrumental. I could not have asked for a more supportive environment to carry out my research during all these years. Special thanks to Arjun Jayaraman, Joshua Leung, Daniel Ng, and Avery Simmons for excellent research support—they truly understand the region inside out and represent a new crop of Asia security watchers with their ears close to the ground. I am especially grateful to David Cruickshank for poring over earlier drafts and for his excellent editorial advice. This manuscript benefitted tremendously from the support of a social science research grant from the Ministry of Education of the Republic of Singapore (IG16-LR105) and the Lee Kong Chian NUS-Stanford Distinguished Fellowship on Contemporary Southeast Asia (2018–2019).

Lastly, at the heart of it all is my family. When I decided to dedicate my working life in pursuit of research, education, and scholarship, my parents and brother supported this unconventional choice without blinking an eye. My dad would have liked—and been very proud—to hold a copy of this book in person; even when he was bedridden until the very end, he would still check in on the manuscript's progress. And, throughout it all, Vanessa's unconditional love and patience in putting up with an egghead kept me grounded. It means the world to have such support and companionship at every step along the way and to know that I did not cross the finish line alone. To hold fast and stay true to one's cause and belief, it takes a village indeed.

ABBREVIATIONS

ASEAN	Association of Southeast Asian Nations
AU	African Union
CCP	Chinese Communist Party
CMC	Central Military Commission
COC	Code of Conduct in the South China Sea
CUES	Code for Unplanned Encounters at Sea
DOC	Declaration on the Conduct of Parties in the South China Sea
DRC	Democratic Republic of the Congo
ECOWAS	Economic Community of West African States
EEZ	exclusive economic zone
EU	European Union
FOCAC	Forum on China–Africa Cooperation
FONOPs	freedom of navigation operations
GDP	gross domestic product
LSG	leading small group
MDT	Mutual Defense Treaty
MFA	Ministry of Foreign Affairs
MONUSCO	United Nations Organization Stabilization Mission in the Democratic Republic of the Congo
NAM	Non-Aligned Movement
NATO	North Atlantic Treaty Organization

ABBREVIATIONS

PKO	peacekeeping operation
PLA	People's Liberation Army
SAM	surface-to-air missile
UN	United Nations
UNCLOS	United Nations Convention on the Law of the Sea
UNMIL	United Nations Mission in Liberia
UNTAC	United Nations Transitional Authority in Cambodia

POWER AND RESTRAINT IN CHINA'S RISE

Chapter One

THE PUZZLE AND ARGUMENT

When does a large, powerful state with increasing material capabilities exercise restraint? Given how prevalent and deeply entrenched power politics is as a starting point of analysis in international relations scholarship and textbooks, it is puzzling that restraint—eschewing the use of force in favor of forbearance in statecraft—should even be a remote possibility as a foreign policy consideration. After all, a state's military strength, economic resources, and technological advancement are some of the most notable measures of strength and power. In turn, a state that commands substantial resources can capitalize on these material advantages to induce change in the behavior of others, often through force and coercion to overcome resistance from weaker neighbors. This is perhaps why scholars like John Mearsheimer have long sounded the warning bells that "conflict is common among states because the international system creates powerful incentives for aggression."[1] Put simply, enlargement of material power drives states—especially ambitious ones—toward rivalry and confrontation as they jostle for security in an anarchic environment.

The core argument in this book advances a theoretical corrective: even with their rapid accumulation of material capabilities, dominant states do not exert coercion as often as expected; nor, in spite of the common assumption of power politics, do they engage in costly conflicts to attain security. Why? The narrative that "might makes right" conflates material power with actual influence.[2] If influence is about attaining the intended outcomes that reflect one's preferences, then the coercive use of threats, sanctions, and military force produces an unintended consequence: it reinforces the perception that a large, rising power with increasing material capabilities portends disruption and danger to the status quo. Moreover, it sows resentment among neighboring states, "creating vicious cycles of repression and resistance" that end up undermining the overall objective of expanding influence.[3] Applying brute force to change the behavior of others is therefore not only costly and difficult to sustain, it generates counterproductive outcomes and is prima facie evidence that influence is not a simple by-product of material capabilities.[4]

Authority relations that underpin the interactions between large, powerful states and their smaller neighbors are more complex and go beyond material considerations alone. How small, weaker actors support or resist large powers is an important aspect of the latest wave of interstate hegemony studies in international relations theory.[5] Large states can and often do exercise restraint as a legitimation strategy because influence is more enduring if it draws on validation from others than if it is derived from military clout. The present book builds on this logic and sets up a testable scope condition for strong-state restraint: When other states—especially small, neighboring ones—collectively articulate their security preferences with a strong, clear consensus, that puts the large, powerful state in a bind. Adhering to the regional consensus clarifies a strong state's cooperative intentions and institutionalizes defensive military postures to mitigate the negative effects of a security dilemma, yielding the concomitant benefit of cooperative security: acceptance and recognition by its peers as a legitimate leader. As will become clear in the chapters to follow, strong-state restraint draws on the ideational rationale of legitimacy and results from a social, interactive process that is the collective influence of strong group consensus.

Empirically, the security dynamics leading to restraint are evident in China's interactions with member states of the Association of Southeast Asian Nations (ASEAN), a crucial test for the present book's theory. In the conflict over the South China Sea—which is highly consequential for states in the region—China's material power far exceeds that of its smaller, rival claimant states, both individually and collectively.[6] Yet, this power differential does not necessarily incentivize China to act on its impulse to satisfy its self-interest as a default option. As Steve Chan observes, "how a powerful country deals with a vulnerable, even defenseless, neighbor can be highly informative of its intentions and motivations. How does it act when it does not have to worry about other countries pushing back? One's character is more likely to be revealed when one can act with relative impunity."[7]

Of course, it is politically expedient for a large state to reject its smaller peers' security preferences and consensus, but doing so reifies the image of a coercive, disruptive, and unpredictable power. As tempting as power politics may be, exercising restraint opens up the possibility for an increasingly dominant state like China to augment its influence through regionally accepted, cooperative means. If the probative argument on strong-state restraint is correct, we are more likely to observe such outcomes in China's foreign policy when ASEAN members share a strong agreement and collectively articulate their security norms and preferences through the regional institution. The level of consensus from the ten-member group would thus have a demonstrable impact on regional security dynamics, incentivizing China to support regional norms and security initiatives that it previously deflected, resisted, or opposed. Evidence of such behavioral change in the direction of restraint delimits the conventional narrative of zero-sum competition or emphasis on material considerations as the modus operandi in an anarchic security environment.

It is important to underscore from the outset that the argument here is not to essentialize China's behavior or to say that a large power's propensity for restraint is a foregone conclusion. In fact, the likelihood for China's militarization and coercive behavior increases with visible signs of regional discord, especially when ASEAN member states disagree on the security norms and initiatives needed to push back on China's unilateral and assertive activities. Thus a key corollary in the analysis is that regional fragmentation incentivizes China to pursue belligerent policies in the South China Sea conflict, especially those that accentuate its increasing material power capabilities. Changes in China's foreign policy are thus bidirectional; the absence of the key scope condition for restraint—strong regional consensus—gives rise to a paradigmatic shift in its approach for attaining security through direct competition with other states instead.

SO WHAT?

That large, powerful states can exercise restraint bears at least three important theoretical and empirical implications. First, it provides a new framework to explain the political phenomenon of China's rise. In the conventional narrative on large, powerful states, the premium placed on material capabilities means that their behavior would almost always be viewed through the lens of competition and confrontation, relegating restraint or noncoercive behavior to an anomalous and undertheorized foreign policy option. As a result, there is no shortage of discussion in the academic and policy-making circles that the region is experiencing an arms race, that the security dilemma is intensifying with an increasing number of regional conflicts, and that military balancing is in the offing as the region turns "ripe for rivalry" in response to China's growing material capabilities.[8]

Scholars have shown time and again, however, that realism as a paradigm is an unfalsifiable collection of assumptions and hypotheses about power politics and competition.[9] There is almost no correct prediction to be derived from any given set of realist principles. Proponents of realism disagree on what comes from their assumptions, which, strictly speaking, should not even be possible unless they are working with an incomplete set.[10] William C. Wohlforth and his collaborators further point out that "mainstream balance-of-power scholarship encompasses nearly every hypothesis ever advanced about when states balance and when they don't. Many of these hypotheses contradict each other. . . . It is antithetical to the purpose of holding theory to empirical account."[11]

Because power is so intrinsically linked to material capabilities in the conventional narrative of power politics, it primes observers to focus almost exclusively on the conflictual tendencies of large state behavior.[12] But interactions among states are not simply about material power, not least in Asia. If we want to explain and understand the statecraft of a large, powerful state like China, we need a different analytical framework that can account for both conflictual and cooperative foreign policy outcomes, not just the former or the latter. The failure to address this variation in foreign policy behavior predetermines the outcome.

Second, if the probative argument that China exercises restraint in the presence of strong regional consensus holds, it delimits the overarching claim that material and narrow self-interests undergird all state behavior in an anarchic environment. Even with territorial sovereignty, access to resources, and power projection at stake in the South China Sea conflict, cultivating a habit of restraint and noncoercion can actually occur without material threats or incentives. China's behavioral change would thus occur as a consequence of action–reaction dynamics, interactions, and deliberations, reinforced by its exposure to such nonmaterial factors as the consensus of regional security norms.

To be sure, strong-state restraint is not the same as capitulating or conceding defeat. In fact, it is more akin to a restraining-to-thrive legitimation strategy. Rather than pursuing militarization, threats, or coercion, adhering to and adopting the security norms borne out of strong regional consensus enable large states to augment their influence. In so doing, they gain the acceptance, recognition, and legitimacy that can only be conferred by others, not least their smaller neighbors and peers.

The argument for strong-state restraint as a legitimation strategy provides a unique and a new explanation for how powerful, nonliberal democracies practice statecraft. Legitimation approaches in grand strategy are not just concerns for modern democracies.[13] As the book will show, legitimacy matters for concentrated authoritarian regimes too, especially when strong, external consensus affects the decision-making process among foreign policy elites. Moreover, the present argument is qualitatively different from the works on strategic restraint that are mostly focused on U.S. foreign policy. G. John Ikenberry's scholarship demonstrates convincingly how a Western, liberal power that had already reached its apex (e.g., the United States) is coping to retain its global outreach.[14] Its analytical relevance for nonliberal powers beyond the Western context is less precise. For instance, the key attributes of China's rise—its rapidly modernizing armed forces, nondemocratic system of governance, and perceived challenges to preexisting institutional arrangements—make it an unlikely case for restraint as a starting point of analysis as per the liberal institutionalist framework. Shifting the argument to a predominantly nonmaterial, ideational explanation can be jarring, not least because observations of China's rise and its fast accumulation of material power rarely include restraint as a foreign policy consideration. This makes studying China's behavior in consequential security conflicts like the South China Sea all the more desirable. As a social scientific exercise, identifying and explaining the variation in its foreign policy behavior between coercion and restraint confirms the analytical value of the relational aspects of power.

Third, strong-state restraint as an observable outcome implies that small states have agency and an important role in inducing such behavior. When they band together through regional institutions, small states become a formidable source of influence with which large, powerful states have to contend. For instance, in Southeast Asia, the claimant and nonclaimant states to the South China Sea engage with one another through ASEAN to propose and develop regional norms and security initiatives aimed at defusing and ratcheting down tension while collectively pushing back on China's material power capabilities and superiority. Even though ASEAN member states are not formally allied, the strong consensus derived from their policy alignment shows they are not as vulnerable to a dominant state like China as many believe.

As Alastair Iain Johnston observes, "despite some controversy over how to characterize and measure the efficacy of institutions in East Asia, the region has grown more peaceful even as structural uncertainties have grown since the end of the Cold War."[15] We know a great deal about how institutions as an exogenous factor affect change in European states' security and economic policies, especially within the context of the socialization processes of the European Union (EU).[16] Less well understood are whether a similar or other distinctive, indigenized process exists in Asia and the extent to which regional institutions at the smaller states' disposal are more or less effective in managing security dynamics that extend beyond military balancing, confrontation, or bandwagoning.[17]

Taken together, what emerges from this book is a novel take on authority relations and state interactions in Asia. Specifically, the research draws on empirical evidence to show more explicitly how small states induce change in a large power's behavior. It is thus a positive theoretical advance with a probative argument on strong-state restraint as a legitimation strategy.

SITUATING THE BOOK'S ARGUMENT AND CONTRIBUTIONS

Whether China's meteoric ascendance and this potential shift in power dynamics will become more or less disruptive to the region and beyond is arguably one of the most important questions in international security. The book's point about strong-state restraint contributes to this timely and topical discussion, and it builds on a number of important studies that have been carried out over the years to help us gain greater analytical clarity on international relations theory and Chinese foreign policy.

In particular, the two bodies of scholarship with which this book is in most direct conversation are Alastair Iain Johnston's *Social States: China in International Institutions, 1980–2000*, and M. Taylor Fravel's *Strong Borders, Secure Nation: Conflict and Cooperation in China's Territorial Disputes*. Both are seminal contributions that examine why and when≈China cooperates, particularly with respect to international security institutions and territorial disputes, respectively. The present book's argument builds on Johnston's and Fravel's works in two specific ways. First, it provides a broader analysis of China's security dynamics and interactions with its neighbors and peers, not simply of China itself or in a vacuum. Second, the book shows how restraint in China's foreign policy behavior has occurred even as it has grown far more powerful, materially speaking, than when both Johnston and Fravel were writing over a decade ago.

Let us first consider Johnston's work on China's socialization into international security institutions. In his book, Johnston explores the question of why Chinese foreign policy decision makers would agree to cooperate in security institutions, given the limited added value such institutions could provide to enhance China's relative power.[18] Extolling the analytical value of socialization processes, Johnston argues that Chinese decision makers' exposure to and participation in a number of security institutions on arms control, disarmament, and nuclear nonproliferation have resulted in notable changes to China's foreign policy, such as mimicking behavior and strategic adaptation. Persuasion, an important marker of change, is arguably the strongest level of state socialization, and Johnston notes that China's acceptance of multilateral approaches to managing regional security issues through the ASEAN Regional Forum as well as its historic decision in 2003 to accede to ASEAN's Treaty of Amity and Cooperation are indicative of persuasion. Put simply, ASEAN–China diplomacy has convinced key Chinese officials to accede to ASEAN's security preferences of the renunciation of the use of force in favor of forging closer regional ties and security cooperation.

The present book's focus on strong-state restraint builds on Johnston's analysis and moves beyond it. If anarchy is really what states make of it, then the ongoing process of state socialization in security institutions implies that changing social structural contexts would have a continuous effect on shaping states' identity and interests. As long as states are engaged with their other players and peers in international institutions, their foreign policy outlook would evolve, adapt, and see continuous change, mirroring the socialization dynamics that occur in Chinese decision makers' experience and involvement in security institutions. While Johnston ends his analysis with persuasion as the strongest indication of change in Chinese decision makers' foreign policy paradigm, the natural follow-up is to examine the extent to which such learned behavior has changed—and, if so, how—since the early 2000s.

The selection of the endpoint in time-series analyses can potentially bias one's analysis and initial conclusion.[19] In Johnston's assessment of China's engagement in international institutions, there has been a gradual shift in its socialization process from 1980 to the early 2000s, culminating in the observation of argumentative persuasion in effect where the causal process has attained a high point. With rapid changes to China's material capabilities in the past two decades, Johnston's preliminary conclusion can benefit from further testing for the robustness and consistency of his theoretical argument.

Specifically, if states can learn the benefits of multilateralism through their social interactions in security institutions, is it possible that they could also *un*learn and see their behavior regress into a more *realpolitik* foreign policy paradigm? What is the causal mechanism that would capture and explain this important variation in behavior? This is precisely what the argument in this book seeks to address. In so doing, the analysis is centered on explaining both restraint and coercion in China's foreign policy behavior. Put simply, if the probative argument is that China's restraint is a by-product of strong ASEAN consensus, the corollary would be that coercive behavior increases when there is regional discord and fragmentation on the security norms governing the South China Sea.

Restraint as a foreign policy outcome is thus a function of strong normative influence and persuasion. To explain and predict when such behavior is more (or less) likely to take place requires an analytical framework that identifies and tests the determinant for restraint. When the condition is missing or not met, one would expect state behavior to shift toward the opposite behavior: coercion. As such, this theoretical expectation accounts for the "two steps forward, one step back" occurrence in China's foreign policy behavior, not least in the South China Sea dispute. This within-case variation is especially important to observe in order to strengthen the book's overall point about the condition for strong-state restraint.

Fravel's research on when and why China uses force or compromises to resolve its territorial disputes has produced an important and counterintuitive finding: China has negotiated almost three times as often as it has used force to settle territorial disputes and, especially on its frontiers, has been willing to offer concessions greater than those it received from the other side.[20] Fravel's insightful research derives from a theoretically driven inquiry, and his explanation rests on two key factors. First, internal threats or domestic instability in China can counterintuitively prompt the state to offer concessions over disputed territory, as it can reduce external support for various ethnic groups inside its territory. Second, Fravel argues that changes in China's relative bargaining position can influence its willingness to compromise, delay, or use force. As its bargaining position in a dispute declines relative to a potential adversary, it may be more willing to use force in order to achieve and secure its claims, a preventive move to deny contested land to its opponent.

Fravel identifies a state's bargaining power to include its ability to project military capabilities over the entire disputed territory, as well as the amount of contested area that it currently occupies. As such, when a state assesses that an adversary is strengthening its bargaining position and material power capabilities, doing nothing becomes more costly and threatening. This logic prompts China to use force to halt or even reverse its decline. Conversely, as China's bargaining position and power improve, it becomes more willing to delay or seek accommodation, knowing that a position of strength is likely to result in a bargaining outcome or settlement that works in its favor.

To expand the explanatory power of Fravel's argument, one would need to carry out further behavioral tests on the validity of the causal logic. Based on his findings, Fravel would presumably not argue the converse: that an absence of internal threats is the main factor that leads to more conflict over territorial claims. Nor would the bargaining logic identified in his book explain all the numerous, ongoing disputes that remain unresolved in the region, not least the ongoing maritime disputes in the East and South China Seas.

Moreover, how resilient is Fravel's theoretical argument when applied to contemporary security issues surrounding state sovereignty? Most observers would agree that China is no longer a weak state. In fact, it is only getting more powerful, materially speaking. By Fravel's account, China's bargaining considerations are largely based on its material capabilities. Internally, as the state apparatus gets stronger, China's central government has been able to exert tighter controls to quell potential internal unrest on the frontiers that border outstanding territorial disputes. Whether greater regime stability translates into China seeking a hardening or flexible stance as its bargaining position and material power increase is not entirely clear.

In fact, China may even be inclined to take on preventive measures because it has the upper hand: the credibility of military threat. Fravel notes two factors that could accelerate this likelihood of coercive behavior. One factor would be the sudden discovery of substantial deposits of natural resources such as oil or gas in the contested disputes. A second factor is that "a much stronger China may decide to use force because, put simply, it can."[21] Given China's trajectory in amassing greater amounts of material wealth and capabilities, two central questions emerge: Does the logic of Fravel's argument still hold? More important, how do we explain the variance in the observable outcomes of Chinese foreign policy behavior in contentious disputes?

In extending beyond Fravel's analysis, the argument here delimits the prognosis that coercion—in the form of veiled military threats or the explicit use of force—would be China's default approach to international security, not least in the South China Sea conflict. Why? The material basis of power is but one facet of a large, dominant state's influence, and it is certainly not a sufficient one to account for restraint. As chapter 2 explains, the relational aspect of power is significantly undertheorized in international relations theory, particularly when applied to a large, powerful state like China. Restraining-to-thrive remains a valid legitimation strategy and a prudent foreign policy consideration, especially if the state in question seeks the identity of a leader in the region and beyond. This recognition cannot be achieved in isolation as legitimacy can be conferred only by its smaller, neighboring peers. Restraint would thus occur irrespective of material capabilities or bargaining power. Instead, the presence or absence of a nonmaterial, ideational factor—regional consensus—can help us infer when and why strong-state restraint as a legitimation strategy occurs.

Other analyses of China's historical and contemporary foreign relations have begun to delimit the logic behind the material-based accounts of power. Three seminal works come to mind. David Kang's analysis of historical East Asia focuses on the stability of Chinese hegemony and preponderance of power between the fourteenth and twentieth centuries. Neighboring entities like Vietnam, Korea, and Japan had no desire to fight because of the benefits derived from trade and tribute with China, cultural exchanges, as well as the broader stability of the Sino-centric, Confucian-based order.[22] In the contemporary period, Evelyn Goh finds China's use of force and coercive practices is rather limited and overshadowed by its use of preference-multiplying and persuasion strategies that "enable others to do something they were not able or willing to do before, despite convergent preferences," or that "constrain and align the preferences of the target actors with those of the powerful actor."[23]

In the same vein, Allen Carlson's research on sovereignty provides an important perspective on how China's understanding and application of this fundamental concept in international relations has changed from skepticism to pragmatic idealism.[24] Carlson shows that sovereignty is malleable, and, like other states, China is constantly modifying, contesting, and redefining it for itself, as well as in relationships with other states and international institutions. The differing degrees of change within the Chinese conception of sovereignty over the past three decades show that sovereignty may not be sacrosanct after all, as positions and policies are in constant flux with competing strategic and security priorities. The underlying theme across these works finds that, when China's leaders exercise power through purely coercive means to prevail over its neighbors and to defend its parochial, material interests, such actions end up undermining its ability to project influence beyond its borders.

More broadly, the scope of this book follows the tradition of other pioneering scholarship that combines theoretical insights with empirical rigor, drawing inspiration from a number of authors. For instance, Samuel Kim's contributions are especially illuminating, forging important links between theory of international politics and deep area knowledge and expertise. His works have shown how China's foreign policy has changed from the 1980s through the early 2000s, particularly in international security arenas.[25] Kim's research is a model for innovative ways to help make comprehensive, convincing, and, most important, falsifiable arguments. Michel Oksenberg and Margaret Pearson have also done similar outstanding work detailing changes in China's participation in international economic and financial institutions.[26] Organizational and material incentives and disincentives are clearly documented, and ideational factors such as reputation and image are also identified as equally important imperatives for the deepening of China's engagement in the intricacies of the global financial web.

Likewise, leading scholars in the field such as Steve Chan, Tom Christensen, Rosemary Foot, Bates Gill, Avery Goldstein, David Shambaugh, Susan Shirk, and Robert Sutter, to name a few, have each contributed important volumes explaining the intricacies of the domestic determinants and external motivations behind China's foreign policy and grand strategy. The broader line of research among China scholars affirms the merits of middle-range theorizing, providing a practical and evidence-based approach to assess and explain the twists and turns, the cooperative and conflictual tendencies in China's foreign policy behavior.[27]

Works on Southeast Asian international relations have been equally important, both inspiring and refreshing. They serve as important foundations from which the present book builds its causal argument about ASEAN's emerging role in the region in terms of change in China's foreign policy behavior. Through their ASEAN-related scholarship, Amitav Acharya, Alice Ba, Mely Caballero-Anthony, Don Emmerson, Evelyn Goh, Jurgen Haacke, Natasha Hamilton-Hart, and Ann Marie Murphy have each offered important insights into the levels of influence the region has amid the rapidly changing power dynamics in Southeast Asia. Their works are refreshing because the empirical focus on ASEAN and Southeast Asia helps us better understand how regionalism and regional organizations operate in a non-European context. We know and have learned a great deal in international relations theory about European institutions such as the European Union, the North Atlantic Treaty Organization (NATO), and the Organization for Security and Co-operation in Europe (OSCE). We can also benefit by being better informed about such regional security preferences as norm localization or omni-enmeshment that have defined Southeast Asia's foreign policy priorities in the post–Cold War era.[28]

This book does not see ASEAN's organizational minimalism, its non-confrontational initiatives, or its reputation as a regional talking shop as a handicap. In fact, ASEAN's decision-making process by consensus and emphases on diplomacy and dialogue merit much closer scholarly attention and treatment. They provide a rare and important opportunity to empirically test how much agency small states have and their role in the causal process for inducing restraint in large, powerful states.

As Amitav Acharya notes, "China's new approach to engaging individual ASEAN members has highlighted differences in ASEAN unity or neutrality. ASEAN will need to respond to these challenges by forging closer personal ties among the region's leaders in more frequent and less formal meetings, and by taking mini-lateral approaches to global and regional challenges."[29] ASEAN consensus, captured through the collective sentiment and threat perception of the maritime dispute, ranges from broad reiterations of general organizational principles and platitudes to a heightened sense of urgency on the unfolding crisis. Using new, original data and discourse analysis to measure the strength of ASEAN consensus, the findings indicate a discernible pattern of behavior: strong levels of ASEAN consensus yield China's restraint, whereas weak regional consensus increases the likelihood for China's aggressive and disruptive activities in the South China Sea.

A key motivation behind the book is to contribute to this debate and discussion on the future direction of China's rise and what that means for regional and international security. The counterintuitive argument here on power and restraint is substantiated by new, empirical data on the South China Sea, identifying and testing the condition under which a large, powerful state like China is more or less likely to show restraint, and determining the influential role of ASEAN consensus in this regard. The goal is to bring greater analytical insights, grounded on both theoretical and empirical rigor, into understanding change in contemporary Chinese foreign policy behavior—especially what has worked in the recent past, what has not, and what is likely to work in the future in incentivizing China to assume the role of a legitimate power.

ORGANIZATION OF THE BOOK

In the pages to follow, the book addresses and elaborates on the overarching puzzle discussed at the outset of this chapter: When does a large, powerful state with increasing material capabilities exercise restraint? This analysis will be carried out in five stages.

Chapter 2 begins with a discussion and critique of power and why states with increasing amounts of material capability show restraint. A large, powerful state's legitimation strategy to enhance its influence cannot be realized through sheer force. Using coercion to demonstrate strength might be convenient and easily achievable because it has the wherewithal to engage in such behavior. But doing so significantly undercuts its own attempts to wield greater influence. In particular, validation, confirmation, and acceptance from others are critical and reflect the importance of the social and relational aspect of power that is much harder to achieve than exerting material force. The acquiescence of smaller states and lesser powers to confer on a large state the recognition of a regional leader comes with expectations that the latter will uphold, or at least not violate, the existing norms of regional and international security and will play its part in reinforcing them. It follows that developing an identity based on the group one seeks to belong to provides a powerful rationale and motivation to accept restraint-to-thrive as a legitimation strategy.

Building on this causal logic, the chapter then articulates the mechanism for strong-state restraint. In particular, the argument for restraint rests on a key causal factor: the consensus of regional security norms. When small states band together and cooperate to develop a strong consensus on their preferred security norms, the clarity in their collective agreement provides a powerful incentive for their large neighbor to consider and adopt foreign policy changes that reflect the shared preference of the smaller states. Hence the presence of strong group consensus is particularly important to observe empirically. The extent to which this condition is met can help account for the variation—restraint or coercion—in the behavior of large, powerful states.

The focus of chapter 3 is to empirically test the book's probative argument for strong-state restraint. The main contribution here is to show how security relations between China and ASEAN are interactional, the effects of which on variation in China's foreign policy behavior have been understudied.

In particular, the ongoing maritime conflict in the South China Sea presents a unique opportunity to determine the extent to which ASEAN is able to cope with the strategic uncertainty in the region and exert its collective influence, especially when it faces a formidable neighbor like China. The logic behind the causal chain begins with the observation of the level of ASEAN consensus. The theoretical expectation is as follows: the stronger and more cohesive the consensus on regional security norms, the more likely it is for China's foreign policy to reflect that consensus and support the regional, multilateral security agreement. Conversely, China's consideration for material power capabilities and power politics becomes more prominent when there is visible regional disunity. A weakened ASEAN consensus due to regional fragmentation means the source of persuasion and normative influence regarding the benefits of multilateral security initiatives would be missing. This provides an opportunity for China's decision makers to capitalize on the regional discord to pursue policies that favor coercion.

ASEAN summit statements enable us to measure the strength of regional consensus. Using discourse analysis, these documents reflect some of the organization's most consequential decision-making outcomes, and as such, they serve as useful proxies to measure the level of ASEAN consensus (e.g., strong or weak). Discourse analysis helps us to look at the text, identify key linguistic properties of the deliberative process, and contextualize the social conditions under which the summit statements are constructed. All of this can help us establish and determine the level of consensus in the regional organization. More specifically, it provides the empirical basis to measure regional consensus with greater precision and identify the intended and actual effects of ASEAN consensus on regional security.

Chapter 3 also focuses on the measurement of change in China's foreign policy behavior. A new quantitative data set helps capture China's foreign policy activities in the South China Sea between 2012 and 2018. These are coded into various categories to determine whether the net outcome for China's activities in the maritime dispute reflects coercion or restraint. The analysis then compares the differing levels of ASEAN consensus with the changes in China's foreign policy behavior in 2012–2018. The results indicate that there is a positive association between China's restraint and ASEAN's summit statements that exhibit strong consensus.

This is especially evident when regional consensus demonstrates a sense of urgency, is aligned on the threat perception, and identifies new diplomatic actions to delimit and push back on China's coercive activities. The analysis is strengthened with process tracing of key developments in the South China Sea to examine the causal significance of congruity in the cases examined. In short, with China seeking regional leadership and acceptance from its peers as a legitimate power, restraint is an appropriate and desirable course of action, not an anomalous behavior. In fact, the likelihood for restraint increases with the presence of strong regional consensus. Similarly, China's coercive behavior becomes more prevalent when we observe that ASEAN is divided in the South China Sea conflict. The chapter will also address why such rival explanations as the bargaining model fall short in accounting for authority relations and security dynamics between China and the Southeast Asian states in the maritime dispute.

To strengthen the book's overarching argument, chapter 4 assesses an alternative explanation for restraint. In particular, this chapter looks at the role of an exogenous factor commonly used in the conventional narrative for explaining state behavior: the distribution of power in the international system. Put simply, the focus here is to examine the role of U.S. military deterrence and its long-standing grand strategy of deep engagement in the region. The alternative explanation posits restraint as a function of U.S. material power and deterrence; as such, China's restraint is explained by the presence of an even larger and more powerful state with superior material capabilities to constrain China's activities in the South China Sea.

Methodologically, a controlled comparison of two notable ruptures in the maritime dispute can help test the causal logic of deep engagement's assumptions and see how it compares with the book's argument for restraint: the Scarborough Shoal standoff in 2012 and the oil rig incident near the Paracel Islands in 2014. In the Scarborough Shoal, the Philippines encountered China's encroachment that led to intensified hostilities in the disputed reef. Likewise, in 2014 Vietnam and China engaged in a tense confrontation over the presence of the latter's oil rig parked near the Paracel Islands. The natures of these two conflicts mirror each other, with one key exception—the level of U.S. military involvement—making it a key rationale for discussion in this chapter.

Analyzing these comparable cases approximates experimental logic to draw causal inferences about which argument serves as the more robust

explanatory determinant for strong-state restraint. If the empirical observations from these recent developments in the South China Sea support
the claims of U.S. deep engagement, then its logic should be considered
robust and consistent in accounting for China's restraint in the maritime
dispute. If not, beyond delimiting and casting doubt on the assumptions
of deep engagement, it reinforces the book's main proposition that the collective influence of ASEAN's regional consensus serves as an important
condition for China's restraint.

The evidence in chapter 4 shows that the more salient explanation for
China's restraint is whether ASEAN member states—both claimant and
nonclaimant states to the South China Sea—share a strong consensus
and are able to articulate their security norms in a cohesive and united
front to push back on China's provocations in the maritime dispute. In
fact, increasing U.S. deep engagement when ASEAN is divided and there
is weak consensus—a development that reflects regional fragmentation—
results in more coercive behavior from China, an unintended consequence
of U.S. deep engagement. The chapter offers some implications for a more
strategic role for the United States in the region and in its partnership with
ASEAN.

Chapter 5 takes stock of China's identity as a legitimate power in a two-
part analysis. The first half of the chapter surveys how China's foreign
policy decision makers view themselves and their position in the region
and in the world, a critical aspect of the analysis on China's rise that is
often missing or underemphasized in the conventional and dichotomized
pessimist–optimist narrative. In opening up China's foreign policy black
box and synthesizing some of the internal debates and discussion on the
future trajectory of China's rise, we notice the significance of external consensus as a legitimation strategy for China's policy elites and foreign policy
decision makers. Put simply, how others view and perceive China's rise
factors quite prominently into the Chinese leadership's foreign policy calculus, especially as it processes and debates the appropriate responses to
the external normative influence and expectations of a legitimate power's
conduct in global affairs.

That external recognition and validation weigh at the forefront of the
country's foreign policy decision-making process provides an important
motivation for restraint in China's statecraft. In fact, its foreign policy is
neither hardwired for power politics with its neighbors nor destined for a

head-on collision with the United States. International relations theories that focus on the material facets of power often come down to dire predictions of rivalry and contestation amid intensifying balance-of-power politics. What has been less well studied and applied to the implications of China's rise is the role of relational power, and in particular how such nonmaterial aspects of power as legitimacy and authority underpin the foreign policy strategy of a large, powerful state.

The second half of chapter 5 presents a plausibility probe case study to trace the remarkable transformation in China's position on peacekeeping, sovereignty, and intervention—pertinent security issues that affect China's parochial and material interests and are thus least likely to engender restraint as a foreign policy outcome. Few issues in international security have seen such a drastic change in China's foreign policy position. From active resistance and fighting against peacekeeping operations (PKOs) that were once seen as excessive U.S. and Western interventions and incursions into state sovereignty, in just two decades, China has emerged as the largest contributor to multilateral PKOs among the permanent members of the United Nations Security Council. Why? Where there is a clear and cohesive consensus on managing or addressing a particular armed conflict through UN peacekeeping operations, the likelihood for China to participate and contribute to the multilateral security initiative increases.

Peacekeeping with robust and expansive mandates that authorize troops to carry out peace enforcement using all necessary means can be construed as a form of external intervention. Voting for these authorizations and committing its own troops on the ground point to a gradual moderation in China's traditional and narrow interpretation of positive international law and the inviolability of state sovereignty. China's support in this regard reflects a cautious and delicate balancing act, but it nonetheless aligns with the majority, consensus view on peacekeeping norms. It is also responsive to growing international expectations of a large, powerful state's tangible contributions toward such multilateral security initiative and global public goods. Rather than pursuing unilateral interventions, China's peacekeeping commitments demonstrate that it is willing to constrain its material capabilities and conform to international consensus regarding UN peacekeeping mandates and security norms.

Consistent with the empirical analyses in the South China Sea, the preliminary findings of cooperative diplomacy and support for multilateral peacekeeping force in the chapter's plausibility probe challenge the prevailing assumptions about the disruptive and unpredictable behavior of large, powerful states in an anarchic security environment. The supplementary evidence for strong-state restraint as a legitimation strategy helps to extend and substantiate the broader analysis on the nonmaterial considerations behind China's rise and identity as a legitimate power. Chapter 5 concludes with suggestions for additional issue areas in international politics and security where the hypothesized mechanism for strong-state restraint can be applied and tested.

Chapter 6 offers a review of the book's probative argument and looks at the broader theoretical and policy implications of the empirical findings. Here, the book's main takeaways are synthesized. Even if the conflictual ramifications of an anarchic security environment persist as constant features in international politics, restraint as a foreign policy option is not an anomalous behavior, not least for large, powerful states with rising ambitions. The argument for strong-state restraint furthers the case that international relations, whether in East Asia or elsewhere, is not simply a function of material power. Dominant states do not exert coercion as often as expected, nor are smaller states in constant fear of existential threats. There are mechanisms and institutions in place that are just as effective for states large and small to ensure survival and achieve security without resorting to such costly measures as military confrontation, balancing, or even capitulation.

In short, the book advances contributions that are theoretically and empirically driven. There are few scholarly works that directly address the variation in China's behavior in the South China Sea dispute, and there are surprisingly fewer books that examine the impact of ASEAN and small states on regional security and in inducing such changes in the behavior of a large, powerful state like China. Understanding why and when China's foreign policy can change in the direction of restraint provides the theoretical foundation on which policy-relevant recommendations can be made to further engage China in ways that strengthen regional and international security.

Chapter Two

THEORIZING ABOUT POWER, LEGITIMACY, AND RESTRAINT

What is power? How is it measured? Is power simply a function of material capabilities? If so, by implication, do states that command a large economy, population, geography, and military force prevail in achieving their preferred foreign policy outcomes? Conversely, if there are other aspects to power than the material, what might they entail? Equally important, how do these nonmaterial facets of power affect the behavior of a large, dominant state and its conduct in global affairs? These are some of the key questions that lie at the heart of the book's theoretical discussion on strong-state restraint as a legitimation strategy.

This chapter proceeds in three stages. First, it provides a critique of power, legitimacy, and restraint. Specifically, we will see why focusing exclusively on the material dimensions of power is insufficient, giving a misleading explanation of what makes a state powerful. In fact, to expand a state's influence and leadership role, there are compelling incentives for decision makers in a large, powerful state to consider legitimation strategies that emphasize restraint and the social and relational facets of power as part of the state's foreign policy statecraft. We will unpack the reasons for why that might be the case.

Second, we will explore when restraint is more or less likely to occur in the behavior of large, powerful states. Put simply, what is the condition that will induce such behavioral change? A key part of the analysis lays out the causal mechanism for strong-state restraint as a legitimation strategy. In brief, when small, neighboring states articulate their security norms with a clear and strong consensus, we would expect to see paradigmatic shifts in the foreign policy of the large, powerful state. The logic and process for restraint will be explained in greater detail in the second section of this chapter.

Third, we will strengthen the hypothesized mechanism for strong-state restraint by addressing an important follow-on question: What might the domestic or internal foreign policy decision-making process of the large, powerful state look like when strong external consensus—the key condition for restraint—in the international security environment is present? Empirically, addressing the nexus between strong ASEAN consensus and change in China's foreign policy decision-making process is important in strengthening the inference and the probative argument on strong-state restraint.

A summary of these three sections concludes the chapter. We will review the puzzle and argument discussed thus far, providing a synthesis of the causal logic and mechanism for strong-state restraint as a legitimation strategy.

POWER AND LEGITIMACY IN INTERNATIONAL RELATIONS THEORY

Power is broadly understood as the ability to affect others to get the outcomes that we want or prefer. In spite of this seemingly straightforward definition, measuring power or articulating what power includes is actually not this simple. In international relations theory, the study of power has largely concentrated on the "threat, use, and control of military force."[1] Scholars tend to place a high premium on the material aspects of power, not least the military dimension.[2] This is demonstrated and reinforced by references to the centrality of force governing interstate relations, identifying the capacity to wage war and the use of force as exemplary measures of power.[3] Indeed, that most—if not all—introductory textbooks on this subfield of political science start with power politics and realism shows how prevalent and deeply entrenched this mode of thinking is in the study of international relations.

If we accept the primacy of material power in the conventional narrative, it is puzzling that any state, let alone a large, dominant one with increasing material capabilities, would consider restraint—forgoing the use of force and other coercive foreign policy measures—in its foreign policy statecraft. After all, the notion that "might makes right" ensures security and survivability in an anarchic environment. Interestingly, this has become the prevailing if not dominant assumption in international relations scholarship.

But it is just as important to recognize that this premise of material power is simply an assumption at best.[4] As Stefano Guzzini observes, "There is no single concept of power applicable to every type of explanation."[5] Unlike a fungible resource such as currency, which can be used to purchase goods and services across different domains—from the stock or housing market to the electronic or farmers' market—power has no similar standard of value that captures all social relationships and contexts. In other words, there is little to no symmetric relationship between power and material capacity. Assuming such a linear narrative is belied by the observation that a large, powerful state with significant material advantages does not always get the outcomes that it wants. A comprehensive analysis of power and influence thus needs to consider the nonmaterial factors that can be just as important, if not more significant, in affecting the behavior of others to attain certain, preferred outcomes.

To address the puzzle for strong-state restraint as a legitimation strategy, we begin by expanding on the way power has been conceptualized in the extant literature. The overwhelming focus on the possessive nature of power—as determined by the material resources and capabilities that a dominant state commands—suffers from a number of shortcomings. As a result, the role of nonmilitary and nonmaterial sources of power has been underestimated, and the field has been impoverished by its insulation from studies of power in other forms. Power does not always, or even generally, rely on violence since "political phenomena are only obscured by the pseudo-simplification attained with any unitary conception of power as always and everywhere the same."[6] As Christian Reus-Smit explains, power "is thought to flow directly from the strings of a purse or the barrel of a gun. Yet power is not so simple, either in its nature or workings. If power is about influence—the ability to produce intended and not unintended outcomes—then it is not a simple by-product of material capacity, even if material resources are an important source of power."[7] To simplify the critique: size, materially speaking, is not the best way to measure power. Instead, determining how much power and influence a state has largely boils down to two factors: (1) the ways in which a large, dominant state exercises its material advantages and capabilities, and (2) whether other states perceive such actions to be rightful and would follow suit to change their behavior to conform to the preferences and desires of the large state.

For instance, in spite of the United States' unrivaled military might and economic prowess, it struggled to attain the political objective of persuading its peers in the United Nations Security Council to support its preemptive military operations in Iraq in 2003. More critically, a number of U.S. treaty allies and security partners in the EU and NATO refused to endorse the U.S. intervention. The U.S. government prevailed in its unilateral approach and relied on its material advantages to demonstrate its war-waging capabilities, but they were insufficient to persuade others to grant it a legal mandate to carry out a military intervention against another sovereign state.[8] Herein lies the paradox of defining and measuring power as a simple by-product of material capacity. The United States had the means to carry out what it desired, but it asserted its capabilities through unilateral military action rather than diplomatic persuasion through UN Security Council authorization.

Legitimacy and Relational Power

Power that draws from a commitment not to exploit represents a kind of influence that embodies and reflects legitimacy. Legitimacy is best understood as leadership that others willingly accept; it is articulated through the social perception by others that one's actions are rightful.[9] In defining power as the "probability that an individual in a social relationship can carry out his own will," Max Weber's discussion on the sources of power and legitimacy extends well beyond the material capacity of power. In fact, the ability to prevail or to carry out one's will is fundamentally embedded within a social relationship.[10] It shifts the possessive view of power to one that is relational. In other words, while possessive power measures power through the sheer quantity of material assets or the capability to wage war and assert control, relational power is based on how others perceive, view, and assess the way those material advantages are executed.

Relational power and legitimacy are thus intrinsically tied. In management and organizations literature, legitimacy is explained as the process through which one justifies to a peer the right to carry out certain activities, whereby conformity with existing norms and rules of behavior is emphasized, as opposed to overt self-justification. John Dowling and Jeffrey Pfeffer observe that legitimacy is derived from a "congruence between the social values associated with or implied by organizational activities and the norms of acceptable behavior in the larger social system."[11] Mark Suchman provides a broad-based definition that encapsulates the essence of legitimacy: "a generalized perception or assumption that the actions of an entity are desirable, proper, or appropriate within some socially constructed system of norms, values, beliefs, and definitions."[12] This emphasis on social audience reveals that legitimacy derives from validation and affirmation by others. In other words, self-legitimation is impossible and an oxymoron. Whether one's actions are deemed rightful depends on the perception and consent of others. Moreover, this support is undergirded by the existing norms and rules of behavior that provide the basis from which to evaluate whether one's actions are consistent with those espoused by the social environment of which the individual is a member or seeks to be a part.

Power, in short, is defined not merely by material resources but by social and relational dimensions and legitimacy. It is possible for a large, powerful state to project its influence without consideration for legitimacy, but such actions that reflect "rule without right" are highly unstable forms of power.[13] As David Lake argues, "Pure coercive commands—of the form 'do this, or die'—are not authoritative. Authority relations must contain some measure of legitimacy . . . an obligation, understood by both parties, for B to comply with the wishes of A."[14] Power that rests on coercion and commands or pure expediency is much less enduring than power that enjoys the value of being considered binding, or, as it may be expressed, of legitimacy. Without legitimacy, relying on coercive actions sows resentment among others, "creating vicious cycles of repression and resistance" that undermine a large power's objective of expanding its influence.[15] Using coercion to affect change in the behavior of others generates counterproductive outcomes and reinforces the observation that influence is not a simple by-product of material power, setting a bound on the applicability of the logic that "might makes right."[16]

To further sharpen the distinction between material and relational power, it is helpful to frame the former as power that relies on and is manifested—implicitly or explicitly—through unilateral threats, sanctions, punishments, or the use of force. A large, powerful state with increasing material capabilities may seek to exert its influence through such measures, but they are costly and difficult to sustain, requiring a large expenditure of material resources to achieve limited amounts of influence over others. In fact, over time, it could generate resistance and subversion. As Edmund Burke notes, "The use of force is but temporary. It may subdue for a moment, but it does not remove the necessity of subduing again; and a nation is not governed, which is to be perpetually conquered."[17]

In contrast, when there is a perceived right to rule or when legitimacy is conferred on a large, powerful state's actions, a deeper and more impactful aspect of relational power emerges that goes beyond material sources and considerations. This makes legitimacy desirable, and especially so for a rising power with leadership ambitions seeking to project, sustain, and enhance its influence in international politics.[18] The probative argument in this book on strong-state restraint as a legitimation strategy is thus built on this fundamental point: a rising power's aspirations for acceptance and recognition of legitimacy become key incentives for restraint, even if the material sources of power—coercion, threats, and the use of force—are tempting and easily within its reach.

Legitimation Concerns for Large Powers

If legitimacy matters, how exactly does it enhance a large, powerful state's overall influence, especially since it does not emphasize material capabilities? Recall that legitimacy is a social and relational form of power that depends on a collective audience. Located within the perception of those who interact with authority, legitimacy derives from a belief that some leadership, norm, or institution should and ought to be obeyed.[19] The legitimate entity is perceived to embody such key traits as predictability and trustworthiness because its actions and behavior are congruent with the shared, prevailing norms and values in the community. Morris Zelditch observes that individuals can be influenced by others, particularly those with legitimacy, because they accept that the decisions made are right and proper and so ought to be followed.[20] The main distinction between coercive power and legitimacy can be explained by the observation that

> resort to either positive incentives or coercive measures by a person in order to influence others is prima facie evidence that he does not have authority over them.... We speak of authority, therefore, if the willing unconditional compliance of a group of people rests upon their shared beliefs that it is legitimate for the superior ... to impose his will upon them and that it is illegitimate for them to refuse obedience.[21]

In international politics, Hedley Bull's notion of "legitimate great powers" stems from this understanding that power is relational. Legitimate great powers are recognized by their peers as having certain privileges, rights, and obligations and as playing a determining role in maintaining peace and security in the international system. More important, in exchange for being accorded these special rights and legitimacy, they are expected to "uphold the core norms of international society and play an active part in reinforcing them."[22] These rights conferred on legitimate powers by smaller states come with an understanding that the former are expected to act with moderation and caution, and that they do not radically change the balance of power or seek to overturn the established norms and institutions at the expense of other states. Like a social compact forged between a large state and its smaller peers and neighbors, legitimacy is bestowed on the former by the latter when the large power provides public goods in such forms as the facilitation of global trade or regional peace and security.[23] Actions as well as nonverbal displays have to be purposeful and produce concrete outcomes that further conform to and support the established practices and norms of the international community. Activities that deviate from such expectations would render aspiring, legitimate powers vulnerable to claims of negligence, irrelevance, and arrogance.

As Gerry Simpson puts it, legitimate great powers reflect "a powerful elite of states whose superior status is recognized by minor powers as a political fact giving rise to the existence of certain constitutional privileges, rights, and duties and whose relations with each other are defined by adherence to a rough principle of sovereign equality."[24] Because legitimacy is a social and relational form of power, it can be neither achieved nor demanded in isolation. Instead, it requires validation and support from others. Likewise, Erik Ringmar observes, "We need recognition for the persons we take ourselves to be, and only as recognized can we conclusively come to establish an identity."[25] Put simply, identification as a legitimate power can only be attained if it is conferred and confirmed by one's peer group.

When a large, powerful state seeks an expanded and enduring form of political clout and influence that bears legitimacy, its activities can thus be influenced and confined by the existing rules and norms governing such authority and by the expectations about the rights and responsibilities of a power with similar capabilities. To be sure, violation of such behavioral expectations is an option and a possibility. But the risks of such a violation would undermine the large, rising state's quest for legitimacy, which would further complicate its desired political objectives and the achievement of a more enduring and accepted form of influence. Unilateralism, the use of coercion and threats, and achieving security through narrow self-interests are actions that signal "might makes right." Most important, they reinforce the perception that a strong state with increasing material capabilities portends danger and disruption to the status quo.

In short, notwithstanding a dominant state's superior material resource capacity, flexing its military muscle in ways that overturn established practices will actually restrict its overall influence and the objective of the right to rule. That restraint remains a viable consideration in foreign policy statecraft puts a limit on the conventional wisdom about a large, powerful state's tendency to disrupt order and stability in the international system. Even as the material power of a large state increases at unprecedented rates, a growing power differential does not necessarily incentivize acting on self-centered impulses. Evidence of change toward restraint would challenge the conventional narrative about a rising power's behavior in an uncertain, anarchic international environment. It shifts the discussion toward identifying and examining the condition under which states with rising military capability might actually forgo unilateral measures of coercion or the use of force and opt for self-constraining commitments and multilateral security initiatives instead. The next section lays out the causal mechanism for restraint.

THE CAUSAL MECHANISM FOR STRONG-STATE RESTRAINT

What is restraint? What is the relationship between restraint and legitimacy? When is a foreign policy outcome of restraint more likely to occur? This section addresses each of these points. We begin by defining the concept of restraint and address its synthesis to legitimacy.

Restraint as a foreign policy outcome requires observing key changes in the behavior of large, powerful states. Whereas the threat, use, and control of military force point to coercion, restraint reflects a fundamentally different foreign policy orientation, especially with regard to the efficacy of the veiled or explicit use of force. At its core, restraint is based on an *idealpolitik* paradigm. It encompasses an understanding that the external strategic environment is benign and that security threats are situational and due less to the fixed nature of rival adversaries than to some changeable condition of mutual interaction. Concrete evidence of foreign policy changes by a large, powerful state in the direction of restraint could include engaging in negotiations leading to multilateral agreements on issues where it had previously deflected or registered clear opposition. Participation in such interactive and deliberative discussions and exchanges of information leads a dominant state to reevaluate its outlook on the nature of its competitors and on conflict.

In particular, such agreements constrain large states' capabilities. They reduce the incentive to prioritize the dominant states' material interests when settling differences with their peers and neighbors. As such, strong-state restraint as a legitimation strategy is premised on the recognition that capitalizing on material capabilities or using coercive foreign policy measures is not always productive. In fact, as discussed in the previous section, power does not always or even generally rely on the use of coercion or force. The oversimplification of power as a by-product of material capabilities thus raises an obvious paradox: large states, in spite of their superior ability to wage and win wars, do not always get the outcomes that they want, particularly when they face collective opposition and resistance from their peers. Instead, powerful states can demonstrate their strength and influence more efficiently through a commitment not to exploit their material advantages. Existing rules and norms that constrain the activities of large states set the expectations about their rights and responsibilities. Violations of such behavioral expectations are tempting and easily within reach because large, powerful states simply have the means, but, as discussed, doing so would undercut their legitimation strategies and further complicate their desired political objective of a more enduring and accepted form of influence.

The primary argument here is that strong, powerful states can be incentivized to exercise restraint as a legitimation strategy. Paradoxically, flexing military might does not make a powerful state strong. Instead, it is the willingness to show restraint that produces the intended outcome and the kind of influence—recognized and accepted by their peers without resistance—that large, powerful states ultimately desire. Put simply, foreign policy behavior that conforms to group norms, or shows restraint, is pertinent for state survival and achieving security in an anarchic environment.

Condition for Restraint: Strong Group Consensus

To ensure that restraint as a political phenomenon is more than a heuristic claim, we would have to examine and test the proximate conditions that makes the restraining-to-thrive strategy more likely to occur in some security contexts than in others. In other words, when do large, powerful states exercise restraint? Drawing from our earlier discussion on the nonmaterial and relational or ideational sources of power, the probative argument on strong-state restraint is predicated on a key determinant: the consensus of regional security norms. In particular, when small states band together and work jointly to develop a strong consensus on their preferred security norms, the clarity in their collective agreement provides a powerful incentive for their large neighbor to consider and adopt foreign policy changes that reflect the shared preference of the smaller states. Hence it is particularly important to empirically observe the presence of strong group consensus. Why?

The collective influence of group consensus is well-established in the extant literature in political and social psychology. The presence of an in-group/out-group dynamic provides a powerful rationale for conforming to group consensus and behavior. What members of the in-group say or do during the interactive process matters, and the stronger the consensus from within the group, the more compelling it becomes for those on the outside to consider it seriously.[26] Developing an identity based on the group to which one seeks to belong provides a sense of acceptance, place, and position in the community.[27] Put simply, the identity of an individual or an entity, however aspirational, is conferred and confirmed by its peer group. In large-scale social experiments, the draw to be part of an "us" or the in-group is supported by key findings that interactions with the group generate strong influence on one's behavior, preferences, and identity.[28]

The incentives for prosocial behavior to fit into the group draw from a mix of both normative and informational conformity. Normative conformity reflects adherence to the group norms and consensus in order to fulfill the group's expectations and to gain acceptance. This type of social influence occurs through a combination of material rewards and punishments.[29] Evidence of rewards or back-patting includes a sense of belonging and conformity with role expectations, while social opprobrium includes naming-and-shaming, exclusion, and loss of legitimacy. Conforming to the in-group identity provides a visible degree of pressure and incentive for behavior that reinforces the group's norms.

Normative conformity can thus be best summed up as strategic adaptation, where "I believe the answer is X, but others said Y, and I don't want to rock the boat, so I'll say Y."[30] Similarly, concerns over social opprobrium incentivize actions that minimize public shaming and sanctions bestowed by the group. According to Oran Young, "Policy makers, like private individuals, are sensitive to the social opprobrium that accompanies violations of widely accepted behavioral prescriptions. They are, in short, motivated by a desire to avoid the sense of shame or social disgrace that commonly befalls those who break widely accepted rules."[31] The change in behavior is thus reflected in consideration of the social costs and benefits of recognition.

The repeated interactions as well as the perennial concerns for social acceptance would lead to and deepen informational conformity. Extending beyond normative conformity, one's belief and understanding change more substantively as a result of acceptance of new information and knowledge adopted and learned from others. Richard Perloff attributes such change to learning, where "an activity or process in which a communicator attempts to induce a change in the belief, attitude, or behavior of another person . . . through the transmission of a message in a context in which the persuadee has some degree of free choice."[32]

A sustained period of reciprocal interaction between states in international institutions can thus lead to changing social contexts that influence and change the identity and interests of those states.[33] Such encounters lead to a greater acceptance of the norms, ideas, and preferences that represent the institution's position and consensus. This shift in behavior occurs beyond simple contact with the group and can take shape even in the absence of gains in material power, other benefits, or coercion. Instead, it stems from persuasion and the quality of engagement with members of the group and their collective views on a particular issue area. Principled debate, argumentation, and deliberation all play important roles in shaping an attitudinal adjustment that reflects a fundamental change in preference.[34]

For large, powerful states, the motivation to take on self-constraining commitments reflects such social dynamics of acceptance and recognition. In particular, they are more likely to do so when there is a strong group consensus on a set of norms to manage a security conflict. Where such convergence in the group is present and clearly articulated, we would be able to observe and trace the large, powerful state's increasing openness to engage with the group. Such interactions reflect principled discussion and argument, whereby the powerful state acknowledges the value of adhering to the emerging security norms that are borne out of the multilateral settings and negotiations, notably with and through the group.

The Hypothesized Mechanism for Restraint

Evidence for strong-state restraint would include a preference shift toward supporting the group's consensus and a preference to de-escalate any conflict or confrontation. Notable foreign policy paradigmatic changes in the direction of restraint would include a move away from unilateral militarization, from coercion, as well as from the veiled or explicit threat and use of force. Instead, restraint would uphold and value the primacy of the group's consensus and clarity on its preferred security norms over sheer material capabilities. The hypothesized condition and mechanism for strong-state restraint as a legitimation strategy can be represented as follows:

H_1: Strong group consensus $\Rightarrow$ Restraint in a powerful state's foreign policy outcomes

Conversely, the consideration of material power capabilities becomes more prominent when there is visible discord and disunity in the group. For instance, a weakened group consensus due to regional fragmentation would mean that the source of persuasion and normative influence regarding the benefits of multilateral security initiatives would be missing. This would render the large, powerful state more likely to practice power politics, where the emphasis shifts toward its material sources of power and a zero-sum view of international security. It would display a higher tolerance for conflict and a stronger preference for the display of material power through offensive, coercive, and unilateral approaches in order to maintain its security. The odds become higher that the large state will defy and deflect multilateral negotiations or agreements that lack strong group backing and endorsement, unless such proposals minimize constraints on its material capabilities while maximizing constraints on others. Increasing levels of bellicose foreign policy actions would thus be the corollary of regional fragmentation:

H_2: Weak group consensus $\Rightarrow$ Absence of incentive for
strong-state restraint

Change in foreign policy is thus bidirectional, and preferences in state behavior can vary from restraint to coercion, depending on the social context, interactions, and the strategic ideology to which the state is introduced and exposed to achieve security.[35] As such, large, powerful states may capitalize on regional discord and fragmentation to pursue policies that reflect their narrow, material self-interests. Or they can conform to consensus and collective agreement among a group and actively pursue the goal of attaining broader influence through such a legitimation strategy. Coercion is thus one of at least two options in foreign policy statecraft, but it is by no means the default preference. This is especially pertinent for a strong state with rising ambitions and where the stakes and implications of its foreign policy actions are significantly higher and more carefully scrutinized by others. Pursuing foreign policy actions that are politically expedient may yield short-term gains, but doing so reduces the likelihood of attaining the kind of recognition that a large, powerful state seeks from its peers. If external validation matters in the formation of identity, it follows that accepting—rather than rejecting—the group's consensus becomes an incentivizing draw as a legitimation strategy, and hence the causal mechanism behind the restraining-to-thrive strategy for large, powerful states.

Theoretical Expectations in the South China Sea

Empirically, in the context of the South China Sea conflict, group consensus emerges from the collective approach of the claimant and nonclaimant states of Southeast Asia in ASEAN, the region's primary security institution. Observing strong levels of regional consensus is thus an important determinant for change in China's foreign policy behavior. The stronger and more cohesive the collective agreement among the member states on a set of norms to ameliorate the security dilemma in the South China Sea, the more likely it is that China's foreign policy will uphold that consensus and constrain China's relative material power capabilities. There would be clear signs of convergence between ASEAN's collective position and China's foreign policy actions, in spite of the relative costs to the latter's material power. We should expect to see official policy pronouncements and practices by China that are consistent with the security norms that the ten-member group prioritizes, as well as a moderation in China's foreign policy approach in the maritime dispute.

Restraint in China's foreign policy behavior would also see an endorsement of the multilateral initiatives it previously deflected or opposed. Such measures would be consistent with ASEAN's preferences for multilateral negotiations and diplomacy. The observable change in the attitude and preferences of China's foreign policy would occur without any threats or sanctioning mechanism from ASEAN. Instead, a strong level of group consensus would provide the basis for identity- and preference-shaping influence on China's decision-making process regarding the South China Sea, as will be shown in chapter 3.

ADDITIONAL INFERENCE STRATEGY FOR STRONG-STATE RESTRAINT

What additional inference strategy might help us discern whether China's behavioral change is a function of its concerns and acceptance of the collective preferences of weaker actors? In other words, how do we know if strong-state restraint as a legitimation strategy is actually at work, and not just tactical adjustments with veiled threats that reflect cheap talk?

Identifying the extent to which strong levels of ASEAN consensus is referenced, discussed, and debated in the foreign policy decision-making discussion in China would strengthen the inference and probative argument for strong-state restraint as a legitimation strategy. Put simply, if there is strong external and group consensus, we would need to see its complementary, knock-on effects on the domestic front that contribute to restraint in China's overall foreign policy behavior.

The influence exerted by a strong external consensus would enable shifts in the domestic thinking on what constitutes power among competing foreign policy actors and elites in China. For instance, the discussion would begin to center on reducing the overall incentive for the use of paramilitary or military force or for adopting coercive, offensive policies that promote China's material interests. Conversely, when the external and group consensus is weak or absent, the visible regional fragmentation in ASEAN would provide China's decision makers with a strategic opening to capitalize on the discord and to advocate for more hawkish and militant policies in the South China Sea, further shifting the emphasis on the material facets of power.

Observing the nexus between ASEAN consensus and change in China's internal foreign policy decision-making process would validate the key condition for restraint: strong group consensus. More important, it would help us gain greater clarity about China's motivations. Yong Deng observes that

> the flourishing of contending views propounded by influential scholars and governmental advisers in and of itself represents a change of great significance, especially in light of the fact that Chinese foreign policy had historically been the most strictly controlled subject. Not all of these new ideas have translated into practice, to be sure. But some have, as manifested in the many foreign policy adjustments China has made [between the mid-1990s and 2010s]. Taken together, they represent an unmistakable sign that China has been under mounting pressure to wrestle with the choices it must make to fulfill its international aspirations.[36]

Through this additional inference strategy, we would learn more about the importance of external perceptions to China. The different responses and articulation of views by China's scholar-officials would uncover insights about the country's shifting positions on the South China Sea, as well as about striking the delicate balance between pursuing hard, material power and the relational, social forms of power, like legitimacy. As such, we could get a better understanding of China's intentions and resolve with regard to the narrative on its rising influence.[37] These are not tangential points but extend directly from the hypothesized mechanism for strong-state restraint. Carrying out this additional analysis is thus an important step to help strengthen the inferences and probative argument for restraint as a legitimation strategy, a point we will explore here, as well as in greater depth in the first part of chapter 5.

Change in China's Decision-Making Process

On the surface, it appears that a single-party and authoritarian regime like China's faces far fewer dissenting views than democracies in determining changes in the decision-making process. Autocracies, however, have a number of openings and internal fissures that allow for policy debate, discussion, and deliberation among different factions, policy elites, and government agencies within the decision-making bureaucracy.[38] This often results in decision-making procedures that are fragmented to varying degrees.[39] The presence of interagency decision-making increases the number of actors and agencies involved in the process of policy formulation.

While the Chinese Communist Party (CCP) retains a firm grip on power, different ministries and government agencies, along with emerging party factions, have distinct policy preferences that are deliberated and negotiated to contribute to the decision-making process.[40] China's current version of fragmented authoritarianism has fairly low barriers of entry into the political process.[41] As in most autocracies, different actors, policy elites, and government agencies have various points of access to and influence in the overall party decision-making process and outcome, as well as the broader Chinese political system.

The interaction among various actors—including but not limited to government ministries, central and local governments, state-owned enterprises, private firms, and civil society—on vital policy issues is already having noticeable impact in the decision-making process. For instance, in the realm of nuclear safety, Amy King and M. V. Ramana find that "whether or not China will enhance nuclear safety will depend on the interactions between, and priorities of, these multiple actors."[42] Political pluralization includes more active "policy entrepreneurs" framing the issues in ways that influence outcomes when it comes to China's hydropower policy.[43] Similarly, others posit that "regulatory pluralism" has also emerged in China on environmental issues, with civic participation from concerned citizens, judges, and prosecutors resulting in more action being taken against industrial pollution.[44] Jessica Teets finds evidence for "consultative authoritarianism," a new model of state–society relationship that encourages the simultaneous expansion of a fairly autonomous civil society and the development of more indirect tools of state control and "challenges the conventional wisdom that an operationally autonomous civil society cannot exist inside authoritarian regimes and that the presence of civil society is an indicator of democratization."[45] In the economic domain, Victor Shih argues that domestic political considerations, especially the preferences of powerful interest groups with access to government officials, determine exchange rate valuation policy in China. "Autocrats are much more concerned with the distributional effects of exchange rate policy than most scholars recognize. Interest group pressures determine whether autocrats will cooperate in international economic affairs or if they will follow beggar-thy-neighbor policies."[46] All this is to say that there has indeed been a broadening of the decision-making process in China that has enabled policy elites—officials, bureaucrats, and scholar-practitioners—to provide input.

China's Foreign Policy Deliberations: More Actors, More Voices

In foreign and security policy issues, the decision-making process has also broadened. Studies on Chinese politics have often pointed to the "complex structure of the state itself as a significant determinant of the political process and policy outcomes."[47] The foreign policy decision-making structure, in particular, has become more pluralized and reliant on the expertise of professional bureaucrats in different functional areas.[48] In such areas as nuclear nonproliferation and arms control, officials and scholar-practitioners with specialized knowledge and technical understanding have an important voice that contributes to the policy debates and discussion.[49]

The shift away from single, dominant leaders has further opened up the foreign policy decision-making space for more interagency competition and participation. For instance, a number of leading small groups (LSGs)—formed by the CCP's Central Committee to focus on interagency consultation on key policy issues—have gained prominence in coordination of the conflicting interests of factions within the party, the government, and the military on foreign and security policy issues. This has been especially significant as China expands its involvement and participation in international security and global affairs. LSGs on foreign affairs, national security, and maritime affairs have all been tasked to provide more effective guidance and to manage competing interests in an increasingly fragmented bureaucracy. The LSGs' deliberations and consensus-building approach provide policy proposals to the CCP's Politburo Standing Committee for final approval, and their interagency coordinating role also enables them to coordinate the implementation of the approved decisions across the different ministries and agencies.[50]

During Hu Jintao's tenure at the helm of the CCP, from 2002 to 2012, the senior leadership widened the stakeholders involved in foreign policy issues to include not just government agencies but also policy advisors, academic scholars, and retired civilian and military officials.[51] Moreover, nearly every government ministry and every local government established an office responsible for international cooperation and liaising with foreign counterparts, effectively creating, mimicking, or replicating the work of the Ministry of Foreign Affairs (MFA). The proliferation of agencies involved in the foreign policy decision-making process in what was once a monolithic, unitary diplomatic system has meant that a significantly larger number of interested actors vie for political influence on the party's senior leadership.

In particular, the People's Liberation Army (PLA) remains a formidable organization in China's bureaucratic structure, vying for influence in the foreign policy decision-making process and outcome. The PLA and its more hawkish allies and militant advisers have been widely seen as an important source advocating for increasing assertiveness in Chinese foreign affairs.[52] While the party still exerts strong control over the military, they have a unique, symbiotic relationship and share vital interests. The

PLA remains the ultimate backstop of the party's grip on power, and it has considerable clout on security-related issues in foreign policy. The military retains significant influence as no Chinese leader since Deng Xiaoping has had any firsthand experience of warfare or military affairs. The need for PLA expertise and advice on military strategy and on foreign and security policy is of key concern and a priority for the party.

From an organizational perspective, there are valid concerns that unchecked military influence could lead to more assertive and conflict-prone foreign policy outcomes. Military officers are predisposed to view preventive war in particular in a more much favorable light than are civilian authorities, for a number of reasons. Owing to self-selection in the profession and socialization afterward, military officials are more inclined to see war as likely in the near term and inevitable in the long run.[53] The professional focus of attention on warfare makes military officers skeptical of nonmilitary alternatives to war, while civilian counterparts often place stronger hopes on diplomatic and economic methods of long-term conflict resolution. Such beliefs make military officers particularly susceptible to "better now than later" logic.

Military officers also tend to display strong biases in favor of offensive doctrines and decisive operations.[54] Offensive doctrines enable military organizations to take the initiative, utilizing their standard plans under conditions they control, while forcing adversaries to react to their favored strategies. Military officers are trained to focus on pure military logic and are given strict operational goals to meet when addressing security problems. As such, achieving victory means undermining the enemy through military activities. For the PLA, its central mission is to secure the fundamental national sovereignty interests of defending the party and the state. Analysts of the PLA have cited security relations on China's periphery, including in Northeast, Central, South, and Southeast Asia, as key foreign policy issues where the military holds significant sway. Likewise, the East and South China Seas have also emerged as a priority for the military in protecting and asserting China's sovereignty interests. This can be seen in the PLA's organizational restructuring and the establishment of the Eastern and the Southern Theater Commands. In so doing, the PLA has doubled down on its effort for strategic and contingency planning. The long-term political, economic, and diplomatic ramifications are secondary and not necessarily of immediate concern for military officers.

These factors combined make military officers strong advocates of preventive war.

The PLA has a distinct advantage in shaping China's foreign policy bureaucracy and decision-making process: it has a clear channel of access through the Central Military Commission (CMC), the PLA's top decision-making body overseeing defense policy and military strategy, to the inner core of the party's decision-making body and to China's leadership. The CMC is chaired by Xi Jinping, who combines the role of commander-in-chief of the PLA with those of president of China and general-secretary of the party. The commission includes eleven generals and admirals representing the armed forces, as well as representatives of the PLA's key organizational departments. The PLA can thus exert its influence on the party leadership. Because it remains an army for the party, on such pivotal foreign policy-related issues as military strategy, defense, and security policy, the PLA's input carries significant weight.

The military's close proximity to the senior party leadership can also come at the expense of sidelining other civilian government agencies, most notably the MFA. As a study points out, the MFA is often caught unawares of developments or positions on foreign and security policy issues. In fact, "many of the foreign policies that have led to allegations that China is becoming more assertive were not actions taken by the MFA, although it has invariably been blamed, but rather by the PLA."[55] Since the power of foreign policy decision-making still rests in the hands of the party, the key objective for the various government agencies, including the military, is to vie for influence with the party's decision-making core.

Domestic Empirical Indicators for Restraint

The involvement in policy formulation of actors and policy elites other than the more militant factions provides additional evidence for restraint in China's foreign policy outcomes. Why? The broadening of the decision-making process to encompass voices and strategies beside those of the military, for instance, allows for other agencies' views and interests, as well as those of reformers or other new thinkers to capitalize on China's substantive integration into regional and international institutions. Different policy elites and actors are thus able to articulate competing foreign policy ideas, interests, and priorities. In contrast, the concentration of the decision-making process in the hands of one entity—especially the military—decreases the odds that counterpoints will be expressed and increases the likelihood of the PLA and those with militant views imposing a narrower set of material prerogatives and parochial interests in defining what constitutes power for Chinese foreign policy. This is especially relevant in consequential security issues like the South China Sea.

Identifying these domestic, empirical indicators would thus further validate the inference and causal mechanism for strong-state restraint. The presence of strong ASEAN consensus as an exogenous factor can incentivize change in China's foreign policy in ways that are more consistent with the norms advocated by the regional institution in which China seeks to gain acceptance and affirmation as a credible and legitimate leader.

SUMMARY

A large, powerful state's aspirations to enhance its influence through legitimacy cannot be realized through sheer force. Nor can it unilaterally demand legitimacy and its right to rule. The acquiescence of lesser powers in conferring such legitimacy comes with expectations that a rising power will uphold the core norms of regional and international security, will play an active part in reinforcing them, and is bestowed with special rights and managerial duties to do so.

Hence, unlike influence based on possession of material power and resources, legitimacy is a form of power that draws from deference, shared values, and expectations of each party's role in a social relationship. This can result in greater stability in international politics, with legitimacy-seeking powers reinforcing the accepted social structures, norms, and values that govern interstate relations. It is precisely for this reason that legitimacy induces restraint in foreign policy behavior, rather than conflict and aggression as the modus operandi for large, powerful states with rising ambitions.

If we know the rationale for strong-state restraint, the natural follow-on is to explain and understand how such a change in foreign policy behavior would occur. To do so, we would have to look at the process. This chapter articulates a key condition behind the causal mechanism for restraint, particularly the level of regional consensus on an emerging security issue.

The extent to which this condition is met can help explain the variation—restraint or coercion—in recent developments in China's foreign policy in the South China Sea, which are explored and tested in the following empirical chapter.

To establish the causal logic of the probative argument, it is critical to observe whether the hypothesized mechanism that connects the condition for change in China's foreign policy behavior is present or absent. The logic behind the causal chain begins with the observation of the level of ASEAN consensus. On the one hand, the stronger and more cohesive the consensus and the regional proposals to ameliorate the security dilemma, the more likely it would be that China's foreign policy would reflect that consensus and support the regional, multilateral security agreement. On the other hand, the consideration of material power capabilities would become more prominent when there is visible regional discord and disunity. For instance, a weakened ASEAN consensus due to regional fragmentation would imply the absence of a source of persuasion and normative influence regarding the benefits of multilateral security initiatives. Hence the level of ASEAN consensus on a particular security issue of debate is important to observe empirically.

It is also critical to be able to trace whether such consensus at the international level on a particular normative or security issue is referred to in the domestic debate and deliberation among policy elites about what constitutes power. References to the risks of and social costs to China's quest for legitimacy that arise from ignoring or deflecting regional consensus would further reflect the identity- and preference-shaping influence of regional institutions like ASEAN. Moreover, evidence for restraint by China would see a preference shift toward supporting proposals and endorsing security initiatives that arise from the normative consensus of regional agreements.

Without such consensus at the regional level, the domestic discourse on what constitutes power would have few reference points about the regional norms, values, and expectations for a legitimate power. The concentration of foreign policy decision-making processes in the hands of more hawkish and militant factions increases the tendency for them to push through their parochial interests and an unchecked pursuit of power politics and material hard power in the South China Sea. Likewise, the odds for defiance and deflection of agreements are also higher, with a general preference for proposals that ensure minimizing constraints on its own material capabilities while maximizing constraints on others. Change in China's foreign policy would thus shift toward coercion or other instrumental, cost–benefit strategies that lead to an increase in foreign policy tension and the overall likelihood of conflict and confrontation.

Put simply, without regional consensus as an important determinant for strong-state restraint, China's assumptions on the efficacy of the use of force, evaluation of the strategic and adversarial environment, and the means of pursuing narrow self-interest would reflect the material sources of power. The next chapter turns to empirically testing the proposition presented thus far. In particular, we will examine the causal role of ASEAN consensus, as well as its effects on China's foreign policy behavior in the South China Sea. China's behavior in the South China Sea conflict provides a crucial test for within-case variation that can help strengthen the inference and the explanatory power of the book's probative argument on strong-state restraint as a legitimation strategy.

Chapter Three

ASEAN CONSENSUS IN THE SOUTH CHINA SEA CONFLICT, 2012-2018

The conventional wisdom points to China's foreign policy behavior in the South China Sea as aggressive, revisionist, and disruptive to regional stability. Since 2012, confrontations between China and other claimant states in Southeast Asia have intensified through such activities as land reclamation, hardening of bases, and fortification of islets; deployment of flotillas of coast guard, paramilitary and naval vessels, and fishing boats; as well as exploration of natural resources in the contested waters and seabed. Observers such as Robert Kaplan argue China's aspirations in the East and South China Seas mirror what other large, powerful states with rising ambitions have done in the past: establishing blue water extensions of its territorial borders to build an oceanic empire.[1] Ralph Emmers writes there is a regional fear in Southeast Asia of China's growing naval capabilities to "resolve the sovereign question militarily." But the claimant states are also taking steps to "extend their sovereign jurisdiction unilaterally to guarantee their access to natural resources," indicating rising tensions, competition, and confrontation.[2] Likewise, Alastair Iain Johnston cautions that "the South China Sea is perhaps the only example where China's diplomatic rhetoric and practice did shift fairly sharply in a more hardline direction in this period."[3]

China's material power dwarfs that of the other claimant states, both individually and collectively. Given this power differential, China's assertiveness ought—according to the conventional wisdom—to center around measures intended to thoroughly minimize the capabilities of other claimant states and thereby sustain its unilateral approach to maritime security. But an all-out, hostile takeover has yet to occur, which seems to be at odds with the prevailing expectations of power politics and state behavior.

In fact, China's activities in the South China Sea thus far have oscillated between restraint—the decision not to capitalize on its preponderance of power or narrow, material interests—and coercion. Even with territorial sovereignty, access to potential resources, and power projection at stake in the South China Sea, there are instances where exercising strong-state restraint pays off. While pursuing material interests may be politically expedient, refraining from doing so as a first resort opens up the prospects for a large, powerful state to reorient its foreign policy paradigm toward cooperative means, rather than prioritizing balancing or relative power considerations. Doing so, as discussed in chapter 2, provides an important means to achieving legitimacy and recognition as a leader and responsible power. Put simply, assumptions about the anarchic security environment as a zero-sum competition are more delimited than conventional wisdom suggests. The question thus becomes: When does a large, powerful state like China back off and when does it double down in a highly consequential conflict?

The focus of this chapter is to test the hypothesized mechanism for strong-state restraint as a legitimation strategy in the South China Sea: that strong ASEAN consensus can induce restraint in China's foreign and security policy behavior in the maritime dispute. When there is unequivocal unity among the ASEAN leaders in the norms and diplomatic initiatives to address China's unilateral activities in the South China Sea, this yields China's restraint. Conversely, if there is regional fragmentation and discord, China would be incentivized to exert more coercive policies in the South China Sea conflict.

We will first delve into the background and context of ASEAN as Southeast Asia's primary regional security architecture, discussing the significance behind the organization's emphasis on decision-making by consensus and the concomitant collective influence that comes with it. The chapter then lays out how ASEAN consensus is operationalized. Specifically, how do we know when there is strong consensus in the regional organization regarding the South China Sea conflict? Equally important, if strong consensus exists, how would we measure it?

ASEAN consensus, as represented by the collective sentiment and threat perception of the maritime dispute, ranges from broad reiterations of general organizational principles to a heightened sense of urgency on the unfolding security crisis. Using a new database and discourse analysis to measure the strength of regional consensus, we will test the hypotheses and causal mechanism for strong-state restraint. In so doing, we will draw inferences from the effects of ASEAN consensus on regional security and stability, identifying the corresponding changes in Chinese foreign policy behavior in the maritime dispute, and show why strong-state restraint is not just cheap talk, a guise for veiled threats, or window-dressing tactics.

By understanding the significance of ASEAN's group consensus as an exogenous factor for China's foreign policy restraint, we are in a better position to examine the extent to which confidence-building diplomacy can cultivate habits of conflict management without formal sanctioning mechanisms, threats, or the use of force. As Amitav Acharya notes, "China's new approach to engaging individual ASEAN members has highlighted differences in ASEAN unity or neutrality. ASEAN will need to respond to these challenges by forging closer personal ties among the region's leaders in more frequent and less formal meetings, and by taking mini-lateral approaches to global and regional challenges."[4] The empirical analysis in this chapter reveals ASEAN as a source of preference- and identity-shaping influence. It also suggests the need to engage with ASEAN consensus when considering how the region can project and implement its security norms in ways that incentivize change in the foreign policy paradigm of an imposing external power like China.

ASEAN CONSENSUS AND ITS COLLECTIVE INFLUENCE

Since the establishment of ASEAN in 1967, the organization has evolved and experienced significant shifts in the region's security environment. In the aftermath of postcolonial border disputes and in the midst of the Cold War proxy wars in neighboring Indochina, it was founded as a diplomacy-centered organization by five states—Indonesia, Malaysia, the Philippines, Singapore, and Thailand—motivated by a fear of communism. The violence in the region culminated in Vietnam's invasion of

Cambodia in 1978. In a more peaceful environment, as the region's economies opened up and the regimes stabilized, ASEAN's membership expanded—first to include Brunei in 1984, then Vietnam, Laos, Myanmar, and Cambodia in the mid- to late 1990s.

In spite of the number of political upheavals over the past five decades, ASEAN retains a distinct role in regional politics and security. The ten Southeast Asian member states have sought a blueprint for a regional security order that emphasizes high degrees of informality and organizational minimalism, or the "ASEAN Way." The establishment of the ASEAN Regional Forum (ARF) reflected ASEAN's aspirations to engage with external powers, retain its relevancy, and contribute to a stable region in the post–Cold War era. Its latest vision for a more united ASEAN community by 2020 across the political, economic, and cultural domains serves as a key litmus test for an emerging regional security community.

ASEAN's approach to regional diplomacy helps shed light on its institutional priorities for mutual respect and dialogue to achieve security and stability in the Southeast Asia. While such milestone achievements as the Treaty of Amity and Cooperation (1976) and the establishment of a formal ASEAN Charter in 2007 may seem to codify ASEAN as a hard, legal institution, it continues to maintain a "soft law approach," which encourages "the internalization and reflexive learning of ASEAN norms" among its member states.[5] At its core, ASEAN was and remains an institution that relies on norms derived from a common understanding of the region's shared history, political dynamics, and cultural practices, as opposed to a set of immutable, iron-clad laws and legal instruments.

As a senior ASEAN official put it, ASEAN may be inspired by the best practices of the EU, but it does not aspire to be like Europe.[6] The hallmark features of ASEAN's approach to regional stability center on consensus, noninterference, respect for state sovereignty, and renunciation of the threat or use of force in regional affairs. Eugene Tan observes that these principles governing ASEAN behavior "generate norms and responsive conduct by member states of ASEAN."[7]

In particular, consensus remains a long-standing and central element of ASEAN's modus operandi. Decisions that affect ASEAN as a whole—for instance, joint statements released at each foreign ministers' meeting or at the heads of government summit—require all ten member states to agree to the content, wording, and substance. Observers have long lamented that such a practice tends to lead to outcomes that reflect the "lowest common denominator."[8] In other words, the statements often contain platitudes, and their content reflects the least contentious and least politically significant issues. Moreover, a decision by consensus invites further criticism of ineffectiveness and delay as it gives every member state a right to veto.

Notwithstanding these criticisms, consensus as the key element of ASEAN's decision-making process has been repeatedly reinforced and was formally enshrined in article 20 of its charter in 2007. The deliberate choice to retain decision-making by consensus demonstrates how pivotal this core principle is to ASEAN and its member states. Consensus helps to ensure that any decision the group makes is demonstrative of the collective will of its member states and the region as a whole. It also reflects the importance of dialogue and deliberation. Through an interactive process of persuasion and principled argumentation between foreign policy officials and leaders, any remaining gaps among the ten member states must be narrowed and addressed before a final decision can be made. While the decision-making process is laborious and time-consuming, it ensures that any outcome and resolution reflects the common stance and preference of the region. ASEAN's collective decisions are thus inextricably linked to its foundation as a diplomacy-centered organization—which it arguably still is today.

A by-product of decision-making by consensus is the centrality of ASEAN. In articulating what ASEAN centrality entails, Acharya identifies the organization as "the leader, driver, architect, institutional hub, vanguard, nucleus, and the fulcrum of regional processes and institutional designs in the Asia-Pacific region."[9] Given that ASEAN's decisions result from collective agreement among all ten member states, ASEAN has the ability to effect change and initiate action in relation to external partners. Although ASEAN generally eschews confrontation, its decisions command region-wide support and endorsement because they are reached through a deliberative process and are strengthened by ASEAN's collective voice and nonalignment with any external power. Put simply, ASEAN member states understand that strength in unity arises when their security outlooks are aligned but not necessarily allied.

Centrality is thus part and parcel of decision by consensus and refers to ASEAN member states acting as a collective body. In situations where there is no consensus, there is no centrality. Likewise, weak consensus also undermines ASEAN centrality. This is particularly evident when decisions in the joint statements contain only the least contentious topics. But when there is strong consensus, the wording and substance of ASEAN's statements reflect a high level of centrality. Here, ASEAN takes a visibly proactive approach in responding to threat perceptions with a sense of urgency, addressing them by putting forward concrete diplomatic initiatives. Strong consensus and centrality would thus be identified when ASEAN member states decide to go beyond common stock phrases in ASEAN statements. Such a breakthrough is achieved when all ten member states engage in principled debate and argumentation to agree on the most sensitive security issues, and it would serve as an indicative measure for strong regional consensus.

Understanding ASEAN's modus operandi contextualizes the broader significance and implications of its consensus-based diplomacy for regional security. In particular, the ongoing maritime conflict in the South China Sea presents a unique opportunity to determine the extent to which ASEAN is able to cope with the strategic uncertainty in the region and exert its collective influence, especially when it faces a formidable neighbor like China.[10]

We turn to the next section to operationalize ASEAN consensus. Specifically, how do we recognize strong and weak ASEAN consensus? Addressing these questions will provide the empirical basis to measure regional consensus with greater precision and identify its intended and actual effects on regional security and strong-state restraint.

INDICATORS AND MEASUREMENT OF ASEAN CONSENSUS

Testing the proposition that large, powerful states can show restraint in the face of strong regional consensus requires us to first measure and observe the key causal factor: group consensus. A proxy measure for the strength of group consensus lies in the content and substance of ASEAN's biannual summit statements, where the ten states' leaders meet and commit the institution's deliberative and most consequential outcomes to paper. Decisions that affect the region as a whole require all member states in the group to agree on the exact wording of each joint statement released at every summit. This effectively gives each ASEAN member state a veto right. As cumbersome as this process may seem, decisions made through this deliberative process reflect and command region-wide endorsement.

In particular, when there is strong group consensus, the wording and substance of ASEAN's summit statements are qualitatively different. For instance, in these cases, ASEAN leaders take a united and proactive approach in proposing new or concrete initiatives that reflect the institutional norms and preferences of diplomacy over conflict. Going beyond common stock phrases in their summit statements, the group takes actionable decisions that entail identity- and preference-shaping initiatives and that draw on ASEAN's collective strength as the epicenter for regional dialogue and diplomacy. The point is not to assume that ASEAN has already become a full-fledged security community. Instead, the exercise here is to use the idea of security community as a framework within which to examine the evolving nature of ASEAN's security role and identify the constraints it faces in developing a viable regional security community in managing its external relations with China in the South China Sea dispute. At a minimum, strong internal consensus would therefore result in at least three key indicators in ASEAN's response to an unfolding security crisis:

- *Sense of urgency*: a heightened sense of urgency on the destabilizing effects of militarization to the region's collective security;
- *Specificity of the threat*: a clear, precise description of the perceived common threat; and
- *Proposal for diplomatic action*: a collective decision to propose diplomacy-based initiatives to manage the regional conflict in question.

Consequently, the discourse analysis of ASEAN summit statements with strong consensus would show three distinctive attributes. First, the leaders would adopt word choices in their statements that indicate a heightened sense of urgency. Strong regional consensus can be observed when the language adopted in the statement is more forceful, substantive, and specific rather than passive, open-ended, and general. Verbs such as "emphasize" or "urge" rather than "reaffirm" demonstrate greater urgency and are more action-oriented in nature.

Second, specificity in the phrases used (e.g., "serious concerns over land reclamation") provide additional clarity on the security threats that are perceived by all ten ASEAN member states. The identification of specific incidents or military activities that are undermining regional stability is akin to a naming-and-shaming approach, with the intended purpose of underscoring an alignment in the group's threat perception to regional security.

Third, clauses in the summit statement would outline new or specific ASEAN-led diplomatic initiatives or proposals aimed at reducing tension and settling the emerging conflict without the use of force or militarization—the region's long-standing security norm and preference.

To be sure, not all decisions and outcomes reflect strong group consensus. For example, when the statement relies on commonly used stock phrases or lofty platitudes, it reflects weak regional consensus. Rather than taking an active stance or calling out a specific activity that is escalating tension in the South China Sea, a decision to use broad statements or oft-repeated principles indicates that certain member states are in disagreement over the nature of the security threat and are thus withholding support for a more proactive, collective action. Agreeing to use such stock phrases still requires consensus, but it is confined to the least contentious aspects affecting regional security. Further, few or no new diplomatic initiatives are included when such calls lack strong group cohesion. This reinforces the visible disagreement among member states over the nature of a particular security threat in the region, as well as over the appropriate collective action to take in response. The absence of unanimous support and a lack of clarity in the member states' views and normative position would all point to a weakened group consensus.

To measure the level of ASEAN consensus in the scope of this study, the focus is on the biannual summit statements from 2012 to 2018. As discussed, ASEAN summit statements reflect the highest policy- and decision-making outcome in the regional body. The ten leaders meet twice a year, usually once in the second quarter (e.g., around April or May) and a second time in the fourth quarter of the year (e.g., around October or November). This was the case for all years between 2012 and 2018, with the exception of 2016, when they only met once, in the third quarter (in September). As such, there were thirteen summit statements in total during the observed time period.

The application of discourse analysis supported the analysis of each summit statement's discussion of the South China Sea conflict. To ensure consistency and accuracy in the discourse analysis, a Python code supplemented the exercise by counting the most frequently used words and phrases, and a longitudinal study contextualized the significance of those key word choices and phrases adopted in the summit statements to reflect the three key indicators for strong consensus discussed earlier: sense of urgency, specificity of the threat, and proposal for diplomatic action. This methodological approach provides the proxy measure for the level of consensus within ASEAN in relation to China's actions in the South China Sea conflict (see table 3.1 for a summary and the appendix for full details).

TABLE 3.1
Discourse Analysis Summary of ASEAN Statements' Consensus, 2012–2018

ASEAN summit and date	Sense of urgency	Specificity of threat	Proposal for diplomatic action	Level of consensus
20th Summit April 2012	No	No	No	Weak
21st Summit November 2012	Yes	Yes	No	Strong
22nd Summit April 2013	No	No	Yes	Weak
23rd Summit October 2013	No	No	No	Weak
24th Summit May 2014	Yes	Yes	Yes	Very strong
25th Summit November 2014	No	No	No	Weak
26th Summit April 2015	Yes	Yes	Yes	Very strong
27th Summit November 2015	Yes	Yes	No	Strong
28th/29th Summit September 2016	No	Yes	Yes	Strong
30th Summit April 2017	No	No	Yes	Weak
31st Summit November 2017	No	No	Yes	Weak
32nd Summit April 2018	No	Yes	No	Weak
33rd Summit November 2018	Yes	No	No	Weak

Note: The appendix expands on the discourse analysis of ASEAN summit statements in 2012–2018.

MEASURING CHANGE IN CHINA'S BEHAVIOR:
COERCION AND RESTRAINT

Given the varying levels of ASEAN consensus between 2012 and 2018, were there corresponding changes in China's foreign policy behavior in the South China Sea over the same time period? If so, what did they look like?

If strong group consensus is in effect, we would see China adhering to the emerging security norms on the South China Sea that result from multilateral negotiations, notably with and through ASEAN. Key preference changes reflecting restraint in China's foreign policy would indicate a move away from such coercive practices as militarization and the threat or use of force in the maritime dispute to address ongoing disputes and differences. China's foreign policy behavior would also shift toward supporting regional initiatives that it had previously deflected or opposed. Such empirical outcomes would be consistent with ASEAN preferences for multilateral negotiations and diplomacy. The observable attitude and preference change in strong-state restraint would occur without any sanctioning mechanisms. Instead, ASEAN security norms and ideology, articulated through a consensus-based decision-making process, would help convey the shared and unanimous concern of the region. A paradigmatic shift in China's behavior consistent with the regional community would reveal ASEAN's preference- and identity-shaping influence on China's interests and policies in the South China Sea.

Conversely, when national interests across the views of the ten ASEAN member states are disparate and irreconcilable, regional consensus weakens. The absence of consensus reveals ASEAN's limited institutional mechanisms, norms, and procedures for conflict management, all of which would incentivize a large, powerful state like China to act unilaterally and pursue power politics. Put simply, absent strong ASEAN consensus, China's fundamental evaluation of the strategic environment does not change. The means of pursuing its material interests in the South China Sea would reflect preferences for highly coercive means to minimize rival states' capabilities and to preserve its unilateral approaches to security. Hence any multilateral or ASEAN-proposed solutions to mediate the dispute will be met with high levels of skepticism and opposition, unless such proposals somehow achieve China's preference for minimizing any costs to its own capabilities while maximizing constraints on the other claimant states.

To capture and measure these key changes in China's foreign policy behavior in the South China Sea with greater precision, a new, comprehensive data set of China's activities in the maritime dispute that were publicly reported and documented between 2012 and 2018 was compiled. The activities were categorized by the interaction between China and the relevant claimant and nonclaimant states to the South China Sea and the nature of the activity (e.g., military, diplomatic, economic) and were subsequently coded as coercion, restraint, or neither.

Several considerations contextualized the variation in China's behavior in the South China Sea. China as the initiator state and the nature of its actions are grouped as categorical data while coercion, neutral, or restraint is classified as ternary data. The actions were further divided into two groups: "active" actions composed of such activities as military exercises and land reclamation activities, and examples of "rhetoric," including diplomatic responses and statements. Dividing the activities into these two categories ensures that similar actions are compared to one another. The following formula determined the outcome in China's behavior in the South China Sea for each three-month period:

$$\text{Outcome (y-axis)}: \frac{\text{Coercion} + \text{Neutral} + \text{Restraint}}{\text{Total number of activities}}$$

In other words, the outcome measures overall net behavior as the average score (in terms of coercion or restraint) of China's activities, giving a data point for each quarter. Figure 3.1 depicts the results with normalized data, where an outcome closer to 1 suggests coercion while a number toward 0 reflects restraint.

FINDINGS AND RESULTS

Between 2012 and 2018 nearly 40 percent of the ASEAN summit statements reflected strong or very strong group consensus (see table 3.1). In those instances, there was a heightened sense of urgency regarding China's destabilizing activities in the South China Sea dispute. This was evident in the 21st, 24th, 26th, 27th, and combined 28th and 29th ASEAN Summit statement outcomes (as labeled in figure 3.1).

If large, powerful states exercise restraint in the face of strong group consensus, particularly when there is clarity in norms and a collective

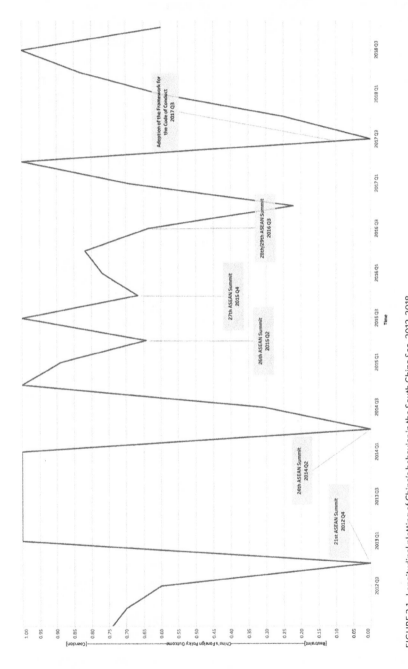

FIGURE 3.1. Longitudinal plotting of China's behavior in the South China Sea, 2012–2018.

Note: The full data set is available for review from the author, including the program file and script in Python used to generate the results in the figure.

concern over the threat perception affecting regional security, then we should expect to see dips in China's coercive activities in the quarters where strong levels of ASEAN consensus are evident in the summit statements. ASEAN summits take place twice a year, in the second and the fourth quarters— generally in April and late October or early November. As there are approximately nine weeks remaining in the same quarter following the release of each ASEAN summit statement, we can observe from figure 3.1 the effects of strong levels of ASEAN consensus on China's foreign policy behavior in the South China Sea.

The results point to a clear pattern of behavior and bear three implications. First, China's restraint closely corresponds with increasing levels of ASEAN consensus. China demonstrated clear or relative restraint in six quarters during the period 2012–2018. Five of these quarters corresponded with an ASEAN summit statement that exhibited strong or very strong consensus. The sixth instance resulted from ASEAN members' unity on the framework agreement for negotiation on a Code of Conduct in the South China Sea (COC), an ad hoc intervention as a direct outcome of the biannual summit arrangements.

Second, a major contribution of the findings here is to show how security relations between China and ASEAN are interactional. Their effects have thus far been relatively understudied to account for variation in China's foreign policy outcomes, not least in the South China Sea maritime dispute. The observation of strong-state restraint as a dynamic process born out of ASEAN–China interactions addresses pertinent questions: If states can learn the benefits of multilateralism through their social interactions in security institutions, is it possible that they can unlearn such behavior and regress toward a more realpolitik foreign policy paradigm? If so, what is the causal mechanism that can capture and explain this variation?

Restraint as a foreign policy outcome would thus appear to be a function of strong group consensus. Explaining when such behavior is more or less likely to take place relies on a casual mechanism that identifies and tests the scope condition for restraint, one that reflects the dynamic security interactions between China and ASEAN. When the condition for strong-state restraint is not met, one would expect state behavior to regress toward coercion. As such, the empirical findings and results account for the "two steps forward, one step back" pattern in China's behavior in the South China Sea between 2012 and 2018. This within-case variation is important to observe to prevent the selection of the endpoint in time-series analyses that would bias the analysis and predetermine the outcome.

Third, and perhaps most important, the empirical results presented here diverge from the conventional narrative that, as China's material capabilities increase, coercive tendencies are becoming the new normal in its approach to territorial disputes, not least in the South China Sea conflict.[11] In fact, restraint as a foreign policy outcome occurred irrespective of China's growing material capabilities. Put simply, the variation in a large, powerful state's foreign policy behavior rests on the presence of a nonmaterial, ideational, and external factor: strong ASEAN consensus. This finding would be in line with what Allen Carlson sees as China's pragmatic foreign policy approach, where even in consequential security issues that involve territoriality, China, like other states, is constantly modifying, contesting, and redefining sovereignty as a concept to itself as well as in relationships with its peers in international institutions.[12]

In addition, to further strengthen the hypothesized mechanism for restraint, what might China's domestic or internal foreign policy decision-making process look like when ASEAN exerts its collective influence? In other words, when there is strong ASEAN consensus, what are the complementary, knock-on effects on the domestic front that contribute to restraint in China's overall foreign policy behavior?

Identifying the extent to which ASEAN consensus is debated and referenced in the foreign policy decision-making process within China helps to further validate the argument for restraint. Such observations would be reflected in the internal deliberations among competing foreign policy elites and stakeholders on what constitutes power, reducing the overall incentive for the use of paramilitary or military force or for adopting coercive, offensive policies that promote material interests. Identifying these empirical indicators would further validate the causal argument that the external group's consensus can incentivize change in China's foreign policy and in ways that are more consistent with the norms and values espoused by the group from which it seeks to gain acceptance and legitimacy.

When there is strong ASEAN consensus, the internal discussion among the foreign policy elites in China on what constitutes power begins to shift. The emphases on legitimacy and diplomatic approaches to navigate the sensitivities around the maritime dispute become more salient and viable as a foreign policy consideration, reflecting regional norms, preferences, and expectations. References to the strong consensus at the regional level sharpen the focus and discussion on the relational aspects of power, reducing the overall incentive for the use force or coercive policies. Observing these empirical developments in China's decision-making process is an additional inference strategy for understanding and explaining the extent to which ASEAN consensus and norms have a preference- and identity-shaping effect on China's foreign policy.

Conversely, when there is regional fragmentation and when the ten ASEAN member states are unable to agree on a collective approach to managing their maritime dispute with China, foreign policy advisers and advocates for asserting China's claims and capitalizing on the country's material advantages become more prominent. Without external pushback or repercussions, regional discord provides an opening through which more hawkish and militant views are able to define what constitutes power. As they expand their influence in the foreign policy decision-making process, more disruptive and coercive actions erupt in the South China Sea.

The following subsections examine a number of crucial tests in the South China Sea. Given the varying levels of ASEAN consensus between 2012 and 2018, can we trace the corresponding effects on China's behavior in the South China Sea more concretely, especially during pivotal moments and test cases in this time period? As discussed, identifying the extent to which ASEAN consensus is debated and referenced in the foreign policy decision-making process in China serves as an additional inference strategy to strengthen the probative causes for strong-state restraint. We will also address in the next section why these observed changes in the direction of restraint go beyond window-dressing tactical adjustments or cheap talk.

2013: Regional Discord and China's Coercion

Let us start with an illustrative case when regional consensus was absent. The corresponding effect would be that China's behavior becomes belligerent. This attitudinal shift is not just a reaction to the anarchical, material structures that incentivize large, powerful states to practice power politics. The theoretical model and probative argument on strong-state restraint expect that change in foreign policy outcomes is a function of the social, interactive process that extends from strong group consensus. If this nonmaterial, ideational factor can explain the cooperative or deviant cases, then its absence should account for the nondeviant cases or conflictual outcomes in state behavior.[13]

In the South China Sea conflict, regional consensus among the claimant and nonclaimant states in ASEAN was conspicuously weak from 2013 through mid-2014. For instance, at the 22nd ASEAN Summit, in April 2013, the ten leaders discussed the situation in the South China Sea but were unable to forge a strong consensus on their priorities in dealing with China in the maritime dispute. They simply reaffirmed previously stated goals for regional stability and left the contentious issue of engaging China to the region's foreign ministers to correspond with their Chinese counterpart. Likewise, at the following ASEAN summit, the region remained divided regarding its collective position and diplomatic response to China. Consensus, while present, was weak and reflected in the two summit statements in 2013, where there was no clear, unanimous agreement on the emerging threat perception or the appropriate diplomatic response. The necessary condition for restraint was thus missing.

The nearly eighteen month absence of strong ASEAN consensus was an opportune window for hard-liners in the People's Liberation Army to advocate for a more militant approach in the South China Sea. Even though China effectively gained control of the Scarborough Shoal in a tense standoff against the Philippines in 2012, PLA strategists thought the government did not go far enough in cementing China's maritime claims. They noted the Philippines' inability to corral ASEAN support and were thus emboldened to recommend policies that took advantage of this division among the claimant and nonclaimant states in the maritime dispute.[14] Indeed, following the Scarborough Shoal takeover, 2013 saw the beginning of a concerted effort by the PLA naval and armed forces to engage in massive land reclamation activities in the South China Sea. Rear Admiral Luo Yuan, for example, was explicit about capitalizing on China's material capabilities and advantages and argued for taking a direct and offensive approach to further protect China's interests, rights, and security.[15] Similarly, another prominent PLA figure, Rear Admiral Yin Zhuo, echoed the need to fortify the islets, turning them into bases for potential combat action.

That these two senior military strategists had a higher risk tolerance was noticeable. In interview discussions with senior colonels specializing in regional security and PLA strategies in the South China Sea, it was clear that they believed any costs to China's regional standing would be contained, given the limited external pushback. They argued that others in the region would eventually come to terms with and accept China's material power and position.[16] A fragmented ASEAN thus allowed for such arguments based on China's self-interest and material power to be more compelling and the dominant narrative throughout 2013. As Feng Zhang explains, "The hardliners thus have a low sensitivity to costs and a higher tolerance for instability. They also have a very low regard of and receptivity toward other countries' views and concerns. Entirely self-centered, they wish only to maximize China's self-interest, regardless of any anxieties and fears of the outside world."[17]

Driven largely by these militant views and emboldened by the lack of regional repercussions, China successfully expanded its claims by fortifying numerous islets in the Paracel and Spratly Islands throughout 2013 and into 2014. In May 2014 China's coercive activities culminated with the China National Offshore Oil Corporation (CNOOC) moving its oil drilling rig, the Haiyang Shiyou 981 (HYSY-981), into waters claimed by both China and Vietnam. Accompanied by a convoy of eighty to a hundred Chinese civilian and paramilitary ships, the HYSY-981's presence within Vietnam's exclusive economic zone (EEZ) raised regional tension.[18] The PLA's navy quickly emerged as a key coordinator behind these military maneuvers to protect China's coercive actions in the contested waters.[19]

Building on the lack of regional unity, Chinese strategists' perception of the South China Sea conflict in 2013 and early 2014 became more focused on unilateral assertions of power politics. In direct response to the limited repercussions from other claimant states during this time period, the PLA and other hawkish scholar-officials adopted an offensive strategy underpinned by a realpolitik outlook that emphasized the highly efficacious uses of China's material capabilities. However, this perception of a highly conflictual external environment was not a linear trajectory. In fact, change was about to unfold as its Southeast Asian neighbors began to mobilize through ASEAN to mount a collective pushback, starting in mid-2014.

2014-2016: ASEAN Consensus in Action

China's fast-expanding land reclamation activities throughout 2013 and its unilateral decision to place the oil rig in Vietnam's EEZ near the Paracels in 2014 heightened Southeast Asian officials' sense of urgency about the unfolding security crisis. In particular, Vietnam sought support and solidarity from its neighbors to protest against China's activities. In the lead-up to the 24th ASEAN Summit in May 2014, Vietnam's deputy foreign minister, Pham Quang Vinh, indicated that "this [oil rig] issue will be high on the agenda of state leaders and ministerial meetings. ASEAN leaders will express their views and urge involved parties to practice restraint, abide by international law, and the UN Convention on the Law of the Sea (UNCLOS), resolve disputes by peaceful means, and refrain from threatening or using force."[20] When he met with regional foreign ministers in May, they issued an unprecedented stand-alone joint statement specifically on the South China Sea. They also called for the "importance of maintaining peace and stability, maritime security, freedom of navigation in and over flight above the South China Sea."[21] It was a timely joint communiqué agreed on and released within days of the breakout of the oil rig crisis.

ASEAN officials at the meeting acknowledged that the statement's intended audience was China, and it sought a united stand within the region to convey the message that the provocations were out of step with ASEAN's security norms and commitment to resolving differences without the use of force.[22] The ASEAN foreign ministers' statement was subsequently endorsed at the highest levels at the 24th ASEAN Summit.[23] Most notably, Vietnam had successfully lobbied for the unanimous support of ASEAN leaders to highlight the urgency of negotiating a Code of Conduct with China to mitigate escalating tensions in the region.

From June through August 2014, ASEAN officials pressed their collective concerns, as outlined in the 24th ASEAN Summit statement, and exerted pressure on China in a number of back-to-back multilateral meetings. These included meetings of senior officials from China and ASEAN on the 2002 Declaration on the Conduct of Parties in the South China Sea (DOC) and meetings of the ASEAN–China Joint Working Group on the DOC and culminated with the 47th ASEAN Foreign Ministers' Meeting. An important breakthrough came with a regional agreement to draft the content for a long-anticipated Code of Conduct and establish a set of security norms and principles governing the behavior of all claimant states to the South China Sea. The ministers tasked senior ASEAN officials to work in tandem with Chinese counterparts on "concrete elements (in the COC) which would promote trust and confidence, prevent incidents, and manage incidents should they occur."[24]

In light of ASEAN's pushback from mid-2014 onward, more moderate views among China's policy elites surfaced to challenge the PLA's hawkish policies. For instance, questions emerged on whether the South China Sea is indeed a core national interest that should be defended at all costs.[25] A number of foreign policy elites advocated that the dispute should be subsumed under China's overall goal of maintaining a positive relationship with its neighbors to secure its right as a legitimate power.[26] According to Yan Xuetong, a leading scholar-practitioner based at Tsinghua University, strategic support from ASEAN is in fact more important than economic resources and island control in the South China Sea, underscoring the significance of working with ASEAN to reduce the likelihood of external containment strategies against China.[27] Put simply, pursuing a militant approach in the maritime dispute amounts to nothing more than a pyrrhic victory. China may be asserting sovereignty and its material power in the South China Sea, but doing so comes at the cost of losing support and credibility as a regional leader from its Southeast Asia neighbors.

ASEAN consensus and collective influence were put to the test again in 2016 following a report of China's deployment of 32 HQ-9 surface-to-air missiles (SAMs) on Woody Island in the Paracels.[28] The report alarmed ASEAN leaders, most notably because it defied and undermined the region's joint statement at the 10th East Asia Summit that called on China to honor its pledge not to engage in activities that would further militarize the dispute in the South China Sea.[29] The deployment of SAMs marked a significant military escalation and once again elevated the region's threat perception of China's unilateral and coercive moves in the maritime dispute. In response, at a special regional foreign ministers' meeting in summer 2016, marking the twenty-fifth anniversary of ASEAN–China relations, Chinese foreign minister Wang Yi sought to divide and exploit differences in ASEAN to prevent it from addressing the latest militarization activities in the Paracels and from issuing a regional statement on the conflict. Wang instead proposed a ten-point statement that merely restated general principles without directly addressing emerging regional concerns with China's South China Sea behavior.

China's initiative, however, was not acceptable to ASEAN members increasingly concerned with China's militarization in the South China Sea. In response, Malaysia released an agreed ASEAN statement stating that China's latest behavior in the South China Sea had indeed "eroded trust and confidence, increased tensions, and . . . may have the potential to undermine peace, security, and stability in the South China Sea."[30] But almost as soon as the statement was made public, Malaysia retracted it for "urgent amendments," noting that certain members, such as Cambodia and Laos, had changed their minds and backed away from endorsing it at the last minute.[31] Singapore disagreed with the retraction; rather than openly disagreeing with Wang in a public forum, Singapore foreign minister Vivian Balakrishnan, whose country held the coordinating role for ASEAN–China relations in 2016, deliberately skipped the joint press conference with Wang after the meeting. Singapore subsequently released unilaterally a summary of the foreign ministers' discussion, indicating that the original draft was indeed an agreed statement that reflected ASEAN's common position and consensus. In spite of the formal (albeit muddled) withdrawal of the statement, the fact that it was initially agreed and issued shows the effects ASEAN consensus could wield.

Bill Hayton, a longtime observer of the South China Sea conflict, pointed out that "what's remarkable is not so much that China wanted to suppress a strong statement on the South China Sea but that ASEAN was prepared to disrupt a major event, the 25th anniversary of China–ASEAN relations, in order to send a message to the Chinese government."[32] The ASEAN statement had dedicated a notable amount of space to the South China Sea, with more than half of the statement detailing the latest developments in the conflict that ASEAN could not ignore. It also stressed the need to maintain "peace, security, stability, safety, and freedom of navigation in and overflight above the South China Sea," as well as "the importance of nonmilitarization and self-restraint in the conduct of all activities, including land reclamation, which may raise tensions in the South China Sea."[33] In the face of China's attempts to divide ASEAN, the region showed clearer signs of pushing back at China's bellicose actions.

Smoking Gun Evidence: Admission of Why ASEAN Consensus Matters

Following the diplomatic fiasco in 2016, there was clear rethinking on China's part to reassess its approach, especially with regard to ASEAN's increasing concerns over its militarization activities in the South China Sea. There was an unprecedented public acknowledgment from Vice Foreign Minister Liu Zhenmin that the brewing discord in the South China

Sea had an unintended, spillover effect on China's broader engagement with its Southeast Asian neighbors: "To be honest, the disputes have affected Sino-ASEAN relations and cooperation ... we hope the Sino-ASEAN cooperation to stay unaffected. China insists on handling the South China Sea issue in accordance with the Declaration on the Code of Conduct on the South China Sea and preventing it from undermining China–ASEAN cooperation. I hope China and ASEAN nations can work in the same direction towards this end."[34]

To date, this remains the most explicit statement underscoring why ASEAN consensus matters to China in the maritime dispute. Prior to this concession, Chinese officials had always insisted on negotiating the conflict bilaterally with individual claimant states, taking a divide-and-conquer approach. But the nature of the dispute had clearly multilateralized, with ASEAN's collective effort and involvement undermining China's strategic partnership with the region as a whole, a development that China had been keen to prevent up to this point.

ASEAN leaders and China were able to reset their ties in subsequent high-level meetings in 2016. In July, for example, shortly after the public acknowledgment from China that it would take heed of ASEAN consensus, Southeast Asian foreign ministers gathered in Laos and issued a joint communiqué reinforcing regional preferences for managing the dispute: through diplomatic means and cooperative agreements. The joint statement called on China to work with ASEAN to commit to "peaceful resolution of disputes, including full respect for legal and diplomatic processes." The ASEAN gathering was convened shortly after the Permanent Court of Arbitration in The Hague issued a ruling that invalidated China's claims to historic rights within the so-called nine-dash line in the South China Sea. While the ruling on China's claims was not directly referenced in the communiqué, Singaporean foreign minister Vivian Balakrishnan observed that "it's unmistakable and unambiguous ... no one is in any doubt it's what we're referring to." Balakrishnan added that the regional consensus articulated in their collective statement "gave us the opportunity to press the reset button and to set ASEAN–China relations back onto a more positive trajectory."[35]

Shortly thereafter, the 13th Senior Officials Meeting on the implementation of the DOC achieved three major breakthroughs, each of which reflected measures that China had previously rejected or deflected. First,

ASEAN and Chinese officials agreed to establish an emergency hotline to manage fishing incidents and disputes in the South China Sea. Second, they agreed to adopt a Code for Unplanned Encounters at Sea (CUES) to reduce risks and accidental clashes on the high seas. Third, and perhaps most important, both sides agreed to fast-track regional negotiations and decided for the first time to set a hard timeline to complete the Code of Conduct in the South China Sea after agreeing to a framework on the regional security agreement aimed at moderating all the claimant states' behavior in the disputed areas of the high seas.

Sustaining strong levels of regional consensus remains a perennial diplomatic challenge for ASEAN member states. As seen in the immediate aftermath of the 2014 oil rig incident through 2016, ASEAN leaders forged a strong and unified approach that sought to constrain China's foreign policy options. To the regional leaders, China's decision to militarize Woody Island with SAM launchers meant that the country was reneging on its earlier promise not to deploy military assets in the disputed features in the South China Sea. It heightened the region's threat perceptions of China's coercive activities. To keep China's coercive behavior in check, ASEAN leaders pursued a concerted and collective effort to restrain China. With closer alignment among the ten ASEAN member states, China tempered its unilateral activities and returned to the discussion table to agree to a number of measures of restraint and to move forward on the substantive negotiations on the COC.

More recently, however, regional consensus appeared to fray again. ASEAN summit statements in 2018 showed that ASEAN consensus had weakened, compared to what was discussed and included in the summit outcomes between 2014 and 2016. Most notably, the Philippines broke ranks with the rest of the region when a senior Philippine official publicly stated what appears to be a growing dissatisfaction with the military involvement of external powers in the maritime dispute: "If there is more than one country militarizing, and it's not only the islands, if huge navies are sailing through the area, is that not militarization?. . . So we [in the region] don't even have a definition of militarization."[36] In spite of ASEAN's previously articulated consensus and support for such freedom of navigation operations (FONOPs) in the South China Sea, the Philippines reversed its position within the group and called for a clearer threshold for defining what constitutes a military threat to regional security in the South China Sea. The visible discord within ASEAN led to a clear fragmentation, and enabled China to capitalize on the weakened regional consensus with limited pushback or repercussion. Throughout 2018, after each of the two ASEAN summit statements reflected weak regional consensus, there was a resurgence in China's coercive actions in the South China Sea, including the redeployment of SAM launchers in the Paracels, as well as resumed efforts to build additional structures in the contested islets in the Spratlys, setting them up as potential militarized bases.[37]

STRONG-STATE RESTRAINT: MORE THAN JUST CHEAP TALK

In carrying out the process tracing of these cases, a counterargument could be made that China actually does not need to capitalize excessively on its material capabilities—at least not yet. From a bargaining perspective, China's restraint between 2012 and 2018 could be well anticipated. In fact, China has even shown a general willingness to negotiate due to its increasing material capabilities. If it were to face increasing instability at home and were to become desperate and vulnerable, it would not go down without a fight. For now, China is "playing nice" as it has the upper hand, with the credibility of a military threat against other claimant states; reliance on the use of force is thus not necessary at this point.

A number of implications and expectations would stem from this counterargument, if the bargaining logic holds. To begin, the empirical indicators for strong-state restraint as a legitimation strategy that we have discussed thus far would be moot; they are nothing more than cheap talk and window dressing because the alleged acts of restraint are occurring under the guise of power politics and China's material power advantages. Veiled threats and the credibility of its material capabilities mean that China does not need to use military force to exert its strategic preferences. Instead, negotiations would follow, albeit on a bilateral basis. Engaging in separate negotiations with each claimant state reflects a "divide and conquer" or "salami-slicing" approach, one that works in China's favor and consolidates its upper hand in the material power asymmetry.[38]

In addition, worried about their own survival and security, the smaller, weaker claimant states would clamor to strike a deal directly with China, jettisoning any false hopes or expectations of securing a better outcome through multilateral negotiations given their competing claims and the clashing interests among the claimant and nonclaimant states in ASEAN. Steve Chan succinctly sums up this instrumental logic and bargaining model of behavior:

> The first [Southeast Asian claimant state] to break ranks and negotiate a separate deal with Beijing is likely to receive the best terms, whereas the last holdout is likely to be left in the cold. Thus, timing seems to be important. This view points to the contesting parties' mixed motives so that all those involved would want to be the first one to strike a deal and none of them would want to be the last. This tendency could of course engender a self-fulfilling momentum to reach bilateral accords with China. At the same time, the prospect of reaching a multilateral deal is hampered by the difficulties of organizing collective action among those contesting Beijing's sovereignty claims, including those difficulties attributable to other claimants' information asymmetries and divergences in their domestic political calendars.[39]

There are several reasons why the empirical observations on strong-state restraint observed in this chapter are not just cheap talk or window-dressing tactical adjustments. First, recall the definition of restraint from chapter 2. Restraint reflects a foreign policy paradigm that has a very clear and distinct assessment of the efficacy of the use of force, either veiled or explicit. The fundamental assessment of the strategic environment is benign. As such, any security threat that arises is seen as situational and due less to the fixed nature of rival competitors than to some changeable condition of mutual interaction. Negotiations leading to multilateral agreements and cooperative security are accepted and emphasized as they help attenuate the effects of security dilemma. Large, powerful states that exercise restraint are thus adhering to foreign policy principles that are antithetical to power politics and the logic of consequences.

As a legitimation strategy, restraint's emphasis is on relational (not material) power. Acts of self-legitimation through coercion or veiled threats based on material advantages are orthogonal to the ultimate goal of attaining the recognition and validation from peers as a credible, responsible leader. Put simply, arm-twisting smaller, weaker states into submission at the negotiation table is not a reflection of strong-state restraint. So while the bargaining model may see China's reliance on the credibility of its military threat as a strategy to "play nice," such actions do not fit the theoretical model for the restraining-to-thrive legitimation strategy for large, powerful states seen here.

The empirical findings for China's restraint when there are measurable signs of strong ASEAN consensus are qualitatively different from mere window dressing or tactical adjustments. The smoking-gun evidence in 2016 furthers this distinction, as discussed earlier. In response to China's militarization in the South China Sea and attempts to pit ASEAN members against one another, ASEAN responded in a way that China had not expected when all ten Southeast Asian states—claimant and nonclaimant states alike—joined forces to lodge their diplomatic protest. That they did so at a high-profile event commemorating two and a half decades of ASEAN–China partnership further revealed their discontent with China's unilateral actions in the South China Sea. The public spat revealed two important observations: First, ASEAN members are not mere pushovers; however small and weak relative to China, they retained a high degree of agency in speaking up with a collective voice. Second, strong ASEAN consensus elicited the kind of reaction that it had been seeking collectively. The response from senior Chinese officials was indeed a public acknowledgment that the maritime dispute has been straining China's strategic partnership with ASEAN as a whole. It was unprecedented because, up to that point, China had denied any spillover effects of the conflict to the region as a whole and had preferred to isolate and contain the dispute and negotiations on a bilateral basis with each of the claimant states. ASEAN's collective pushback pointed to a larger concern at stake for China's decision makers: the possibility of losing support, credibility, and legitimacy as a regional leader among its Southeast Asia neighbors.

If such public admission were simply cheap talk on China's part, it would not have followed ASEAN's lead to accept the terms and preferences for multilateralizing the conflict. These ranged from making substantive headway on the content and timeline of the Code of Conduct in the South China Sea, setting up an emergency hotline for the disputed waters, and acceding to CUES, a regional code for mitigating accidental encounters on the high seas. The counterargument that China is simply "buying time" or adopting a "just wait" response without specifying a time frame amounts to an unfalsifiable exercise. We cannot deny that the conduct of China's policies shifted, so much so that it defies a core tenet of the bargaining model: negotiations should have been taking place bilaterally to retain China's upper hand. Instead, the empirics show that these were all diplomacy-centered and cooperative security agreements advanced through ASEAN that reflected the collective preferences of the smaller, weaker neighbors in the region and sought to enmesh China into a broader multilateral framework for dispute and conflict management.

Moreover, the Southeast Asian claimant states have neither engaged in a "race to the bottom" nor clamored to strike a deal with China separately. The instrumental logic expects a claimant state to break ranks with its peers as soon as it can to secure the best possible deal on the South China Sea dispute. But, rather than ASEAN claimant states collapsing like dominoes at China's enticement, to date no claimant state has a bilateral deal in place. With the credibility of China's material threat growing stronger over time, it is puzzling that the widening power gap has not induced the weaker, smaller Southeast Asian states to capitulate, in line with the bargaining model's expectations.

As discussed earlier, the Philippines is a good case in point. In 2012, when faced with a near-existential threat in the Scarborough Shoal, the Philippines abandoned any hopes of a regional resolution to the crisis. President Benigno Aquino doubled down on his tough rhetoric against China and sought maximum security deterrence and protection from the United States, its long-standing ally. Aquino's government also lodged legal proceedings with the Permanent Court of Arbitration to rebuff China's historical claims to the disputed waters.

Bilateral relations saw a "reset" of ties when Rodrigo Duterte won the presidency in 2016.[40] There was a dramatic reduction in the Philippines' balancing efforts against China, leading to the high expectation that the Philippines would strike the first bilateral deal of a claimant state with China on the maritime dispute. The cultivation of political, diplomatic, and economic ties with China since 2016 has advanced to a point that the costs of extricating Manila from Beijing's orbit would become so high that the Philippines would simply sign any bilateral deal with China. Yet, four years later, Duterte remained adamantly resolute that he would not cede "an inch of Philippine territory or sovereign rights to other states."[41] His administration, including senior defense and foreign policy officials, has echoed his calls, reiterated the importance of ASEAN centrality in managing the ongoing disputes to push back against China's unilateral provocations in the South China Sea, and at one point even indicated that it will adhere "without any possibility of compromise" to the 2016 international arbitration results annulling China's historical claims.[42]

Likewise, Vietnam's approach toward China in the maritime dispute stands out. It is the only claimant state in the South China Sea that has faced off with China in direct combat on three separate occasions: the Paracel Islands in 1974 (as South Vietnam), the Spratly Islands in 1988, and a three-week border war in 1979. At the same time, Vietnam remains the only claimant state that has had any prior experience (and relative success) in engaging directly with China in bilateral negotiations over sensitive sovereignty issues: the land border settlement in 1999 and the maritime boundary demarcation in the Gulf of Tonkin in 2000. The South China Sea dispute remains the last unresolved territorial issue between the two countries. There are, however, no signs of capitulation, and officials in Hanoi are in no hurry to sign a bilateral deal with China. Instead, Vietnam's negotiation position has been to maintain a steadfast policy of neutrality, captured by what observers call the "three noes": no foreign bases on its soil, no formal alliances, and no strategic leaning to third parties to oppose another country.[43] Maintaining its political independence is thus vital to Vietnam's foreign policy strategy.

Incidentally, the "three noes" embedded in Vietnam's foreign policy principles have ensured its visibility and strategic importance in the region. For instance, as discussed earlier, in the oil rig incident with China in 2014, the success of Vietnam's strategy of multilateralizing the conflict through ASEAN cannot be understated: it was able to corral all nine other ASEAN member states—including rival claimant states such as the Philippines and Malaysia, as well as nonclaimant states such as Laos and Cambodia that tend to be sympathetic to China's cause—to issue a formal statement through ASEAN on the incident, as seen in the 24th ASEAN Summit. The statement was directed at China and called for restraint. It marked the first time that ASEAN had forged a strong and unequivocal consensus on the Paracel Islands, a purely bilateral dispute between China and Vietnam. This collective approach sent a clear signal to China regarding the region's concerns and its preferred security norms of dialogue and diplomacy, as opposed to unilateral acts of coercion. That we subsequently saw a dip in China's coercive activities (see figure 3.1), including a pullback of its oil exploration activities ahead of schedule, was neither a coincidence nor cheap talk. In addition, as mentioned, domestically we saw moderate views among China's scholar-officials and the delimitation of the PLA's militant policies in the maritime dispute. While one can question the intention behind these internal decision-making considerations, the deliberations produced a concrete outcome: a recognition that attaining diplomatic support from ASEAN was far more consequential than securing economic resources in the South China Sea, the motivation that set off the oil rig dispute with Vietnam in the first place.

Taken together, the empirical observations between 2012 and 2018 reveal that none of the claimant states capitulated to China's demands in the South China Sea with any bilateral deals. Instead, the claimant states' approach was to band together whenever they could, recognizing that there is strength in numbers. We have seen ASEAN rallying together on at least six occasions during this time period. We know from the findings in this chapter what strong regional consensus looks like and its intended effects in inducing strong-state restraint in China's behavior in the South China Sea dispute. Most important, the region's perception of legitimacy matters to China's narrative as a rising power, making the latter think twice before doubling down on coercion when there is strong ASEAN consensus and pushback.

In fact, ASEAN member states have increasingly taken steps in this direction by emphasizing the importance of adhering to international law and by asserting diplomacy-based negotiations and the nonuse of force in the Code of Conduct in the South China Sea.[44] As a senior Malaysian official noted, "China has always preferred to talk separately with individual countries, so that when the countries group together there is no more need for discussion and they would just endorse what China puts on the table."[45] Southeast Asian states, no matter how small and insignificant in their material capabilities, clearly do not want to settle the maritime dispute through bilateral channels. Instead, they continue to emphasize the centrality and continued relevance of utilizing ASEAN as the key platform for negotiations with China.[46]

The probative argument on strong-state restraint is not to say that there is a linear development or trajectory in China's foreign policy behavior in the direction of restraint (or coercion); instead, it is about identifying patterns of behavior and observing the conditions under which a large, powerful state would resort to restraint as a key part of its foreign policy strategy. Observing that coercion occurs in some of the outcomes (as seen in figure 3.1) is not a shortcoming of the theoretical model here. In fact, capturing both restraint and coercion is important precisely because it demonstrates that the variation in a large, powerful state's foreign policy behavior is contingent on a nonmaterial, ideational, and external factor: strong group consensus.

Authority relations between China and ASEAN are thus multifaceted and more complex than material considerations alone, even when we see coercion in action. Why? Recall that the propensity for China to rely on its material capabilities becomes greater when there is weak external consensus constraining its options. This incentivizes decision makers in China to articulate their policy preferences through unilateral means. As discussed, we observed this firsthand with China's aggressive approach toward the Philippines in 2012. Likewise, we also noticed that, in the period leading up to China's decision to deploy SAMs on Woody Island in the Paracels, we can trace and observe that regional consensus and regional threat perception of China's activities were relatively weak. Periods of regional fragmentation allow Chinese decision makers to capitalize on these developments to define and pursue power in material terms, leading to greater reliance on material threats and coercion. As long as regional discord persists, China would continue to test the limits of ASEAN centrality and unity until the region decides to respond with a more coherent alignment of threat perceptions and is able to exert its collective influence through strong consensus again.

The variability in the probative argument here demonstrates how ideational factors can account for both deviant and nondeviant cases in international behavior. As Alastair Iain Johnston puts it, "There is no a priori reason to believe an ideational account of realpolitik [behavior] is epiphenomenal to a material structural account."[47] Likewise, if strong-state restraint as a legitimation strategy is not simply cheap talk, it further delimits the material constructs of power politics as the basis for explaining foreign policy statecraft.

SUMMARY

The implications and effects of regional security norms cannot be understated. ASEAN consensus matters more than we think in providing the kind of legitimacy that China cares about as it seeks an expanded leadership role in the region. In particular, ASEAN security norms—the organization's emphasis on diplomacy, deliberation, and decision-making by consensus—have served as the building blocks for regional stability for over five decades, and Southeast Asia has managed its regional conflicts through these shared values and principles without having to resort to the use of force. When applied to the South China Sea context, the very same norms and principles that have served ASEAN well in the past continue to have salience in its security relations with an imposing, large power like China.

When ASEAN acts as a collective bloc, its strong consensus becomes particularly effective in inducing change in the behavior of a large, powerful state like China. Between 2012 and 2018 we observed six instances in which strong ASEAN consensus and its collective influence yielded clear or relative restraint in China's foreign policy actions in the maritime dispute. In particular, strong levels of regional consensus were grounded on substantive measures, such as proposing new diplomatic actions to delimit China's coercive activities, elevating the region's concerns over specific threats like the unilateral deployment of military assets, and calling for new agreement and initiatives to regulate the behavior in the maritime dispute.

Given the conventional narrative in international politics about the behavior of large, powerful states with rising ambitions, China's military preponderance of power makes it a hard and least likely case for restraint. But this case is also all the more desirable from a social scientific perspective, as finding a positive association between ASEAN consensus and change in China's foreign policy behavior can provide substantial corroboration to the hypothesized mechanism for strong-state restraint as a legitimation strategy. It further validates the undertheorized significance of relational power in foreign policy statecraft.

Indeed, the empirical data in this chapter show that, when there is strong ASEAN consensus that enables the group to take a cohesive and collective diplomatic approach, it can legitimize cooperative behavior and restraint while delimiting the material and parochial interests for power politics in China's behavior in the South China Sea. We observe China's behavior conforming to regional concerns, particularly when ASEAN summit statements express strong consensus and the centrality of ASEAN. With China seeking regional leadership and acceptance from its peers as a legitimate power, exercising restraint becomes an appropriate and desirable course of action. The findings from this chapter shed important light on the analysis of ASEAN as a source of preference- and identity-shaping influence, especially on the ways in which China's security interests and behavior in the South China Sea are regulated and redefined through its interactions with an emerging regional security community like ASEAN.

To be sure, ASEAN member states may not be able to match China's material power head-on, but the regional organization is able to exert its collective strength through a stronger convergence of views. The pragmatic approach of ASEAN leaders means that they are preparing to cope with a rapidly changing regional security environment as it is, not as ASEAN wishes it to be. Relying on preference-shaping norms of consensus and centrality, ASEAN's response is not to retaliate with sanctions but to consistently push through a rules-based outlook to defuse tension in the maritime conflict. As Singaporean defense minister Ng Eng Hen puts it, "ASEAN has taken a practical approach to work on the Code of Conduct to constrain if not bind behavior."[48] The process may have been halting and frustrating, but persistence paid off when ASEAN committed China to a hard timeline for the completion of the COC agreement, a breakthrough that had previously proven so difficult to achieve. The significance behind ASEAN's strategy lies in its collective approach to multilateralize the conflict and to enmesh China into regional security norms, preferences, and priorities, which further raises the stakes for China to reject or deflect the consensus that matters most to the regional organization.

The next chapter looks at another important rival explanation for restraint in China's foreign policy behavior in the South China Sea. In particular, we will turn to a key exogenous factor that lies in the international distribution of power: the United States, the role of U.S. military deterrence, and its long-standing grand strategy of deep engagement in the region. If the claimant states in Southeast Asia are not rushing to sign bilateral deals with China in the maritime dispute, are they holding out for the prospect of U.S. intervention? We will assess how the causal logic behind this alternative explanation stacks up against the ideational and nonmaterial construct that underpins the book's probative argument for strong-state restraint as a legitimation strategy.

Chapter Four

A CAUTIONARY ASSESSMENT OF U.S. DEEP
ENGAGEMENT IN THE SOUTH CHINA SEA

Deep engagement is arguably one of the most commonly asserted proposi-tions for a grand strategy for the United States. Its proponents argue that increasing U.S. power projection and military presence overseas is the optimal strategy for keeping potential adversaries at bay, maintaining global security, and leading the liberal institutional order.[1] By extension, without strong levels of U.S. military presence in conflict areas, large, powerful rivals like China would emerge and behave with increased coercion and aggression and hence destabilize the status quo and under-mine U.S. material interests and relative power.

This chapter examines whether U.S. deep engagement in the South China Sea conflict, rather than ASEAN consensus, has a causal role. Empirically, the validation of deep engagement implies that changes in China's behavior in the South China Sea would be attributed to the activi-ties of a stronger and more powerful state in the region: in this case, the deterrence extended through U.S. military and security engagement—or deep engagement—in the Pacific theater. Carrying out this analytical exercise helps to assess how U.S. intervention as an alternative explanation compares to the book's probative argument on strong-state restraint. Spe-cifically, we will be able to better determine how much agency small states in Southeast Asia actually have in inducing China's restraint, and the extent to which their collective influence hinges on U.S. preponderance of power in the region.

The logic of deep engagement stands in stark contrast to the relational or social aspects of power, such as legitimacy, a central part of the present book's argument for strong-state restraint. As discussed in chapter 2, the rationale for strong-state restraint as a legitimation strategy is not materially driven. Instead, the ideational concerns for validation and acceptance by one's peers are the key social markers for an expanded and enduring form of influence, all of which are much more difficult to attain than simply relying on or exerting material force.

If the proposition that increased U.S. military presence leads to China's restraint is empirically founded, it has profound theoretical and policy implications for understanding and explaining the mechanism for restraint. These implications are not diminished by the great potential for military confrontation involving the United States, China, and ASEAN member states that comes out of the intensifying maritime dispute in Southeast Asia. For one, it reinforces the view that in a zero-sum security environment, large, powerful states with increasing material capabilities need to be kept in check with more, not less, forward deployments of military assets, as well as a doubling down on military deterrence and force posture.[2] Constraining potential adversaries, in other words, is a byproduct of deep engagement. At a time of increasing U.S.–China rivalry and competition, it undermines those calling for a reorientation in U.S. grand strategy and security priorities abroad.[3] Deep engagement provides the policy justification that maintaining and expanding U.S. security presence abroad secures and promotes U.S. interest in retaining global primacy, which concomitantly leads to regional peace, order, and stability.

Moreover, if U.S. deep engagement is actually keeping the peace and deterring China from exercising brute force in the maritime dispute, it has ramifications for the bargaining position of the Southeast Asian claimant states. The choice for these small, weaker states is clear: defer negotiations with China and bank on a better pay-off with U.S. intervention. As discussed in chapter 3, China is consolidating its material capabilities and bargaining position. By holding out, Southeast Asian claimant states will be in effect wagering that the United States will come to their aid, with U.S. deep engagement offsetting any increase in China's advantage.

But this process can likewise reverse course, whereby Southeast Asian states find themselves increasingly beholden to the uncertainties in great power relations between the United States and China. Small states can thus be easily side-stepped, with their interests undercut in the process. As such, the region has a relatively narrow space to maneuver. If it wants to avoid being caught in a lopsided conflict with China, it needs the sustained and deepening involvement of the United States.[4] Put simply, if the logic of deep engagement holds, then internationalizing the conflict remains the ideal backstop plan to prevent China from overwhelming the smaller, weaker states in Southeast Asia. As such, without U.S. deep engagement, the region would fall like a house of cards.

To determine the validity of deep engagement, this chapter begins with a discussion of the theory's logic and premise. Attempts at critiquing the theory often fall prey to the rebuttal that retrenchment entails a high-risk experiment speculating what the world would look like without an engaged superpower like the United States at the helm.[5] To circumvent the problem of counterfactuals, this chapter then carries out an empirical test to examine how deep engagement compares with the book's primary argument for strong-state restraint. The empirical data and analysis in chapter 3 show that, when there is strong ASEAN consensus to push back on China's coercive actions in the South China Sea, China responds with restraint in support of regional diplomacy to defuse tension. The next section takes the premise of deep engagement at face value and asks a basic question: To what extent does the empirical evidence in Southeast Asia support the claim that increasing U.S. military involvement—a core tenet of deep engagement—deters and restrains China's provocations in the South China Sea conflict?

Methodologically, a controlled comparison of two notable ruptures in the South China Sea assesses the logic of deep engagement: the 2012 Scarborough Shoal standoff and the 2014 oil rig incident near the Paracel Islands. Why is this pairing of events important? These two conflicts approximate an experimental logic as they mirror each other in terms of the intensity of the confrontation in all but one key aspect: the level of U.S. military involvement. This would allow us to test the saliency of U.S. deep engagement and its intended effects of constraining China's behavior in the South China Sea. If the empirical observations show that increased U.S. military presence leads to a successful pushback of China's assertiveness, then the logic of deep engagement would be robust and consistent. If not, beyond impugning the theoretical assumptions of deep engagement, it reinforces the book's main probative argument that the collective influence of ASEAN's regional consensus serves as an important determinant for China's restraint.

As will become clear, the evidence underscores the observation that the more pertinent exogenous factor for constraining China's behavior is whether ASEAN members—both claimant and nonclaimant states to the South China Sea maritime dispute—share a strong consensus, with the proxy measure being their threat perception of China's coercion. When there is unanimous regional alignment, the expectation is that ASEAN's collective influence would incentivize China to pare down its unilateral provocations, regardless of the level of U.S. military involvement in the conflict. Put simply, deep engagement is neither necessary nor sufficient for constraining China's actions in the South China Sea. In fact, China's bellicose behavior appears to correlate with increasing levels of U.S. military presence in the maritime dispute, especially when there is a visible fragmentation of regional threat perceptions.

The purpose of this chapter is not to conclude prematurely that U.S. grand strategy based on active military deployment in Southeast Asia to deter and constrain potential adversaries like China is never useful, but rather to caution that deep engagement needs to be situated with a deeper understanding of the ASEAN's collective position and threat perceptions of China. If the expansion of U.S. military power projection alone is neither necessary nor sufficient for constraining China, and by extension maintaining stability in the South China Sea, then a more nuanced assessment of how ASEAN leaders view their security relations with the United States and China along with a recognition that Southeast Asian institutions and interests matter would provide a more targeted and effective U.S. security strategy in the region.

THE LOGIC OF DEEP ENGAGEMENT

The logic behind deep engagement fundamentally rests on the conventional narrative of power politics, specifically the structural effects of the international system.[6] Simply put, the distribution of material capabilities in an anarchic security environment incentivizes states to stay on the offensive in order to increase their relative power and to ensure their survival at all costs. States that are relatively weaker are coerced or forced to pare down their foreign policy activities due to the threats and looming presence of larger states, which command a more robust military force as a form of deterrence.[7] This emphasis on material capabilities is indicative of the notion that "might makes right." The weaker states are constrained and kept in check by the material power and advantages of the larger and more powerful states.

This deterrence-based logic has underpinned an important aspect of U.S. grand strategy for seven decades: that an active and vigilant U.S. military presence abroad is critical to minimizing any disruptions by adversaries and any security challenges to U.S. national security. At its core, deep engagement is concerned with the dominant U.S. security presence that allow it to issue threats and enforce military actions and punishments to constrain a potential adversary's behavior. As Stephen Brooks, G. John Ikenberry, and William Wohlforth, explain, such a strategy is meant to ensure continued U.S. primacy because "leadership facilitates cooperation to address security challenges and expand the global economy, and moves the cooperative equilibrium closer to U.S. preferences."[8] Even scholars who call for a more prudent application of power acknowledge the importance of the United States maintaining a robust security dominance to ensure its position at the helm of the current U.S.-led security order.[9] By extension, without sustained levels of power projection abroad, U.S. security interests would be undermined, and potential adversaries would respond to a leadership vacuum with more direct challenges and hence destabilize the status quo.

Given this premise, how might we observe the logic of deep engagement—specifically the increase in U.S. military presence and involvement in security conflicts abroad—and its intended effects in the South China Sea? The variable outcome of interest here is China's foreign policy behavior in the maritime dispute. Empirically, a deterred China would pare down its unilateral provocations as a direct consequence of U.S. military involvement in the maritime conflict. Conversely, the absence of a U.S. military presence to constrain China would mean that the latter would act with increasing belligerence. We should thus observe a stronger tendency for China to initiate threats, intimidation, and coercion in the South China Sea in relation to Southeast Asian claimant states. Such actions emphasize the efficacy of the use of force and a preference to increasingly rely on material power capabilities in the maritime dispute.

There are, however, several assumptions embedded in the logic of deep engagement that undermine the causal effect in the theory, especially when applied to Southeast Asia. For instance, proponents of deep engagement assume conflict as a constant feature in international security and minimize the importance of nonmaterial incentives and compromises as effective alternatives to managing security threats.[10] As Stephen Walt observes, a "paranoid frame of mind" underpins the strategy, whereby "U.S. leaders sell deep engagement by convincing Americans that the nation's security will be fatally compromised if they do not get busy managing the entire globe."[11] Little has changed in this mindset in the three decades since the end of the Cold War. The George H. W. Bush administration's controversial "Defense Guidance" of 1992 that was leaked to the press boldly asserted that the United States was now the most powerful state in the world.[12] To retain its global primacy, the United States would not tolerate any peer competitor.

Ten years later, in October 2002, the same security outlook was echoed in George W. Bush's "National Security Strategy," where "preemptive war" became a strategic priority and the United States would keep any rising powers in check to maintain its commanding position in the global balance of power.[13] Similarly, the priority list of Barack Obama's new defense strategic guidance, announced in 2012, called for the United States to deter and defeat aggression globally. The strategic guidance identified and invoked concerns with states such as China and Iran and emphasized the need to continue power projection in areas where U.S. access could face disruption.[14]

Putting the United States on a constant state of alert is meant to keep rising challengers in check in order to maintain its commanding position and material advantage in the global balance of power. For example, the Department of Defense's *Indo-Pacific Strategy Report* has drawn the foregone conclusion that China is a revisionist power.[15] In response to China's emerging threat to U.S. national security, the U.S. Indo-Pacific Command (INDOPACOM) has made a $20 billion special funding request from the U.S. Congress for the necessary resources to implement a strategy of active deterrence by 2026. The fund would pave the way for the establishment of a new "Pacific Deterrence Initiative (PDI)," similar to the Pentagon's

European Deterrence Initiative that funds projects focused on deterring Russian aggression in Europe. Voices outside the defense and military establishments have also expressed concerns about the emergence of a large, powerful state like China to challenge U.S. preponderance of power. In a report issued by senior U.S. policy elites in 2018, China's growing regional and global influence was deemed a serious threat undermining U.S. national security and democracy.[16] In a dissenting opinion on the report, Susan Shirk finds that an overstatement of such threats "risks causing overreactions reminiscent of the Cold War with the Soviet Union."[17]

But a security strategy that is underwritten by deterrence and containment is rather limiting in helping us understand the diminution of conflict and the long stretches of stable relations, not least in Asia.[18] Policy and theoretical scholarship that begins by assuming another rival must be contained, and that assumes doing so is the only possible course of action, unnecessarily restricts the full range of foreign policy statecraft and results in potentially misleading analysis. Doing so can have the effect of determining the outcome before even starting the analysis: if one balances, then the other state is a threat and must always be deterred.

Moreover, deep engagement presupposes that moving the equilibrium of power dynamics closer to U.S. security preferences is essentially what other countries around the world desire. This is reminiscent of the ethnocentric underpinnings of U.S. officials' thinking throughout the Cold War. Robert Jervis warns that,

> like most theories of international relations developed by Americans and West Europeans, it is grounded on the experience, culture, and values of the West; deterrence theorists usually assume that while countries differ in the goals they seek, they see the world in the same way. Others may hold a strategic doctrine that lags behind that of the United States, but they will eventually come around to the "correct" way of seeing things.

Perhaps more pointedly, Jervis warns that "although deterrence theory leads us to see that it is sometimes in a state's interest to pretend to reject a doctrine whose validity it actually accepts, it does not consider that people from other cultures might develop quite different analyses."[19]

While deep engagement through military deterrence and containment worked and continues to be a priority for the United States to retain its global preeminence, it may not necessarily apply to the increasingly complex power dynamics in Southeast Asia. As David Kang explains, relying so overwhelmingly on the Anglo-Saxon experience and history to understand international politics elsewhere in the twenty-first century risks "getting Asia wrong."[20] Actively confronting and deterring China with power projection activities might make sense for officials in Washington. But for those witnessing China's rise at the frontlines in Singapore, Hanoi, or Jakarta, a security strategy based on military assertions to settle an ongoing dispute with a formidable neighbor makes less sense. In fact, it is an oversimplification of the complex manner in which a state's foreign and security policy is crafted. Situating the security factors alongside economic and social domains of interaction among countries is important for creating a fuller analysis of a state's priorities in a particular region or with another state.[21] As referenced in the preface, Ambassador Chas W. Freeman, Jr., identifies a key problem with the logic of a security strategy based primarily on active deterrence and containment, pointing out that "we have a copious literature of coercion. We have almost no literature of persuasion, and yet in ordinary life, when we have a problem with our neighbor, if we're wise, we don't pull the gun and say submit or else."[22]

Southeast Asian decision makers have always engaged in what Evelyn Goh calls complicity with and resistance to external powers, particularly the United States and China.[23] This position is perhaps clearest with Indonesia, a pivotal member of ASEAN. Even though it has no territorial disputes in the South China Sea, Indonesia has seen increasing levels of China's incursions in the EEZ of its Natuna Islands. One would expect that engaging in closer security cooperation with the United States would be part of Jakarta's foreign policy priorities. Yet in October 2020 Jakarta publicly rebuffed a proposal by the United States that its P-8 Poseidon patrol aircraft land and refuel in Indonesia while carrying out maritime surveillance in the South China Sea.[24] When U.S. secretary of state Mike Pompeo visited Indonesia and sought clarification, Indonesian officials did not budge. Like their peers in Southeast Asia, Indonesian officials prefer resolving differences through diplomacy. In fact, Indonesia has never allowed foreign military operations in the country, a reflection of its long-standing commitment to neutrality.

Simply put, the logic of consequences derived from material capabilities and distribution of power that is at the center of deep engagement is but one lens to view and understand state interactions, particularly between large powers and smaller actors in a region. To assume that a region shares identical concerns as the United States obscures the possibility that two neighboring states in the same region may hold different views on the efficacy of the use of force. The United States and China may be facing off in competition for regional hegemony, but few in Southeast Asia feel the necessity to choose sides. As Jeffrey Bader explains, from a U.S. perspective, "our security, and that of our partners, will not be aided, however, by a strategy that suggests we have decided that China is, or inevitably will be, an adversary. Our allies and partners in Asia certainly welcome our presence, security and otherwise, in the face of a rising and more assertive China, but they do not welcome hostility toward China."[25] It is not surprising that, so far, few Southeast Asian leaders appear willing to make the costly domestic and economic tradeoffs that would be required for major and sustained investments in their offensive military capabilities, preferring not to be "trapped by this [U.S.–China] rivalry."[26]

Calls for outright balancing against China's rise are thus more reflective of a longer-term U.S. concern and strategy to preserve its position in the region than ASEAN member states' immediate security concerns. The Malaysian defense minister emphasized the significance of regional consensus and unity in the South China Sea by underscoring that "as a coalition of ten countries, I am confident that even China cannot take us lightly or ignore our stand."[27] If Southeast Asian states are not resorting to their militaries as first responders to China's activities in the South China Sea, then a more muscular U.S. military role and involvement, one that is premised on the logic of deep engagement, needs to be considered with caution and placed in the broader context of understanding Southeast Asia's security approach.

INFERENCE STRATEGIES

What inference strategies might help us assess the noticeable effects of the two exogenous factors on China's activities in the South China Sea? If the proposition for deep engagement holds and is empirically supported, we would expect to see China's restraint as an observable outcome. Such a change in foreign policy behavior would be a function of the high levels of U.S. military presence and involvement in the conflict in an effort to push back on China's activities in the South China Sea that are seen as challenging or undermining U.S. security strategy. Most visibly, these U.S. activities might include carrying out joint military exercises with affected claimant states in the region, holding high-level security dialogues, and deploying military assets to carry out freedom of navigation operations (FONOPs). All these would demonstrate U.S. resolve to maintain its security commitments and overall leadership in the region and to promote and protect U.S. national security. The logic of deterrence and the overwhelming presence of superior material capabilities would induce a potential adversary like China to reduce and scale down its unilateral activities (see figure 4.1).

As such, empirical evidence in support of the argument of deep engagement would expect China's restraint as an outcome, regardless of the level of regional unity among ASEAN members. Simply put, whether ASEAN is united or divided—on its threat perceptions of China or on a set of preferred security norms in response to the emerging threat—would bear little to no consequential impact on China's behavior. At most, ASEAN unity would be a secondary or supplementary factor. What would be most important and would serve as the main determinant for constraining the activities of a potential adversary is U.S. military presence and involvement. This is observed in figure 4.1, where we take the logic of deep engagement at face value to look at the expectations of its effects on China's

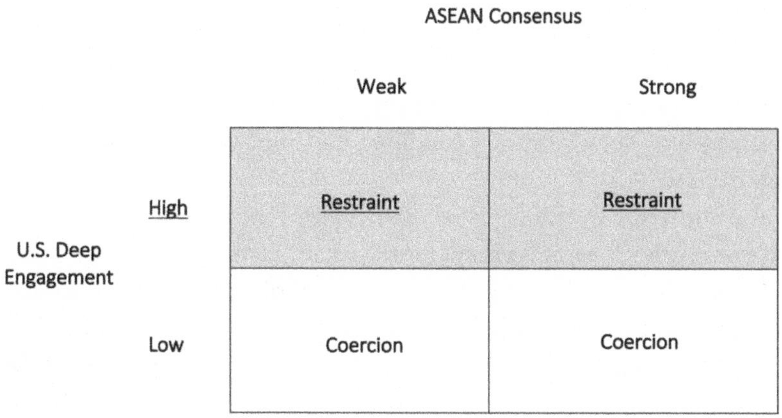

FIGURE 4.1. Expectations of deep engagement's effects on China's behavior in the South China Sea conflict.

behavior in the maritime conflict, and where China's behavior is independent of ASEAN consensus. Consequently, if the U.S. military factor were removed or absent in the South China Sea conflict, the theoretical expectation and inference would be for China's assertiveness and coercion to continue unabated, leading to instability and rising security tensions in the region.

This contrasts with the book's probative argument, which focuses on ASEAN consensus and delimits the logic of U.S. deep engagement. In this approach, the level of regional consensus on the threat perception is the more likely factor for observing change in China's foreign policy, in the direction of either coercion or restraint in the South China Sea. When ASEAN members do not share a strong, collective threat perception, we would expect to see increasing belligerence and coercive activities by China. This would occur especially when the Southeast Asian claimant and nonclaimant states are divided on the security norms and diplomatic approaches needed to respond to the emerging security threat emanating from China's exertion of its material capabilities in the maritime dispute. But when ASEAN member states are united, the strong group consensus in itself would be expected to constrain and push back against China's bellicose behavior.

As a direct extension of this inference strategy, the expected foreign policy outcomes in figure 4.2 further suggest that, if China's coercive behavior results from weak ASEAN consensus in spite of increasing U.S. military involvement in the South China Sea, then deep engagement is not a sufficient condition for inducing China's restraint. Moreover, if China's restraint is a direct function of strong ASEAN consensus and occurs even when U.S. military involvement in the conflict is absent, then U.S. deep engagement is not a necessary condition for China's restraint in the maritime dispute.

A comparison of two "most similar" cases—the cases that are comparable in nearly all aspects except for the causal factor in question—allows us to gauge how variance (e.g., the presence or absence of that key variable) may explain the difference in outcome.[28] The controlled comparison in the pairing of the cases here achieves this objective by identifying the difference in the level of U.S. security involvement and its corresponding impact on the outcome in each of these two similar events in the South China Sea. It helps us test the logic and validity of deep engagement and assess how its

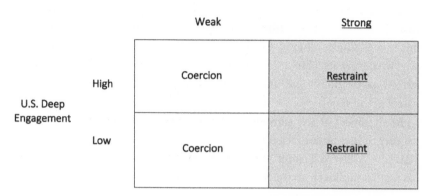

FIGURE 4.2. Expectations of ASEAN consensus's effects on China's behavior in the South China Sea conflict.

explanation compares to the present book's core argument, that is, ASEAN consensus in the maritime dispute. The following two subsections turn to this exercise.

Behavioral Test I: The Scarborough Shoal Standoff in 2012

The logic behind deep engagement in the Scarborough Shoal standoff in 2012 between the Philippines, China, and the United States does not appear to operate as stipulated by theory's assumptions. The empirical evidence in this first behavioral test suggests that, contrary to the claims of deep engagement, increasing and expanding U.S. military involvement in the conflict does not deter China, nor is it a sufficient condition for inducing restraint and stability in the maritime dispute. Moreover, the problem is exacerbated by the lack of a strong, cohesive regional unity regarding the threat perception of China's activities in the Scarborough Shoal.

In April 2012 a Philippine Navy surveillance aircraft detected eight Chinese boats fishing illegally near the Scarborough Shoal. The Philippine Coast Guard deployed a cutter to arrest the fishermen but did not realize that Chinese maritime surveillance vessels were also in the area. These intercepted to prevent the Philippines from detaining the fishermen. Chinese maritime vessels in the Scarborough Shoal demanded that Philippine forces withdraw and used a rope barrier across the reef, effectively taking over the area and blocking Filipino fishermen from accessing it for over two months. In mid-June U.S. officials helped broker what they thought was a deal for a mutual withdrawal between Philippine and Chinese forces in the reef. Outnumbered and lacking viable alternatives, Manila eventually withdrew its ships. China, in contrast, failed to comply with the agreed-on deadline, and its maritime vessels remained on near-constant patrol at the shoal.

At the onset of the standoff, the Philippines took steps to clarify the validity of its Mutual Defense Treaty (MDT) and alliance with the United States. A twelve-day joint exercise—the Balikatan—took place less than 150 nautical miles from the Scarborough Shoal as a sign of U.S.–Philippine solidarity. The war-gaming portion of the joint military exercise was in fact expanded at the last minute as an "important warning signal" to China.[29] Shortly thereafter, in the bilateral U.S.–Philippine "2+2 Meeting," Secretary of State Hillary Clinton and Secretary of Defense Leon Panetta met with their Philippine counterparts to reiterate the security alliance, with Clinton stating firmly and unequivocally that the United States will honor its treaty obligations under the MDT.[30] Within weeks of the high-level meeting, the U.S. Navy deployed a fast-attack, nuclear-powered submarine, the USS *North Carolina*, to the Philippines' Subic Bay. The presence of robust U.S. naval forces amid the Scarborough Shoal stand-off reinforced the deterrent aspect of the military involvement of the United States in the conflict. When Philippine president Benigno Aquino visited Washington in June 2012, the summit was meant to further signal U.S.–Philippine alliance in the face of China's belligerence in the Scarborough Shoal, with President Obama reaffirming the centrality of the MDT that binds the two countries in a security partnership.

Even with the high and visible levels of U.S. military engagement throughout the conflict in the Scarborough Shoal, China appeared largely undeterred. With each step that the United States took to reaffirm and support its Southeast Asian treaty ally, there was a reciprocal, counterbalancing reaction from China. For instance, almost immediately after the Balikatan exercise, China and Russia conducted their own joint exercise in the Yellow Sea, focusing on maritime defense and the protection of navigation rights. In addition, following the U.S.–Philippine 2+2 Meeting,

China announced a unilateral ban and trade sanctions targeting the Philippines' agricultural products. Additionally, China issued a travel advisory leading to the cancellation of scheduled Chinese tour groups and flights to the Philippines. Further economic pressure was exerted when China announced a fishing ban in the Scarborough Shoal, warning that foreign fishing vessels that violated the ban would face severe consequences. In other words, repeated invocations of the MDT and enhanced U.S. security commitment and direct involvement in the conflict were thoroughly ignored by China. Not only did Chinese government vessels maintain and increase their deployment and presence in the shoal, they effectively took over control when the Philippines withdrew its ships.

At the regional level, ASEAN member states were divided on their response to China's behavior and the Philippines' position. Most prominently, ASEAN failed to rally around a common stance at its regional high-level meeting in early July 2012 where, for the first time, no joint communiqué was issued at the 45th ASEAN Foreign Ministers' Meeting. A close reading of an important primary source—the meeting's transcript—reveals that a majority of Southeast Asian countries, including Brunei, Indonesia, Laos, Malaysia, Singapore, and Thailand, preferred to focus the discussion on developing a Code of Conduct for the South China Sea as a way to defuse regional tension, rather than dwelling on the divisive and contested nature of territorial sovereignty. The Philippines, in contrast, insisted that the communiqué mention China's expansionism in the Scarborough Shoal and put on official record the gross violations of the Philippine's territorial sovereignty by China's maritime activities.

A detailed account of the discussion among regional leaders illuminates the clear absence of regional consensus. Cambodia, as the rotating chair of that meeting, objected to Manila's request, explaining:

> When you say violation of Scarborough Shoal, we have to know to whom it belongs. We are not a tribunal. Maybe it belongs to the Philippines, I don't know. I still don't understand, when we said disputed areas that covers all the areas disputed. Why should we add the shoal and EEZ and continental shelf? Before we go to the concluding session, I propose we delete the South China Sea in the joint communiqué, and proceed without paragraph 16. I have no other recourse. Or claimant states will deal directly with China.[31]

While the statement from China-friendly Cambodia was expected, it is important to underscore that other countries at the meeting also had major reservations about the Philippines' proposal for the substance and wording of the joint communiqué. Regional fragmentation stemmed in large part from the competing and overlapping sovereignty claims in the South China Sea among Southeast Asian states themselves. For instance, Malaysia's foreign minister insisted that "the violation of regional norms is happening. Nowhere did we mention that it [Scarborough Shoal] belongs to one country or another. Instead of 'affected shoal' we put it as 'disputed area.'"[32] Malaysia's proposal, however, was rebuffed by the Philippines with the clarification that the Scarborough Shoal was not a disputed area, underscoring again its territorial sovereignty. Indonesian foreign minister Marty Natalegawa attempted to break the deadlock and explained that the term "disputed areas" is preferable as there is no prejudice to national claims, adding, "We don't think that this issue is impossible to resolve."[33]

The negotiated compromise aimed at forging regional unity fell through when Vietnam broke ranks. Hanoi has a different set of ongoing disagreements with China over the Paracel Islands in the South China Sea, particularly over oil rights in its EEZ. Vietnam rejected the usage of the term "disputed areas" in the communiqué, explaining the "EEZ is not a disputed area, certainly not. Some countries try to turn an undisputed area into a disputed area."[34] The meeting eventually concluded without any final joint statement from the region, an unprecedented situation for ASEAN. As Carlyle Thayer observes, "The Philippines may have overplayed its hand with misguided expectations of receiving support from fellow ASEAN members and its U.S. alliance. Some ASEAN members and even Filipino activists have expressed misgivings about how Manila confronted Beijing. In the words of one Filipino senator, the Philippines found itself an orphan."[35]

In short, the Scarborough Shoal standoff serves as the most likely case where the logic of deep engagement would have applied. U.S. involvement—in the forms of staging joint military exercises, holding high-level security dialogues, publicly reaffirming a bilateral security alliance, deploying naval assets to the conflict area, and hosting a summit to demonstrate its resolve and unequivocal commitment throughout the Scarborough Shoal crisis—was meant to deter and push back against China's bellicose behavior. We should thus have observed a more constrained China as a result of the direct and prominent role of U.S. engagement in the conflict. In fact, the empirical observations suggested otherwise. Rather than backing off, China doubled down on its presence in the Scarborough Shoal, stationing more patrol boats and surveillance vessels that harassed and rammed Philippine fishing boats. It also imposed unilateral fishing bans and trade sanctions on the Philippines. That deep engagement at face value was not a sufficient factor for inducing stability and restraint in the South China Sea meant that it fails to explain this most likely case, further raising doubts about the theory's logical consistency and persuasiveness.

The absence of strong regional consensus on China's destabilizing activities and the Philippines' cause in the Scarborough Shoal also meant that ASEAN did not exert timely and sufficient collective political and diplomatic pressure on Beijing. The visible discord within ASEAN prevented any meaningful resolution and facilitated China's continued militarization in the Scarborough Shoal without any regional pushback or repercussions. As U.S. involvement did not restrain China, the absence of strong regional consensus enabled China's belligerence and its ability to make provocative unilateral actions that heightened tensions throughout the Scarborough Shoal standoff in 2012.

Behavioral Test II: The Oil Rig Incident in 2014

According to deep engagement's logic, the absence of robust U.S. military involvement in regional hotspots means that potential adversaries like China would act without restraint, increasing the overall likelihood for regional instability and the latter's aggressiveness. The oil rig conflict between Vietnam and China in 2014, however, does not appear to operate as stipulated by the corollary argument of U.S. disengagement. Nor does the available evidence in this case support the claims that deep engagement is a necessary condition for regional stability. Moreover, the lack of U.S. military involvement in the oil rig incident actually points to the significance of ASEAN unity and collective response in constraining China's unilateral provocations.

China's abrupt deployment of the forty-story oil rig Haiyang Shiyou 981 in the disputed Paracel Islands of the South China Sea in early May 2014, along with an armada of nearly a hundred fishing and coast guard vessels, shocked the region and particularly Vietnam, a rival claimant to these islets in the South China Sea. Like the Scarborough Shoal confrontation, this particular incident reflected an equally coercive behavior. Vietnam protested the oil rig deployment and confronted the Chinese armada with its own coast guard and fishing fleets. Tensions ratcheted up, with both sides keeping count of the repeated ramming of boats and other damage from the confrontations at sea.

The United States stayed largely above the fray throughout the incident, limiting its involvement to diplomatic outreach shortly after the confrontation broke out. For instance, Secretary of State John Kerry spoke to his Chinese and Vietnamese counterparts, expressing concern over the incident as early as May 2014. But, beyond Kerry's phone conversations, the United States did not provide more substantive forms of military presence or support in the Paracels, a stark and important contrast to its involvement in the Philippines–China conflict in the Scarborough Shoal in 2012. U.S. officials invited Vietnam's foreign minister to visit Washington at the height of the dispute, but Vietnam turned down the offer.[36] Instead, it concentrated on regional efforts to help resolve the conflict.

Shortly after the oil rig entered Vietnam's EEZ, Vietnamese officials sought support and solidarity from neighboring countries to push back against China's actions. In the lead-up to the 24th ASEAN Summit hosted by Myanmar in May 2014, Deputy Foreign Minister Pham Quang Vinh indicated that he would elevate the oil rig crisis in the agenda and push for a collective agreement with his peers on defusing the conflict through international law, nonuse of force, and diplomacy.[37] The Vietnamese delegation to the regional summit lobbied for widespread support and sought unanimous consensus from both claimant and nonclaimant states to the South China Sea. When the region's foreign ministers met in May, they issued an unprecedented stand-alone joint statement specifically on the South China Sea. The statement expressed "serious concerns over the ongoing developments in the South China Sea, which have increased tensions in the area."[38] Officials at the meeting underscored the importance of regional norms that included maritime security and freedom of navigation in and flights above the South China Sea. It was a timely joint communiqué, agreed on and released days after the oil rig incident broke out.

The ASEAN Foreign Ministers' Statement was subsequently endorsed at the highest levels by regional heads of state at the 24th ASEAN Summit. Most notably, Vietnam had successfully solicited the unanimous endorsement of ASEAN leaders to support an early conclusion of the COC to mitigate escalating tensions in the region. There was clear convergence from both claimant and nonclaimant states alike on the emerging threat of China's unilateral provocations, and Vietnam made a persuasive case about the danger that China's oil rig activity portended for regional security. As discussed in chapter 3, Vietnam's strategy of multilateralizing the oil rig crisis was unprecedented. The direct call for China's restraint and for returning to the COC negotiations saw ASEAN's strong consensus coalescing for the first time on the Paracel Islands, a bilateral issue between Vietnam and China.

With strong ASEAN consensus on Vietnam's diplomacy-centered approach during and after the oil rig incident, China appeared keen to prevent the conflict from spiraling into an all-out confrontation and diplomatic fiasco. In addition to stepping up its negotiations with ASEAN counterparts regarding the COC, in June 2014 Chinese state councilor Yang Jiechi paid a visit to Hanoi for the Joint Steering Committee for Bilateral Cooperation, a long-scheduled annual meeting between the two sides. In public, Yang expressed disappointment with the increasing number of anti-Chinese riots across Vietnam. But Yang's discussions behind closed doors with senior Vietnamese officials, including Nguyen Phu Trong, general-secretary the Communist Party of Vietnam, were aimed at containing the spillover from the oil rig incident and working with Hanoi's proposals broached earlier at the ASEAN summit.[39] In turn, Vietnam's collective leadership decided to reciprocate the gesture by not lodging legal actions against China at that point and to focus instead on working toward the COC with ASEAN counterparts and China.[40] The crisis came to an end with the withdrawal of China's oil rig in mid-July 2014, a month earlier than planned. The regional pressure and diplomacy saw step-by-step measures toward restraint and paved the way for the timely and face-saving exit of the Chinese oil rig.

The oil rig incident from May through July 2014 revealed Vietnam's preference for strong ASEAN consensus, a stark contrast to the Philippines' reaction in the 2012 Scarborough Shoal standoff. Hanoi sought and received support from its neighbors, with ASEAN displaying a united front in responding to China over the oil rig dispute. Likewise, Vietnam's adroit regional diplomacy was supplemented with its cautiousness toward involving the United States in the conflict. Asked whether Hanoi was moving into the U.S. strategic orbit, Vietnamese deputy defense minister Chi Vinh Nguyen responded pointedly, "I don't think so. We are standing alone. We don't stand on one side or the other side."[41] Even without any direct U.S. military involvement throughout the conflict, China eventually pared down its bellicose actions.

According to the logic of deep engagement, the turn of events that unfolded in the oil rig crisis would seem least likely for China to exercise restraint. U.S. military involvement was virtually absent throughout the conflict. Without U.S. deterrence and military support to defuse the conflict and respond directly to China's provocative behavior, the logic for deep engagement dictates that China would have responded with increasing belligerence. Yet regional tensions de-escalated as a result of strong regional consensus and ASEAN's collective pushback against China. Vietnam rallied the regional organization in a series of high-level meetings to help ensure that both claimant and nonclaimant states in Southeast Asia understood the broader implications for regional security of China's provocations in the South China Sea. ASEAN's threat perceptions about China aligned, and its collective influence induced China to commit to regional negotiations on the Code of Conduct and to withdraw the oil rig from the Paracel Islands ahead of schedule. Remarkably, a deterred China occurred in spite of U.S. noninvolvement in the conflict, indicating that deep engagement in itself is not a necessary factor for restraining China.

U.S. DEEP ENGAGEMENT WITHOUT ASEAN CONSENSUS: MORE TURBULENCE AHEAD

Sustaining strong levels of regional consensus remains a perennial challenge and opportunity for ASEAN member states. As discussed earlier with the oil rig incident, ASEAN member states were able to overcome internal differences and their competing claims to forge a strong and unified diplomatic response and approach to China's unilateral and coercive activities in the Paracel Islands.

More recently, however, regional consensus appeared to unravel. The discourse analysis of ASEAN summit statements for 2017–2018 (see appendix) reveals that ASEAN consensus has weakened compared to what was discussed and included in the summit outcomes from 2014 to 2016. Most notably, the Philippines broke ranks with the rest of the region when a senior Philippine official publicly stated what appears to be a growing dissatisfaction with excessive U.S. intervention in the regional dispute, and specifically at the increasing frequency of U.S. FONOPs.[42] As a senior defense official in Manila explained, referring to the United States, "They have the luxury of sailing through the South China Sea to make their point about freedom of navigation in international waters, but the vessels come and go quickly. The region, however, is stuck in this quagmire and has to live with the consequences. Each time a FONOP occurs, we see tensions inch up and have to wonder who and what is this for after all."[43] In other words, the Philippines' concerns over FONOPs target the lack of clarity of purpose in these operations. Rachel Odell's research on U.S. FONOPs since 1991 shows that such naval operations are fundamentally carried out to sustain U.S. command of the sea, with selective engagement in areas that would ensure continued access to strategic straits and littorals.[44] As Nick Bisley explains, the controversy surrounding FONOPs and their implications for territorial claims and state sovereignty—sensitive topics for all claimant states to the maritime dispute—are not unfounded: "A FONOP should not happen because of a sense that something must be done to push back against a country that seems to only understand the currency of force. Such a rationale massively increases the risks of miscalculation and escalation, badly overstates the ability of such an operation to achieve the lofty goals of pundits and politicians, and needlessly increases the temperature in a region which is already pretty febrile."[45]

With the Philippines wary of excessive U.S. naval sail-bys and FONOPs in the region, the weakened ASEAN consensus allowed China to capitalize on the regional fragmentation with limited pushback or repercussions. Throughout 2018, after each of the two ASEAN summit statements that produced weak regional consensus, there was a resurgence in China's coercive actions in the South China Sea, including the redeployment of SAM launchers on Woody Island in the Paracels, as well as resumed efforts to build additional structures in the contested islets in the Spratlys, setting them up as potential militarized bases over time.[46]

The security dilemma in the South China Sea has again intensified with regional fragmentation and with increasing levels of U.S. military activity in the region, particularly FONOPs. Barack Obama's two-term administration carried out six publicized FONOPs in the South China Sea. Within the first eighteen months of the administration of Donald J. Trump, there were already seven such operations. In fact, the continuation of and increase in U.S. FONOPs in 2018—three such operations bimonthly within the first six months—were strong security concerns for Chinese foreign policy decision makers. Two U.S. warships, for example, sailed within the territorial waters of the Paracels in May 2018, an unprecedented military maneuver reflecting a doubling-down of the logic of U.S. deep engagement in the South China Sea. As a Chinese security policy specialist puts it, "The Nansha [Spratlys] region faces severe military pressure, especially since Trump took office and increased freedom of navigation patrols. So, China has raised its threat assessment."[47] The tit-for-tat militarization in the South China Sea supports the analysis in chapter 3 regarding the uptick in China's assertive behavior in 2017–2018 and reflects a new empirical reality: with ASEAN divided and its collective consensus weakened, an increasing frequency of U.S. FONOPs over the same time period appeared to track closely with China's increasing turn to coercive activities in the South China Sea (see figure 4.3).

SUMMARY

The findings of this chapter show that deep engagement is neither necessary nor sufficient for constraining China's provocative behavior in the South China Sea conflict.

On the one hand, taking the logic of deep engagement at face value, increasing U.S. military involvement should have deterred China's destabilizing actions in the Scarborough Shoal standoff in 2012. Instead, we saw the opposite, unintended consequences of deep engagement—continued bellicose behavior by China throughout the conflict. Hence, U.S. involvement was not a sufficient condition for restraining China from taking unilateral actions disrupting the status quo. Moreover, ASEAN fragmentation—due to competing and irreconcilable national interests among its member states—meant that the lack of strong regional consensus on China's provocations in the Scarborough Shoal led to raised tension in the South China Sea.

On the other hand, in the wake of China's deployment of the Haiyang Shiyou 981 oil rig in Vietnam's EEZ in 2014, ASEAN took the unprecedented step of responding to the dispute with a unified, common position. Regional leaders, including those from claimant and nonclaimant states

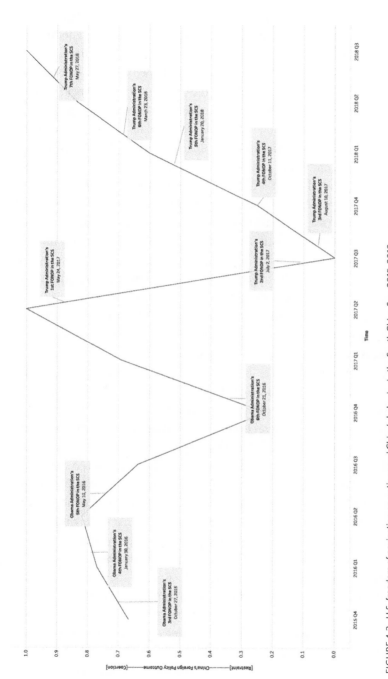

FIGURE 4.3. U.S. freedom of navigation operations and China's behavior in the South China Sea, 2015–2018.

Note: Measure of China's behavior from 2015 to 2018 is based on data from figure 3.1. The full data set is available for review from the author, including the program file and script in Python used to generate the results in the figure.

alike, were determined not to repeat the diplomatic fiasco in Cambodia in 2012 when its foreign ministers failed to issue the customary joint communiqué. While the region's states were not formally allied, their concerns about China's provocation were more closely aligned. A series of high-level regional meetings between ASEAN and China throughout the oil rig incident banded the region together to collectively press China to rekindle multilateral negotiations on the Code of Conduct. Vietnam's regional diplomacy paid off, with China withdrawing its oil rig ahead of schedule.

Most significantly, the conflict between Vietnam and China in 2014 eventually ratcheted down with the conspicuous absence of any form of U.S. military involvement. In fact, Vietnamese officials publicly insisted that they did not see the need for U.S. security engagement. China's restraint, however reluctant, demonstrated two empirical observations: U.S. military involvement is not a necessary condition for deterring China; and ASEAN consensus, especially with regard to a closer alignment of its threat perception, provides an effective pushback against China's provocations.

The latter finding, in particular, demonstrates that the smaller, weaker states in Southeast Asia retain a large degree of agency, especially when they band together and exert their collective influence. That there is strength in numbers further underscores that the region may not be in such a dire predicament as proponents of deep engagement would argue. Even if the Southeast Asian claimant states do not settle and accept Beijing's terms on the South China Sea on a bilateral basis, it does not mean that their bargaining position has weakened or that their prospects for securing a better deal by holding out has diminished. Neither are the Southeast Asian states clamoring for U.S. intervention to improve their odds of survival and security against a formidable giant like China in the maritime dispute. Instead, working through and with their peers in ASEAN's diplomacy- and consensus-based approach remains the preferred security strategy in managing Southeast Asia's security dynamics with external powers.

Moreover, as discussed, the security dilemma in the South China Sea tends to intensify when regional fragmentation is exacerbated by increasing levels of U.S. military activities in the region, as seen in 2017–2018. Increasing U.S. FONOPs—at least half a dozen of them at that time—when the region is divided and lacks a cohesive approach toward China's provocations in the South China Sea invites the opposite and unintended consequence of deep engagement: increasing belligerence and coercive activities in China's behavior in the maritime dispute. In fact, the empirical findings and data show that there is a tit-for-tat dynamic between China's behavior and increasing levels of U.S. military involvement in the region through its FONOPs—these end up increasing China's coercive actions in the South China Sea. Put simply, the empirical findings show that deep engagement's emphasis on the material basis of power is neither necessary nor sufficient for inducing restraint in a potential rival's foreign policy behavior.

The findings discussed here make a careful evaluation of the intended—and unintended—consequences of deep engagement in one of the most consequential security disputes and provide a firmer empirical basis from which to gauge the conditions under which U.S. deep engagement is a force stabilizer. That China's restraint has little to do with U.S. preponderance of power and its military involvement in the South China Sea delimits and impugns the argument for deep engagement in Southeast Asia (see the summarized argument in figure 4.4). This is not to say that the United

ASEAN Consensus

		Weak	Strong
U.S. Deep Engagement	**High**	**Coercion** (Example: 2012 Scarborough Shoal standoff)	**Restraint** (Examples: 2016 Code for Unplanned Encounters at Sea signed; emergency hotline established; and draft of Code of Conduct timeline set)
	Low	**Coercion** (Examples: 2017 and 2018 unilateral deployments; fortification; and land reclamation)	**Restraint** (Example: 2014 Paracel Island oil rig incident)

FIGURE 4.4. Why U.S. deep engagement is neither necessary nor sufficient for China's restraint in the South China Sea.

States should opt for a complete withdrawal from the region. On the contrary, the United States is and will remain a pivotal power in the Pacific theater, but it can do more with less. This would require that the United States relies less on a strategy that fundamentally rests on the logic of military deterrence and does not expend its material capabilities as a first resort for every security problem in the region. As Hal Brands explains, "The durability of U.S. pre-eminence, in other words, depends not just on how much power America possesses, but on how benign and broadly beneficial that pre-eminence is seen to be."[48]

Instead, a recalibration of U.S. security strategy as a force multiplier requires a more effective display of leadership and authority. The U.S. role in addressing the demands of regional security can benefit from a more thorough understanding of Southeast Asia's evolving threat perception of China. As the empirical findings in this chapter demonstrate, Southeast Asian regionalization has a distinct approach toward curbing China's increasing material power capabilities in the South China Sea. ASEAN may not always be successful in confronting China, especially when there is regional fragmentation. But when there is strong regional consensus, ASEAN's unity and collective influence have been shown to counter and moderate China's behavior in the maritime dispute. By throwing its weight behind ASEAN's diplomatic preference for a rules-based approach to managing the South China Sea conflict, the United States would be in a much stronger position to enhance its standing and role in the region. This is particularly acute for the new U.S. administration in Washington. Future scholarship and policies that call for more a robust U.S. military involvement in the South China Sea would thus need to be considered with prudence and placed in the broader context. First and foremost, this requires understanding of the significance of Southeast Asian countries' preferences, threat perception, and security priorities.

Having tested the book's probative argument against this alternative explanation of U.S. deep engagement, in the next chapter we apply the hypothesized mechanism for strong-state restraint to the broader contours of China's foreign and security policy.

Chapter Five

CHINA'S IDENTITY AS A LEGITIMATE POWER

When a large, powerful state jostles for regional and global influence, concerns often arise about the implications for order and stability in the international system. The political phenomenon behind the rise of China is without exception. Much of the uncertainty and anxiety stem from an overarching question: How will the power represented by China's expanding influence in global affairs be defined?

On the one hand, the unprecedented growth in China's economic and military capabilities for over three decades suggests that an impending struggle in the current international order is all but inevitable.[1] As China actively carves out and widens its spheres of influence, it could take the necessary steps to define a "new type of great power relations" aimed at, and in direct competition with, the United States. This would change the balance of power in the region and the broader international system in potentially disruptive and unpredictable ways.[2] On the other hand, conflict between China and the world can be minimized through an interlocking web of international institutions, economic interdependence, and invocation of deep historical-cultural ties, all of which are aimed at incentivizing constructive engagement and ensuring mutual gains and reassurance.[3]

The jury is still out on the kind of power that will eventually define China's surge. While power politics, unilateralism, and coercion could become the new normal in China's grand strategy, cooperative diplomacy cannot be ruled out altogether either. Neither narrative is a fait accompli, nor are there foregone conclusions with regard to the ongoing debate on the future direction of China's rise.

In this chapter we focus on two analytical observations to expand on the book's probative argument on strong-state restraint. First, we will explore in greater detail the broad contours of change and continuity in China's contemporary foreign policy and strategy. Moving beyond a dichotomized pessimist–optimist debate on the implications of China's rise, it is important to look at a key part of the analysis that is often missing in the conventional narrative: how China's foreign policy decision makers view themselves and their position in the region and in the world, with the important recognition that such debates and discussion are deeply affected by and interact with incentives and constraints from outside. Understanding how China's scholar-practitioners assess authority relations between large and small states can help us gain greater insights into what kind of power China seeks to attain. In so doing, we will highlight the significance of external consensus as a legitimation strategy for a large, powerful state like China. Put simply, how others view and perceive China's rise matters, especially as the country's leadership and policy elites process and negotiate the different responses to the external normative influence and expectations of a legitimate power's behavior and conduct in global security.

Second, we will test and apply the book's probative argument for strong-state restraint in other security issues, especially in areas that affect China's parochial interests and material capabilities and are thus least likely to engender restraint as a foreign policy outcome. Beyond the crucial test case of the South China Sea discussed in chapters 3 and 4, how and where might the causal mechanism apply in other consequential cases and issue areas? A plausibility probe case study is discussed in the latter half of this chapter to look at the changes behind China's position on peacekeeping, sovereignty, and intervention. Perhaps no other issue in international security has seen such a drastic change in China's foreign policy position. From actively resisting and fighting against peacekeeping operations that were once seen as excessive U.S. and Western interventions and incursions in state sovereignty, in just two decades, China has emerged as the largest contributor to such multilateral security initiatives among the permanent members of the UN Security Council. Why and how has this happened? To what extent does the probative argument for strong-state restraint discussed in this book capture this dynamic change in China's foreign policy behavior?

Carrying out this additional probing exercise to examine how and why strong-state restraint as a legitimation strategy explains this remarkable transformation helps extend the analytical value of the book's argument beyond China's security dynamics with ASEAN in the South China Sea dispute. If the presence of strong, external consensus incentivizes a large, powerful state to accept restraint in other domains in international security, we are then able to conclude with a greater degree of confidence that cultivating habits of noncoercion can indeed occur without material threats, retaliatory measures, or formal sanctioning mechanisms. As such, behavioral change in the direction of restraint can be attributed to an action–reaction dynamic, reinforced by exposure to the consensus of regional and international norms.

CHANGE AND CONTINUITY IN CHINA'S FOREIGN POLICY STRATEGY

The increasing gap in material capabilities between China and its neighbors is regularly cited as a factor likely to disrupt or destabilize the status quo. By most measures, China has all but completed a regional power transition, with the distribution of material power and wealth changing rapidly over the past generation. For instance, China's share of Asia's gross domestic product (GDP) grew from 11 percent in 1990 to 43 percent in 2016, while Japan's share shrank from 62 percent to 28 percent.[4] Over the same time period, China's GDP increased thirtyfold to more than $9.5 trillion, and its economy is now widely recognized as the world's second largest. China's GDP per capita approaches $10,000, and its defense spending currently accounts for nearly 15 percent of total global military expenditure.[5] Most remarkably, unlike other large, powerful states with expansionist policies in the twentieth century, China's ascendance to regional dominance has occurred in the absence of an all-out war with its neighbors or with the United States, the current superpower.

Even with this widening material gap in the region, continued reassurance and emphasis on stability remain important foreign policy priorities for China. Qin Yaqing, a prominent international relations scholar-practitioner and past president of China Foreign Affairs University, cautions against the Chinese leadership adopting impetuous foreign policy pronouncements, arguing that "a strident turn from one strategy to the other is inadvisable, and indeed continuity through change is a realistic description of China's present international strategy."[6] That China's foreign policy strategy stems from a balance of continuity and change in the Chinese leadership's priorities and goals means the regime continues to be guided by a long-standing central tenet in the country's grand strategy: maintaining a peaceful and stable external security environment is critical for continued domestic growth and development. Domestic stability is of utmost priority for a developing state like China, and much of the leadership remains focused on maintaining and sustaining the developmental take-off at home as its primary responsibility. This core principle builds on Deng Xiaoping's vision in the early 1980s, when he observed that with the world tending toward peace and development, the prospects for major, global wars were diminishing. As such, China could expect to benefit from a long and stable stretch of relative peace and stability in the international environment to carry out much-needed domestic reform and ensure a more balanced growth to narrow the widening urban–rural divide and developmental gap.

In early 2000 Chinese leader Jiang Zemin effectively presented the country's "new security concept," which followed Deng's advice of maintaining the nexus between external stability and internal development in China's overall foreign policy approach. Chinese foreign policy elites also began to comment on and discuss publicly the idea and vision of China's "peaceful rise." Zheng Bijian, a senior adviser to the Chinese leadership, articulated this notion in an article in *Foreign Affairs* in late 2005 that acknowledged China's expanding influence and posited that its emerging role on the global stage would be conducive to regional peace and international security.[7] Similarly, an editorial in *Liaowang*, a widely read and influential CCP domestic and foreign affairs journal, pointed out:

> Compared with past practices, China's diplomacy has indeed displayed a new face. If China's diplomacy before the 1980s stressed safeguarding of national security and its emphasis from the 1980s to early this century is on the creation of excellent environment for economic development, then the

focus at present is to take a more active part in international affairs and play a role that a responsible power should on the basis of satisfying the security and development interests.[8]

In other words, the message regarding China's newfound power and influence was articulated to reassure its peers and neighbors in the region and beyond: that China intends to augment its own economic growth and influence through securing mutually beneficial outcomes. The underlying objective behind the notion of a peaceful rise or development was to advance China's foreign policy prerogatives that would mitigate apprehensions about any sudden changes or disruptions to the global balance of power, and to "put its relations with the United States on more solid footing and deflect lingering U.S. concerns about China's emergence as a more powerful player."[9]

Reaffirming these preceding concepts in contemporary Chinese foreign policy goals, Xi Jinping put forward the concept of the "Chinese Dream" upon taking over the helm of the CCP. The Chinese Dream has been linked to Xi's call for the "great rejuvenation of the China nation," achieved through maintaining stable external conditions for China's reform, development, and stability.[10] This vision promotes two major aspirations that are of significance for the legitimacy of the CCP and the Chinese state: first, the aspiration to build a "moderately well-off society" by 2021, the hundredth anniversary of the founding of the CCP; and, second, the vision of becoming a fully developed nation by 2049, coinciding with the hundredth anniversary of the establishment of People's Republic of China. Undergirding Xi's vision is the confidence in what China has already accomplished—a tenfold increase in its GDP per capita in under three decades. Assuming a trajectory of steady (albeit slower) growth in the next thirty years, China's income level would be on par with the United States, Japan, and most of the European Union's advanced economies.

The implications of the Chinese Dream for the country's emergent identity as a legitimate power are manifold. It consolidates such enduring themes as the "new security concept" and "peaceful rise" into a new ideological foundation that Xi coined upon consolidating his power base. In a major policy document in late 2013 penned by China's state councilor Yang Jiechi, Xi's Chinese Dream is a cornerstone vision and guiding ideology that represents "a continuation and development of the important thinking of China's peaceful development in the new era." Most important,

Yang underscored that the concept reaffirms—rather than negates or undermines—past goals and strategies, all the while crediting Xi's contribution in linking principles with practice. The socioeconomic objectives behind the Chinese Dream, when achieved, would strengthen and augment China's wealth and position in the region, placing it on a level competitive playing field with the United States and Japan in the Pacific realm. Yang reassured that, in spite of China's growing material capabilities, "promoting healthy and stable relations with the United States, as well as with Beijing's other major diplomatic partners, is the inherent requirement of the 'two centenary goals' and the inevitable demand for our overall strategy of peaceful development."[11]

To clarify how China intends to exert its newfound material capabilities, additional emphasis has been placed on deepening China's regional leadership and global diplomacy. At a major policy study conference in October 2013, Xi reaffirmed some of the core visions and principles of China's foreign affairs, including the "period of strategic opportunity" through the 2020s for China's continued growth and development. He also reminded party cadres of the importance of maintaining a stable external environment to attaining its goal of building a well-off domestic society. More notably, the emphasis on the nexus between domestic growth and international stability has been repeated and validated at every party congress since 2007, as well as in the country's national defense white papers since 2000. In a report assessing Chinese foreign policy strategy, Christopher Johnson explains the significance behind the revalidations of these domestic–international linkages and the enduring and understated importance of the nonmaterial sources of China's power:

> With China's rapid military modernization and sizeable year-on-year defense budget increases, it is easy to lose sight of the fact that the "period of strategic opportunity" acts as an important conceptual brake on a runaway military buildup. Implicit in its characterization of China's priorities is the notion that economic development—and not the path of arms races and military adventurism followed by the Soviet Union—is paramount in securing the country's return to global pre-eminence. As long as the concept remains in force, there will be hard limits on Beijing's willingness and ability to set out on a truly revisionist course aimed at fundamentally reshaping the balance of power in East Asia.[12]

External recognition—especially regional and global perceptions of China's rise—matters, as it continues to weigh at the forefront of the country's foreign policy calculus. Xi, for instance, has underscored that China must strive to make its neighbors "more friendly in politics and economically more closely tied to us," to treat regional neighbors as "friends and partners, to make them feel safe and help them develop," and to forge a stronger sense of "common destiny" between China and its neighbors in the regional community.[13] This approach reflects an active foreign and security policy strategy to secure the support and validation from its peers as a credible security and economic partner. It also appears that China's leadership believes the country's outreach and focus on mutually beneficial outcomes will in due course convince and persuade its neighbors that there is more to gain from working with China than from deterring and challenging it, all with the added benefits of preventing the formation of a containment coalition against China on its periphery.

Subsequently, at the CCP's Central Conference on Foreign Affairs Work in November 2014, Xi called for a "new great power diplomacy with Chinese characteristics," one that would include a "new type of great power relations with the United States."[14] The signal was clear: that China intends to have a more even-keeled relationship with Washington in which the parties can complement each other and compete on an equal footing in the region and beyond. To achieve this, China would need to adopt the strategy of "striving for achievements" within and beyond its borders. In addition to strengthening its material sources of power through continued economic reform at home, there remains a strong emphasis on the benefits and urgency of increasing bilateral and multilateral diplomatic and economic activities in and around the region. This dual approach builds on China's long-standing strategy of strengthening its domestic development while actively carving out its own space in regional politics and global diplomacy through multilateralism. Johnson observes that China's perceivable "less awestruck view of U.S. power also has the important side effect of imbuing Xi with greater confidence to more deliberately court contributions from China's other important foreign partners rather than pursuing a single-minded focus on the United States."[15] Such a policy pursuit would deter neighbors in the region from enacting policies that run counter to China's interests, with the larger and longer-term goal of delimiting U.S. influence and rebalancing efforts in Asia.

Herein lies the potential danger and disruption associated with a large, powerful state emerging on the international stage. As China's leadership strives for achievement and seeks power parity with the United States, the rapid increase in the country's material capabilities will continue to occur in tandem with its desire for external recognition as a legitimate power. This requires a delicate balancing act, not least because of the nationalistic tendencies to exert China's newfound and increasing levels of military prowess to defend such core interests as sovereignty and territorial integrity.[16] As long as the material power differential between China and its neighbors persists and continues to widen, there will be concerns about China's intentions and resolve. At worst, continued uncertainty over power redistribution and an intensifying security dilemma could trigger a balance-of-power politics and thus increase the overall likelihood for conflict and confrontation.[17]

WHY DOES EXTERNAL CONSENSUS MATTER FOR CHINA'S RESTRAINT?

Although the strategic rationale behind "striving for achievements" is often externalized and characterized as a form of power play, the imperative for international recognition and legitimacy could arguably be the single-most important foreign policy priority for China's leadership. Yong Deng's analysis reflects the fact that China's foreign policy behavior thus far has excluded the extreme options of being "systematically confrontational" or "wholesale pro-Western." Any impulse for revisionism is "balanced by the need to seek acceptance from, and interdependence with, the dominant great power group, neighboring states in Asia, and other key players in world politics."[18] Even as China's material capabilities grow at an astounding rate, the desire for legitimacy and recognition from its neighbors and peers remains a powerful impetus and incentive for taking on self-constraining commitments and supporting international institutions. Simply put, if what its peers and neighbors think about China's rise matters and continues to be among the foremost of China's foreign policy objectives, then restraining power politics in order to achieve recognition and validation as a legitimate power remains an important underlying facet of its foreign policy statecraft.

To be sure, striking the right balance between material power and international recognition remains a challenging task. As discussed, to a large extent the external projection of China's newfound power mirrors the ongoing debates and discussion among Chinese scholars and policy elites on how best to define the sources of the country's comprehensive national power. This diversification of views helps us glean how China's leading strategists and policy elites are thinking about the kind of power—material or relational—that will define the country's growth trajectory. For instance, a number of influential Chinese scholar-practitioners, such as Liu Mingfu and Yan Xuetong, contend that China's ultimate foreign policy goal is to replace the United States, and, as such, confrontation and rivalry between the two are inevitable.[19] Likewise, they stress the primacy of material power, defining it as economic, technological, and military strengths, as well as governmentality and national cohesion, all of which are critical for China to restore its rightful place in the region and the world as it vies for global influence and leadership.

Other scholar-practitioners caution against such overreliance on China's nascent and untested material capabilities. For example, Wang Jisi, a prominent member of the Foreign Policy Advisory Committee of China's Ministry of Foreign Affairs and former dean of international studies at Peking University, calls for the country's leadership to maintain a low-profile approach in its external affairs. While China may have ascended to become the world's second largest economy, it lacks buy-in, widespread support and recognition, and legitimacy in the eyes of its neighbors. Wang notes that China "still lags far behind the United States, Japan, and Europe as regards innovation, quality of life, and soft power influence."[20] Recognizing this inherent weakness in China's regional and international standing, Wang Huning observes that culture and values are indispensable to a country's comprehensive power.[21] Wang was one of the first political theorists to introduce the concept of soft power in China's political discourse. His influence has been elevated in the CCP, where he chairs the party's central policy research office and its Central Guidance Commission on Building Spiritual Civilization and currently ranks as one of the seven most powerful leaders in the Politburo Standing Committee. It is expected that his emphasis on the relational aspects of power will be widely considered in future foreign policy decision-making processes as the collective leadership determines the kind of power that would help with the successful implementation of Xi's vision for "national rejuvenation" and the Chinese Dream.

In examining how China can ascend peacefully without disrupting the international system, a number of leading Chinese scholars have pointed out the significance of maintaining a reinforcing pattern of interaction between its material power and international recognition. For instance, Qin Yaqing observes that China's identity as a responsible great power can "expand its security interests and promote good interaction between China and international society."[22] Qin's previous portfolio as head of the primary institution responsible for training China's diplomatic corps adds significant weight to this important call for continued reassurance and to heed the concerns of China's neighbors. Similarly, in Liu Feitao's influential scholarship on China's foreign affairs, he identifies the linkage between power and responsibility in constructing a rising country's identity, noting that there needs to be "an adequate exertion of power."[23] Even Zhang Ruizhuang, a scholar who has been a frequent advocate for a more realpolitik foreign policy approach, acknowledges the need for strategic restraint, especially at the critical juncture where the country's material power is becoming more formidable: "China's rise has generated strategic uncertainty and anxiety in the West (especially in the United States), and that China must now be extremely cautious and prudent."[24]

The emerging domestic debate among some of the leading policy elites on China's power and identity points to at least two important implications. First, it suggests that China's foreign policy decision-making process has become more varied, whereby a "more complex decision-making process has created space for diverse voices to emerge."[25] This may seem counterintuitive, given Xi Jinping's consolidation of power in the decision-making process in China's domestic and foreign policies. In October 2016 Xi was awarded the title of "core" leader, after becoming leader of the party, the military, and the state, as well as heading at least a third of the key decision-making groups within the CCP. Subsequently, the National People's Congress eliminated the two-term limit for the presidency, opening a pathway for Xi to extend his stay in power after 2023, when his second presidential term ends.

Nonetheless, evidence of the proliferation of advisors involved in the decision-making bureaucracy is very much present in China. While Xi has enhanced his consolidation of power by holding key positions in the CCP, the military, and the state apparatus much more quickly than expected, it remains an open question whether he enjoys the same kind of authority that previous leaders like Mao Zedong and Deng Xiaoping commanded. The party communiqué that awarded Xi the title of "core" leader was equally careful to emphasize that the collective leadership system "must always be followed and should not be violated by any organization or individual under any circumstance or for any reason."[26] Likewise, even with the elimination of term limits in March 2018, there were clear signs that the retirement age of 68 and the "longstanding norm of institutional balancing in the Politburo" remains in effect and will not be altered.[27] As Yan Xuetong puts it, "Power refers to control or impact on others by coercive force, while authority means leadership that others willingly accept."[28] Xi's leadership is thus qualitatively different from Mao's or Deng's, precisely because the country is "no longer principally led by one strong individual."[29] It reflects and continues to resemble a "fragmented authoritarian" regime,[30] where consensus among select members, committees, and factions in the party and in the state apparatus remains the key prerequisite for determining the outcome of any major policy decision.

Given the contending voices and points of view about how China should exert its newfound power and project its influence abroad, the second key implication is clear: There is no foregone conclusion internally—as of yet—about the future direction of China's grand strategy. Surveying and monitoring how China's leadership and some of the country's leading policy elites continue to address the differential between the material and nonmaterial sources of power can help us gain important insights and greater clarity on the latest thinking about China's trajectory. The debate and discussion appear to be oscillating between two major and distinct foreign policy paradigms: continue to augment material capabilities and exert those advantages unilaterally, with the understanding that external concerns and perceptions are orthogonal to the pursuit of China's material power and interests; or maintain a path of cooperative diplomacy, with the expectation that China would conform to international norms that have widespread support and strong consensus to achieve the long-sought recognition as a legitimate great power.

Behavioral changes between coercion and restraint are thus continuously reflected in China's evolving foreign policy strategy. As discussed in chapter 3, strong-state restraint is very much a dynamic process, reflective of a "two steps forward, one step back" approach. The likelihood of China exercising restraint in the South China Sea increases when there is strong ASEAN consensus as an incentivizing, causal factor. Clarity and unity in ASEAN's threat perception, security concerns, and diplomatic initiatives to reduce tension in the South China Sea provide a collective pushback against China's unilateral and coercive policies. Such strong levels of regional consensus to defuse tension through diplomatic means give pause to decision makers in China who might wish to double down on the use of force or capitalize on material capabilities. When smaller, weaker actors speak with one collective voice, their concerns are amplified, further reminding China of the social costs and repercussions of ignoring or deflecting the interests and priorities of its neighbors at a time when it is seeking their support and validation as a legitimate leader in regional security.

As such, the presence of strong external consensus sets the stage for shifts in China's foreign policy calculus so that it becomes more attuned to and consistent with the security norms, preferences, and values espoused by ASEAN, the collective group from which it seeks to gain deference and acceptance. By extension, the internal discussion among foreign policy elites in China on what constitutes power changes. The emphases on legitimacy and diplomatic approaches to navigate the sensitivities around the maritime dispute become more salient and viable as a foreign policy consideration, reflecting the primacy and impact of regional norms and expectations. References to the strong consensus at the regional level sharpen the focus and discussion on the relational aspects of power, reducing the overall incentive for the use of paramilitary or military force or for adopting coercive, offensive policies that protect and promote China's material interests. As discussed in chapters 3 and 4, observing these empirical developments in China's decision-making process becomes important, additional inference strategies for understanding and explaining the extent to which strong ASEAN consensus has a preference- and identity-shaping effect on China's foreign policy.

Furthermore, recall from earlier discussions that coercion can also occur as a foreign policy outcome. In particular, the odds for China's belligerent activities increase when there is regional fragmentation—where the ten ASEAN member states are unable to agree on a collective approach to managing their maritime dispute with China. As such, foreign policy advisors and advocates for asserting China's claims and capitalizing on the country's material advantages become more prominent. Without external pushback or repercussions, regional discord provides a strategic opportunity through which more hawkish and militant views—such as those emanating from the People's Liberation Army—are able to assert the benefits of flexing China's material power. As such voices dominate the narrative and expand their influence in the foreign policy decision-making process, more disruptive and coercive actions erupt in the South China Sea.

It is important to look at the discussion and debates that shape China's outlook on its position in the region and in the world. Doing so enables us to understand the competing views on power and influence and provides insights into how China's leadership and policy elites are responding to external pressure and to expectations of a legitimate power's behavior. In short, these deliberations further underscore the extent to which adhering and conforming to external consensus matters for China's rise and identity as a legitimate power.

Beyond the South China Sea, where else might we see strong-state restraint as a legitimation strategy in China's foreign and security policy? We turn next to look at other pertinent security issues: peacekeeping, sovereignty, and intervention. Carrying out a plausibility probe case study helps with the sharpening of the hypothesis and the refinement of the operationalization of the key causal factor.[31] As will be discussed in the next section, authorization of and participation in UN peacekeeping operations touch on key, sensitive foreign policy issues that often seem incompatible with core principles of China's foreign policy, namely, noninterference in other states' internal affairs and state sovereignty. Applying and testing the argument on strong-state restraint here is thus challenging but all the more desirable from a social scientific point of view to substantiate and expand the explanatory power of the book's probative argument for strong-state restraint.

CHINA'S POSITION ON PEACEKEEPING, SOVEREIGNTY, AND INTERVENTION

China's deployment of uniformed personnel to UN peacekeeping operations has steadily expanded more than twentyfold in the past three decades. With nearly 2,500 troops—in the form of contingent troops, engineers, military experts, logistical support units, formed police units, and medical staff—China deploys more peacekeeping personnel in the field than all the other permanent members of the UN Security Council combined and ranks higher in overall peacekeeping contributions than any European or NATO country.[32]

This reflects a significant and puzzling development: Why would a large, powerful state with increasing material capabilities cede control of key aspects of its military to a multilateral peacekeeping force? Existing studies that argue peacekeeping contributions grow out of national security prerogatives have notable shortcomings.[33] If the motivation were primarily driven by material interests, then there would be concomitant efforts to minimize constraints on its military forces placed under broad UN managerial oversight. Troop deployments would likewise be ad hoc and result from political expediency, rather than increase steadily in both qualitative and quantitative terms over time. Put simply, sending critical military assets to far-flung and hostile security environments in the absence of tangible, material gains would be relegated as an anomalous behavior, not the norm.[34]

Recent research has also found that peacekeeping participation tends to expand as the level of democracy increases within troop-contributing states. The logic is that elected governments are more well-disposed to supporting democratic principles and ideals as a means of achieving international peace and security.[35] But this finding does not account for why nondemocracies, especially those that happen to be large, powerful states with increasing material capabilities, might make long-term contributions to such multilateral security initiatives.

As Alex Bellamy and Paul Williams put it, "to understand variation in peacekeeping contributions we must understand variation in the way states construct their interests."[36] Relational and ideational factors like legitimacy are not mere afterthoughts for foreign policy decision makers, nor are they epiphenomenal when weighed against material considerations. For instance, the level of international consensus on peacekeeping norms and intervention among member states of the UN Security Council or regional bodies like the African Union (AU) affects troop-contributing countries' outlook on supporting and contributing to such multilateral security initiatives. Consistent with this book's probative argument on strong-state restraint, where there is a clear and cohesive consensus on managing or addressing a particular security conflict, the odds of a large, powerful state rejecting or deflecting such agreements decrease, in spite of the relative costs to its own material power. We should expect to see official policy pronouncements and practices consistent with those agreed on by regional or international security institutions and the deployment of its armed forces and other resources to support the established agreement and consensus on peacekeeping as well as greater pragmatism and flexibility on issues of sovereignty and intervention.

The likelihood for restraint in foreign policy orientation is thus premised on identifying and observing the strong consensus that helps forge and incentivize a large, powerful state's positive-sum and cooperative behavior in UN peacekeeping, mitigating the negative effects of conflict and violence in an anarchic international security environment. Exercising restraint provides a more enduring form and display of power and influence, precisely because it is augmented by legitimacy and acceptance from others. Large states are more sensitive to such concerns: for a rising power aspiring to global leadership, exercising restraint enables further recognition from its peers. The privileges and rights that are conferred on large, powerful states also mean that they have an additional responsibility and obligation to pull their weight in contributing to peace and security in the international system. Moreover, the authority relationship between a large and a small state comes with an understanding that the former is expected to act with moderation and caution, and that it does not radically seek to overturn the established norms and institutions at the expense of others. In sum, as a social compact between a large, powerful state and its smaller peers, legitimacy is bestowed on the former by the latter when there are clear and consistent provisions of public goods in such forms as the facilitation of conflict mediation and resolution through UN peacekeeping.

Empirically, examining China's expanding engagement in UN peacekeeping operations bears a number of theoretical and empirical implications. That restraint remains a viable consideration for China's foreign policy statecraft delimits the conventional wisdom about a large, powerful state's tendency to disrupt order and stability in the international system. Even as China's material power increases at unprecedented rates, the growing gap and power differential do not automatically incentivize it to act on narrow self-interests or unilateral approaches to security. Evidence of change toward restraint and support for multilateral security initiatives like UN peacekeeping challenges the prevailing assumptions about its behavior in an anarchic security environment, not least in defending the sanctity of state sovereignty and in rejecting external interventions.

Most important, carrying out a plausibility probe on strong-state restraint as a legitimation strategy here helps substantiate the broader analysis in this chapter on the considerations that factor into China's narrative and identity as a legitimate power. We will apply and test the book's conceptual and theoretical framework on strong-state restraint and identify how, why, and when cooperative security strategies and self-constraining commitments take form in the context of China's position on peacekeeping, sovereignty, and intervention.

THE CONTEXT OF CHINA'S CHANGING APPROACH

Since the founding of the People's Republic in 1949, China's views toward, and ultimately participation in, UN peacekeeping has seen significant twists and turns in policy and practice. In the first decade after China was admitted to the United Nations in 1971, its foreign and security policy decision makers viewed UN peacekeeping operations with a significant degree of skepticism, maintained a low profile on peacekeeping issues, and refrained from taking substantive actions in the Security Council debates on the subject.[37] This cautious approach reflected a traditional and narrow interpretation of positive international law and its application with regard to sovereignty: China maintains the inviolability and sanctity of the principle of state sovereignty, often questioning the necessity of external interventions in areas of conflict, even if a particular operation was sanctioned by the Security Council and was operating under the auspices of international peacekeeping forces. Undergirding this long-standing skepticism were China's earlier experiences and encounters, particularly during the Korean War in 1950–1953, where the PLA fought UN forces under U.S. command. It thus harbored serious concerns about the nature and legitimacy of interventionist operations, particularly those that are driven and led by Western states.

A shift in China's position on peacekeeping became more evident in the late 1980s. In 1988 China became a member of the UN General Assembly's Special Committee on Peacekeeping Operations (known as the C34), which paved the way for a gradual increase in its engagement in multilateral peacekeeping initiatives. It started with the deployment twenty military observers to the UN Transition Assistance Group (UNTAG) to help monitor elections in Namibia. This was followed by contributing five military observers to the UN Truce Supervision Organization (UNTSO) in the Middle East. Perhaps the most significant break with past practices came with the decision to deploy four hundred engineering troops and forty-nine military observers to the UN Transitional Authority in Cambodia (UNTAC) in 1992, in spite of its relatively underdeveloped power-projection capabilities at the time. As one senior Chinese official put it at the time, all states should lend "powerful support" to peacekeeping, setting a new tone for Chinese pronouncements in support of the UN peacekeeping regime.[38] Chinese decision makers were likely concerned with China's image and reputation, particularly after the Tiananmen crackdown in 1989, and sought external confirmation as a peaceful neighbor.[39]

Throughout the 1990s and early 2000s, China's participation in peacekeeping activities expanded and diversified. Following the UNTAC deployment, China's contributions to UN peacekeeping ranged from fifty to one hundred peacekeepers per year in the decade from 1993 to 2002 and then quickly grew in 2003 (see figure 5.1). In 2014 China made an unprecedented decision to send combat troops to UN missions. This included 170 infantry personnel to Mali to provide security to the eastern headquarters of the UN Multidimensional Integrated Stabilization Mission in Mali (MINUSMA). It was followed by a seven-hundred-strong infantry battalion deployment to support the UN Mission in South Sudan (UNMISS). At the Peacekeeping Leaders' Summit in New York in 2015, Xi Jinping announced that China would set up a permanent peacekeeping standby force of eight thousand troops ready for rapid deployment whenever necessary.[40] The Chinese troops on standby registered with the UN include infantry battalions, sapper units, transportation and logistical detachments, and helicopter units. In addition, Xi pledged that China would contribute $100 million in military assistance to the African Union over the following five years to help support the operationalization of the African Peace and Security Architecture, building the AU's capacity to respond to humanitarian emergencies and crises. If China continues on its current trajectory and maintains its level of commitment, it could be an "important peace broker in conflicts around the world," as António Guterres noted in 2016 in his meeting with senior Chinese officials shortly after taking over as UN secretary-general.[41]

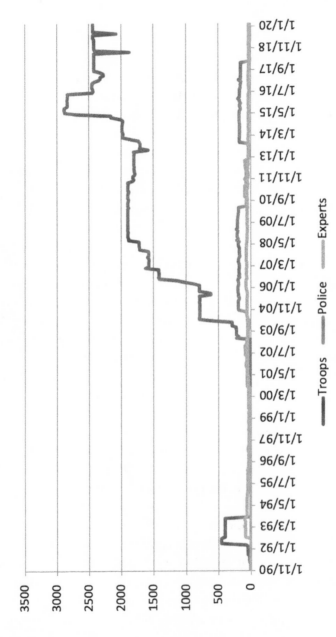

FIGURE 5.1. China's uniformed personnel in UN peacekeeping operations, 1990–2020.

China's participation in UN PKOs demonstrates just how far its foreign policy has shifted from initial opposition and skepticism to the latest deployment of critical assets like infantry battalions. Given China's increasing material power and military capabilities, ceding command and control over a key part of its armed forces to a multilateral peacekeeping bureaucracy delimits the country's sovereign right to national self-defense. In fact, it transfers that right to the United Nations, where collective security outweighs national security and where the interdependence of states' security is prioritized over attaining security through unilateral means.

This transformation in Chinese decision makers' foreign policy paradigm on multilateral security and UN peacekeeping operations is remarkable. The key rationale for the plausibility probe is to identify how the new ideas that underpin this transformation were introduced by the emergence of a global consensus on the security norms related to peacekeeping, sovereignty, and intervention. The next section looks at precisely how the book's causal logic for strong-state restraint has induced changes in the direction of restraint in China's foreign policy calculus.

EMERGING SECURITY NORMS ON PEACEKEEPING
AND CHINA'S RESPONSE

Following the atrocities of ethnic cleansing and genocide in Rwanda, Bosnia, and Kosovo in the 1990s, there was a growing sense of frustration in the international community that the UN had fallen short in meeting its Charter's fundamental principle of "saving succeeding generations from the scourge of war." In particular, the gap between rhetoric and action is most evident when the UN is politically constrained from taking preventive action on governments that fail to halt targeted violence against their own population. In response, the UN embarked on a number of pivotal reviews to reform the way it carries out peacekeeping operations.

One of the key documents for peacekeeping reform was produced by a high-level panel headed by Lakhdar Brahimi, a veteran statesman and member of The Elders. Brahimi and the panel were tasked with assessing and recommending practical steps the UN could take to institute more effective PKOs. The panel's findings and recommendations, released in November 2000, highlighted the need for PKOs to have clear and robust mandates to facilitate UN personnel's abilities to carry out their tasks.

This meant the rules of engagement would need to allow for peacekeeping troops to be active defenders and enforcers of the operation's mandate, as opposed to being passive bystanders when local parties incontrovertibly violate the terms of a ceasefire or peace agreement. Even as the centrality of UN impartiality was reaffirmed, the report warned that "no failure did more to damage the standing and credibility of United Nations peacekeeping in the 1990s than its reluctance to distinguish victim from aggressor."[42]

The Brahimi report underscored that UN peacekeeping forces must increase their field intelligence capabilities, be better equipped, and streamline decision-making processes. Perhaps most important, the report recommended the need for clearly articulated preauthorization when it comes to the use of force for credible and effective deterrence.[43] In short, the findings and recommendations called for UN peacekeepers to have the resources and the mandate to stop violence against civilians in order to avoid the fate of previous UN peacekeeping operations—such as those in Rwanda and the Balkans—that failed to deliver on the UN Charter's fundamental principle.

By and large, the UN Security Council supported the Brahimi report, albeit with some skepticism among some council members at the time about the nature of its ambitious changes.[44] India and Russia, for instance, differed on the extent of peacekeeping reform that was needed. India cited the report as a "dangerous simplification of a complex problem," pointing to the larger crisis within the extant structure of the Security Council decision-making process, as seen in the political inaction that led to the Rwandan genocide. Russia, in contrast, defended the actions of the Security Council, deeming it the singular legitimate body that can authorize the use of force. As such, its deliberations, however painstakingly slow, need to be carried out judiciously in order to establish the justification for preventive actions through PKOs. Russia also saw the concept of humanitarian intervention as problematic, where attempts to solve complex security problems by an interventionist force could end up undermining the UN's impartiality.

Most important, the Brahimi report's findings and recommendations were endorsed by African states, where three-quarters of UN PKOs are deployed. Nigeria's representative, for example, highlighted the prospects for closer integration between regional organizations like the Economic Community of West African States (ECOWAS) and the UN. Key African members of the Non-Aligned Movement (NAM) such as Kenya, Botswana, and Tanzania also voiced support for the role of UN peacekeeping in preventive diplomacy, for stronger peacekeeping mandates, as well for closer coordination between the UN and regional entities like the Organization of African Unity (OAU, the predecessor to the AU).

Speaking in response to the Brahimi report's findings and recommendations, China's envoy to the UN Wang Yingfan pointed to the significance of the coalescing views, indicating "on the basis of the work of the Working Group, the Security Council has reached consensus on strengthening peacekeeping operations. This is an important first step in strengthening United Nations peacekeeping operations and lays down foundations for future actions." Wang further identified that the success of future PKOs hinges on the collective support of member states to "make lasting political commitments and provide sufficient and dependable resources and support."[45]

The Security Council subsequently unanimously adopted a resolution that endorsed the Brahimi report's calls for future PKOs to have clear provisions on the use of force to protect all mission components and personnel, and that the rules of engagement should support the accomplishment of the mission's mandate, including the protection of civilians.

China's position upheld and supported the majority view in the Security Council that civilian harm in armed conflicts affects stability and development, posing a threat to international peace and security. At the same time, strong cognitive priors also meant that China maintains a degree of wariness about excessive and unwarranted intervention and external interference. Instead of threatening to use its veto, the Chinese representative left the door open for China's conditional support for UN PKOs to intervene in ongoing conflicts in order to protect civilians. In particular, the hard lessons from past atrocities were an important rationale, with the Chinese representative underscoring that "the Security Council should handle the issue of protection of civilians in armed conflicts on a case-by-case basis. It was necessary to take timely measures in response to cases like the Rwandan genocide."[46]

Nearly a decade later, the UN launched the "New Horizon" process to review progress made since the Brahimi report of 2000, and to identify possible solutions to ensure peacekeeping operations continue to adapt to meet current and future challenges. One of the most pressing recommendations in the New Horizon's report was a renewed call for troop-contributing countries to support rapidly deployable peacekeeping forces. Having such strategic reserves would enhance existing operations that are already stretched thin, as well as allowing them to respond to new crises that are time sensitive. As the report points out, "Even the best plans are ineffectual in the absence of a credible response. When a political crisis erupts or serious violence breaks outs, UN peacekeeping must be able to react rapidly and effectively. . . . Without a reliable mechanism for responding to crises, the authority and credibility of the peacekeeping partnership are vulnerable to challenges from spoilers on the ground."[47]

In discussing the findings and recommendations of the New Horizon report, China sided with a number of NAM and sub-Saharan African states in expressing concerns about the expansive scope of peacekeeping activities that could in turn delimit state sovereignty. But it was also through a number of deliberations that differences between the developed and developing states narrowed. There were at least five open session debates in the Security Council, thirteen Security Council working group meetings, two internal consultations, a Security Council summit, and one UN General Assembly session with all member states to discuss the report's findings and recommendations on furthering peacekeeping reform. In these deliberations, the tone and rhetoric shifted toward identifying common ground that underpinned the core finding in the New Horizon report: to prevent and mitigate mass atrocities, UN peacekeeping operations need to have a streamlined and time-sensitive decision-making process, a clear and robust mandate with the financial and logistical wherewithal, and the ability to draw on professional troops on standby from member states for rapid deployment. These fundamental principles form the basis on which more nimble UN PKOs would carry out their tasks and responsibilities. Most critically, where such operations invoke a mandate under chapter 7 of the UN Charter, UN peacekeepers would no longer be passive bystanders; instead, they were to be authorized and obligated to protect civilians under imminent threat of violence in armed conflicts. In recent years the Security Council has adopted the practice of citing chapter 7 when authorizing the deployment of UN peacekeeping forces in volatile conflict and postconflict settings where the host state is unable to maintain security and public order. The Security Council's invocation of chapter 7 in these situations, in addition to denoting the legal basis for its action, can also be seen as a statement of firm political resolve to restore peace and security using all means necessary. This shift toward supporting peacekeeping forces operating with clear authorizations and more robust mandates reflected an emerging consensus that there are extenuating circumstances—as well as legal justification—for UN peacekeeping troops to take all necessary measures to prevent and mitigate humanitarian tragedies.[48]

The Chinese representative eventually supported the New Horizon's key findings, indicating that China would "support continued efforts by the Secretariat to enhance its rapid deployment capacity and enhance its communication with troop-contributing countries."[49] Predictably, it also cautioned that more robust strategic reserves for peacekeeping must be tempered by the way that UN peacekeeping engages with the use of force, issuing a cautionary note against excessive reliance on the military intervention as a first resort for conflict resolution.[50] In short, while tepid about granting blanket calls for UN peacekeeping to intervene to protect civilians at all costs, Chinese officials prefer to weigh in on a case-by-case basis, balancing the merits and challenges of each PKO's mandate and the evolving situation of the security conflict on the ground.

Important to note is that, where there is clear regional or international consensus, China has been supportive in joining the majority to authorize PKOs that include chapter 7 mandates. As adamant as it had been—and continues to be—about the inviolability of state sovereignty, China exhibits foreign policy preferences that can and do change to allow for flexibility when it comes to interventions to protect civilians and mitigate humanitarian disasters through peacekeeping forces.[51] One of the clearest manifestations of China's preference alignment with the consensus view is its decision to vote for a slew of UN PKOs that sought to implement the necessary reforms identified in the Brahimi and New Horizon reports. In fact, in the cases of the Democratic Republic of the Congo (DRC), Liberia, and Darfur, China has supported each of these operations where chapter 7 mandates were considered, deliberated, and authorized. More significantly, in addition to voting with the consensus view, China's has significantly expanded its contributions in qualitative and quantitative terms to include infantry battalions in some instances and come at a time when UN peacekeeping forces are stretched thin and in need of critical material support and rapidly deployable forces. In the following subsections, we will take a look at China's evolving position and involvement in each of these three security conflicts and at China's expanding security dialogue with the AU.

Democratic Republic of the Congo: Authorizing an Intervention Brigade

In the DRC, UN peacekeeping forces have been present since 1999 to help monitor a national ceasefire and enforce a peace accord between armed militias and the Congolese army. For more than two decades, UN peacekeepers in the DRC have been carrying out disarmament and demobilization of armed groups to protect civilians and humanitarian personnel under threat of physical violence and to support the stabilization and peace consolidation efforts in the country (see table 5.1).

With the conflict at a standstill in eastern DRC, the UN Security Council received an unprecedented request in 2013 tabled by key regional actors—namely, the chairs of the African Union, the Southern African

TABLE 5.1
Key UN Security Council Decisions on the Democratic Republic of the Congo and China's Position on the Security Conflict

UN Security Council resolution (year)	Key points of deliberation on peacekeeping operation	China's position
1291 (2000)	Take all necessary measures to protect UN personnel and facilities; ensure the security and freedom of movement of all personnel and protect civilians (invokes chapter 7 of UN Charter).	Voted for the resolution.
1565 (2004)	Increase operational strength to ensure the protection of all civilians, including humanitarian personnel, under imminent threat of physical violence.	Voted for the resolution; Deployed 219 troops and has maintained its troop levels since 2004.
1856 (2008)	Attach the highest priority to address the crisis in the Kivus (eastern DRC), especially on the protection of civilians under harm in the conflict.	Voted for the resolution.
1925 (2010)	Use all necessary means for the "protection of civilians, humanitarian personnel and human rights defenders" under imminent threat of physical violence.	Voted for the resolution.
2098 (2013)	Authorize a specialized "intervention brigade"—one artillery and one special force and reconnaissance company—under direct command of the MONUSCO force commander to "neutralize and disarm armed groups."	Voted for the resolution.

Development Community, and the International Conference on the Great Lakes Region, along with the latter's eleven member states. Undergirding the regional leaders' call for a new peace framework in the DRC was the proposal for a new "intervention brigade" under the existing UN peacekeeping operation in the country.[52] The regional leaders argued that such a brigade would be critical in addressing the threat emanating from the M23 militia group and stem the recurrent waves of conflict in eastern DRC and in the wider Great Lakes region. The specialized brigade would be established for an initial period of one year and operate within the troop ceiling of 19,815 authorized for the United Nations Organization Stabilization Mission in the Democratic Republic of the Congo (MONUSCO). The proposal consisted of three infantry battalions, one artillery, and one special force and reconnaissance company for the primary purpose of preventing the expansion of all armed groups, including neutralizing and disarming them to reduce their threat to state and civilian security in eastern DRC and to make space for stabilization activities.

As the Security Council deliberated on the merits of this intervention brigade, China's ambassador to the UN, Li Baodong, indicated initial reservations about the worsening humanitarian situation in eastern DRC and the spillover effects the conflict was having on the wider Great Lakes region. In response to the consensus already forged among key African leaders, Li subsequently expressed China's approval for authorizing such a unique intervention brigade: it voted in favor of the resolution because the specialized force would not create a precedent, and it had the buy-in and support from local actors directly affected by the conflict.

Put simply, given the collective agreement and demand among key regional leaders for such a specialized force, China was ready and willing to endorse the action, even if the force was to take on an offensive role of peace enforcement to neutralize and disarm armed groups. As long as it operated under the auspices of the existing UN peacekeeping mandate and could help implement the Framework Agreement in eastern DRC, Li indicated China's support for such an initiative. As a veteran UN observer put it, the key factor here was strong regional endorsement on the urgency and necessity of the intervention brigade.[53] That it was an African-led proposal made a noticeable difference. Absent this important criterion, China would have voted against such a specialized intervention brigade.[54]

Liberia: Supporting ECOWAS Initiatives

China's peacekeeping contributions in Liberia from 2003 to 2018 reflect a similar trend line of supporting the consensus view adopted by its peers in the UN Security Council as well as from ECOWAS, the regional organization in sub-Saharan Africa most directly affected by the unfolding security crisis. An ECOWAS-led observer force had been set up in 1990 to help negotiate an end to Liberia's civil war and to settle a peace agreement. After more than a decade, in 2003 the ECOWAS force transitioned into a UN-led peacekeeping force, the UN Mission in Liberia (UNMIL), with the support and endorsement from ECOWAS members for more troops, training, and international support to stem the recurring violence and broker a peace agreement in Liberia.

China established diplomatic recognition with Liberia in August 1993. Interestingly, for ten years Liberia maintained formal ties with both Beijing and Taipei. Liberia only dropped its recognition of Taiwan in October 2003. It may seem like a quid pro quo arrangement, whereby China's diplomatic headway with Liberia coincided with the authorization of UNMIL forces. But such a narrative would have seen China's peacekeeping role in Liberia taper off, reflecting political expediency. If the objective was to whittle down Taiwan's allies and to reward the Liberian government for switching recognition, China's peacekeeping involvement in Liberia and support for UNMIL should have decreased following Liberia's derecognition of Taiwan. After all, there would be limited material incentives to deploy troops to far-flung places and put its own troops in harm's way, given the volatile situation and continued social unrest in Liberia. In the initial troop deployment phase, China deployed 4 troops to support UNMIL in October 2003, and this subsequently ramped up to over 350 troops within five months. By May 2004 its peacekeeping forces in UNMIL, primarily engineering and medical units, almost doubled in number. In October 2013, in addition to its troop contributions, China deployed for the first time 140 formed police units to UNMIL, responsible for law enforcement and public order. China's overall troop and police deployments continued to expand for fifteen years until the mission's official completion, in 2018.

Throughout China's involvement in UNMIL, it supported and adhered to the input derived from Nigeria, Gambia, Senegal, and other ECOWAS troop-contributing countries most affected by UNMIL's activities. For instance, China voted for Resolution 1509, which invoked chapter 7 of the UN Charter and included specific recommendations from ECOWAS. The resolution paved the way for a sweeping peacekeeping mandate that authorized UNMIL troops in the field to take all military and nonmilitary actions necessary to implement and enforce ceasefire agreements, protect civilians and UN staff and facilities, support security-sector governance and reform, and carry out voluntary disarmament and collect and destroy weapons and ammunition from armed groups.

With considerable improvement in Liberia's security and stability following over a decade of UNMIL presence in the country, there were calls to draw down UN forces. In 2016, as the Security Council debated a possible scaling back, China joined the majority view in extending UNMIL's mandate through early 2018 to support the general elections in Liberia in 2017.[55] Among the permanent members of the UN Security Council, France, Russia, and the United Kingdom abstained from the measure, while China voted in favor of the extension, citing strong ECOWAS support and Liberia's preference and request for the continued, stabilizing presence of UNMIL during the critical transitional and election periods.

Darfur: Testing the Concept of the Responsibility to Protect

The humanitarian crisis in Darfur in Sudan in the early 2000s provides another example of the significance of regional and international consensus, as well as its influence on China's foreign and security policy toward Sudan and the international peacekeeping force in Darfur.

In 2003 an armed conflict between Sudanese government forces and armed rebel groups broke out in Darfur in the west of the country. The rebel groups took to arms in response to the Sudanese government's oppression of Darfur's predominantly non-Arab population. The ensuing violence between the two sides saw heightened tensions when the government launched a campaign of ethnic cleansing in Darfur. The African Union attempted to intervene and broker a ceasefire in 2004–2005, deploying an AU-led monitoring force with troop contributions from Nigeria, Rwanda, and South Africa. Throughout the conflict, a large number of sub-Saharan African leaders found the actions of the Sudanese government and its president, Omar al-Bashir, in Darfur offensive on human rights, religious, and racial grounds. Moreover, al-Bashir dragged his feet on a proposal by

UN secretary-general Kofi Annan that would have allowed for a swift and unprecedented deployment of a hybrid UN–AU peacekeeping force of twenty thousand troops to help stabilize the crisis in Darfur.[56] Sudan's reluctance to accept external intervention also meant that AU forces were under grave strain and placed at considerable risk for failing to mitigate the humanitarian tragedy in Darfur. China, for its part, became vulnerable to being called to account within Africa and internationally for abetting and enabling Sudan's intransigence, given its traditional stance on the inviolability of state sovereignty and its close economic ties with Sudan.

Responding in a large part to mounting criticism of its relations with the Sudanese government, in 2006 China began exerting pressure on Sudan to consider a hybrid UN–AU peacekeeping force in Darfur.[57] With reports of hundreds of thousands of internally displaced persons and the casualty count rising from hunger, malnutrition, famine, and violent clashes in the armed conflict, the Chinese ambassador to the UN, Wang Guangya, was widely credited for his shuttle diplomacy between AU leaders and Sudan that eventually paved the way for Sudanese acceptance of the international peacekeeping force. In response to the deteriorating humanitarian crisis, China also became the first permanent member of the UN Security Council to deploy more than three hundred troops to the conflict zone, a move that was critical in its rapid deployment and widely applauded by African leaders.[58]

In February 2007 China's president, Hu Jintao, visited Sudan and met his Sudanese counterpart, al-Bashir. The summit drew widespread criticism internationally, not least because Beijing was due to host the Olympic Games the following summer, and human rights activists were ramping up their efforts to label it the "Genocide Olympics," where China was seen as abetting gross human rights violations committed by the Sudanese regime in Darfur. With mounting opprobrium from the AU and regional leaders in sub-Saharan Africa, Hu reportedly intervened personally during the visit to press al-Bashir to abide by international commitments.[59] Prior to leaving Sudan, Hu also delivered a rare public statement that outlined "four principles" as the basis for a diplomatic approach to Darfur.[60] The first, not unexpectedly, reaffirmed the principle of non-interference. But the fourth principle appeared to contradict the first, saying: "It is imperative to improve the situation in Darfur and living conditions of local people." Senior officials involved in the drafting of the public statement acknowledged that while the last point may not be headline-grabbing, it was about as close as a Chinese leader has come publicly to supporting the notion that national governments have a "responsibility to protect" their citizens from harm.[61]

Furthermore, in March 2007 the National Development and Reform Commission (NDRC), China's main economic planning agency, released a public document in conjunction with the MFA and the Ministry of Commerce, noting that Sudan had been removed from the latest list of countries with preferred trade status.[62] According to the announcement, Beijing would no longer provide financial incentives to Chinese state-owned companies to invest in Sudan. The decision was a signal of China's disaffection with al-Bashir's reluctance to provide the international peacekeeping force with full and unfettered access to monitor and implement a ceasefire in Darfur.

China subsequently appointed Ambassador Liu Guijin as its special envoy to Africa, complementing the role that its UN ambassador was engaged with on the crisis in the Security Council. Liu, a seasoned diplomat, took on Darfur as his top priority. Liu's primary role was to carry out diplomatic consultations with his counterparts and key policy stakeholders in Addis Ababa, Brussels, Paris, and Pretoria to garner regional views and international support and to liaise and negotiate with the Sudanese government. In July 2007 Sudan finally accepted an expanded international peacekeeping force in Darfur. Liu explained that the months of intense negotiations and consultations with regional and international partners had seen some direct language between him and his interlocutors that persuaded China to get Sudan to accede to the joint AU and UN proposal for the deployment of a hybrid peacekeeping force.

The African Union's Influence on China's Peacekeeping Considerations

An important consideration behind China's growing commitment toward UN peacekeeping lies in its increasing levels of interactions and consultations with African leaders. With nearly two thousand troops in the continent, four-fifths of China's total peacekeeping contributions are based in sub-Saharan Africa, specifically Darfur, South Sudan, Côte d'Ivoire, Liberia, the Democratic Republic of the Congo, and Western Sahara. China's position on UN peacekeeping operations largely follows the debates and consolidating views on how African states and the international community are reconciling the imperatives of global stability and justice. Regional collaboration and views on peacekeeping are particularly important, as reflected in one senior Chinese diplomat's remarks:

> It is necessary for the United Nations to strengthen coordination with the regional organizations in the field of PKOs. The Security Council undertakes the primary responsibility of maintaining world peace and security and has the final say in peacekeeping operations. At the same time, regional organizations can play an active role in peaceful settlement of conflicts, a useful complementarity for PKOs. Regional PKOs should also be conducted in accordance with the UN Charter and the relevant PKO norms and guiding principles. Cooperation between the United Nations and the regional arrangements must strictly abide by the provisions of Chapter VIII of the Charter. Since PKO missions are mainly in Africa, PKOs should attach greater importance to Africa. Increased support to the African regional organizations should be a top priority on the agenda of peacekeeping reform.[63]

Since 2000, Chinese officials have stepped up security and peacekeeping engagement and coordination with their counterparts in Africa. Every three years the two sides hold a major summit, the Forum on China–Africa Cooperation (FOCAC). With each successive FOCAC summit, the substantive content, deliberations, and action plan on peace and security issues have focused more sharply on African leaders' concerns and priorities. This need-based approach reflects African leaders' emphasis on developing a more comprehensive and balanced partnership and identifies the key areas where China can play a contributing role on a bilateral and multilateral basis, as well as through the AU and the UN Security Council.

In 2009, for example, the FOCAC Sharm-el-Sheikh Action Plan for 2010–2012 laid out specific activities for cooperation in a number of security areas.[64] The highlights focusing on deepening political and security cooperation include increasing the number of high-level visits between the two sides to increase mutual trust and understanding; establishing a regularized China–AU Strategic Dialogue Mechanism as a formal channel for greater political consultation; and China's support for an increasing African voice and representation in the Security Council. The establishment of the Strategic Dialogue Mechanism was critical in regularizing and institutionalizing a platform for joint discussion on security issues, addressing conflict mediation efforts and the role of UN peacekeeping. This effort further complements the multilateral process at the UN, where Chinese and African foreign ministers jointly decided to launch a political consultation mechanism at the UN headquarters in September 2007 to ensure a more calibrated approach in addressing regional conflicts. Such mechanisms have increased regular exchanges, opening the door to greater consultation on areas of convergence and divergence between African and Chinese officials. More important, these interactive processes have introduced Chinese foreign policy makers to regional security norms that are pertinent to bringing peace and stability to Africa, allowing China to become more attuned to the sensitivities and concerns of the Global South as it seeks external confirmation of its role as a legitimate power.

Security consultations between China and Africa intensified in July 2012. Under the "Initiative on China–Africa Cooperative Partnership for Peace and Security," a new action plan was established whereby China would contribute more financial, technical, and capacity-building support to strengthen AU peacekeeping operations in the continent.[65] Closer policy coordination on preventive diplomacy would also be strengthened between the two sides. Additionally, the initiative expanded the quality of contact through increased military personnel exchanges and training on peacekeeping, conflict prevention and management, as well as postconflict reconstruction and development.

Most recently, at the FOCAC high-level gathering in 2018, both sides focused on further operationalizing the African Peace and Security Architecture, an AU-driven effort on conflict prevention, conflict management, and peace building in the continent.[66] African leaders have indicated continued support for and appreciation of the sustained levels of peacekeeping contributions from China. Senior Chinese officials have pledged to provide peacekeeping and police training and to support peacekeeping missions with force multipliers and enablers. At the high-level meeting, Chinese officials moved to implement a $100 million military assistance program to support the African Standby Force and the interim African Capacity for Immediate Response to Crisis. Furthermore, they will continue to "work with Africa to raise the voice and influence of developing countries in the field of UN peacekeeping," as well as support AU-led solutions and proposals for peacebuilding and postconflict reconstruction initiatives in the Lake Chad Basin, the Sahel region, the Gulf of Aden, and the Gulf of Guinea.[67]

CHANGING DOMESTIC VIEWS ON PEACEKEEPING, STATE SOVEREIGNTY, AND INTERVENTION

It is critical to identify the extent to which consensus at the international level is referenced and discussed among policy elites in China. Observing such indicators would reflect the preference- and identity-shaping influence the emerging consensus and security norms on peacekeeping, sovereignty, and intervention have on China's internal foreign policy decision-making process.

At a major international conference commemorating the fiftieth anniversary of the Universal Declaration of Human Rights, Qian Qichen, the late senior foreign policy statesman, stated there was a global recognition of the "universality of human rights" and all nations "observe the same international norms on human rights." Qian also underscored, "We all recognize that no country's human rights situation is perfect, and that all countries are confronted with a weighty task of further promoting and protecting human rights."[68] Qian's statement reflected a recognition of the need to better integrate the emerging international consensus and understanding on human rights and peacekeeping norms into the Chinese foreign policy lexicon.

Although China was a relative newcomer, and latecomer, to the debates related to peacekeeping and intervention, these security issues have gained considerable traction within the country. A number of policy elites, international law experts, scholar-practitioners, and military advisers have increasingly commented and written on the changing circumstances in international security that call for a more flexible interpretation and understanding of the normative principle of state sovereignty, as well as the importance of supporting peacekeeping as a legitimate and accepted form of conflict prevention.[69] Most critically, China's long-standing position of nonintervention in the internal affairs of other states is seen as impractical and undercutting the image of a legitimate power that it is seeking to project in international security.[70]

For instance, the journal *Zhongguo faxue* (Chinese legal science), a widely read and influential source of legal studies in China, has featured a number of papers discussing a state's obligations to its citizens and how a failure to uphold these responsibilities warrants the international community to intervene to protect individuals. Other, similar journals such as *Xibu faxue Pinglun* (Western law review), *Fazhi yu shehui* (Legal system and society), and *Wuda guojifa Pinglun* (International law review of Wuhan University) have also argued that human rights is a moral issue increasingly shaped by the international community and that all states have a right to monitor these concerns.[71] Allen Carlson's research has led him to conclude that a growing number of Chinese researchers, scholars, experts, and policy makers have adopted more flexible views of sovereignty and intervention as a result of these debates and discussion.[72]

Equally important, some of the policy elites have gained access to key policy makers and top leaders within the Chinese foreign and security policy apparatus and have shaped and influenced the foreign policy discourse on peacekeeping.[73] In 2005, for example, President Hu Jintao announced that China would endorse a "comprehensive strategy featuring prevention, peace restoration, peacekeeping and post-conflict reconstruction."[74] Speaking on the role of the Security Council in responding to humanitarian crises, a senior Chinese official underscored that "in areas emerging from conflict, ensuring the rule of law and justice should become an integral part of the overall effort to achieve peace and stability, protecting the fundamental interests of local populations and serving the overall interests of social stability."[75] These policy pronouncements from the senior-most levels appear to reflect the proliferation of opinions penned by policy elites and scholar-practitioners calling for greater foreign policy pragmatism and flexibility when it comes to such sensitive issues as peacekeeping, sovereignty, and intervention.

THEORETICAL AND EMPIRICAL IMPLICATIONS

Over the past two decades, China's engagement with international institutions, particularly those in the developing South like the African Union, has exposed its foreign and security policy decision makers to normative values concerning human rights and conflict resolution that are gaining traction and factoring into its foreign policy calculus and discourse. It is still at too early a stage to determine how far China's foreign policy decision-making officials have accepted and internalized these normative values.

What is clear, however, is that China's policy outcomes have been shaped and influenced by the measures taken by other external actors, particularly in Africa in the areas of peacekeeping, sovereignty, and intervention. When there was strong international consensus regarding a specific intervention, as most recently seen in the DRC, Liberia, and Darfur, China has lent its support and doubled down to commit its forces in support of these operations. China's foreign policy calculus has thus shifted, pointing to a gradual moderation in its staunch defense of state sovereignty. This is particularly acute when the mandate for these operations calls for the use of all means necessary, including military and non-military options, to carry out peace enforcement. The changes in China's position are reflective of the emerging consensus for PKOs with more robust authorizations and are consistent with the international expectations of a large, powerful state's contributions to such multilateral security initiatives. Rather than pursuing unilateral interventions, China's peacekeeping contributions demonstrate that it is willing to constrain its material capabilities and conform to international consensus regarding UN peacekeeping norms and mandates.

As a plausibility probe, the preliminary findings discussed in this section help to confirm the key causal factor for strong-state restraint: a cohesive, common position and consensus on peacekeeping norms coalescing in the relevant international institution such as the UN Security Council or the African Union. This is observed when there is general agreement on the nature of the threat to regional or international security, as well as on the urgency and need to authorize a peacekeeping force with a clear and robust mandate to protect civilians, deter violence, and provide stability and security for humanitarian efforts on the ground.

The observation of such strong external consensus in turn has an impactful consequence on China's foreign and security policy behavior, not least with the alignment of its policy outlook and preferences with the multilateral security agreements related to PKOs that command collective regional and international support. To reduce uncertainty and avoid being cast as an outlier, there is an increased likelihood that it will defer to and accept the consensus achieved by external experts and peers in key regional organizations most closely affected by the conflict, overcoming cognitive priors that would have otherwise seen heightened levels of defiance, threats of veto, or normative contestation. For instance, this resulted in China's close support of and interaction with the African Union to mediate or de-escalate an existing or emerging conflict, significant troop contributions in the continent, and endorsement of multilateral security initiatives where it was previously ambivalent or saw only limited, direct unilateral gains or material benefits.

SUMMARY

The purpose of this chapter is twofold. First, it seeks to bring further clarity to the broader contours of continuity and change in China's foreign and security policy. Second, it identifies where the book's probative argument regarding strong-state restraint as a legitimation strategy fits into the narrative of China's rise. The key takeaway is that, even as China's material capabilities are increasing at unprecedented rates, there is no foregone conclusion about the trajectory of its grand strategy. The conventional wisdom tends to see that China will define its power in purely material terms and pursue more direct confrontation that would upend the global balance of power in its favor. But such narratives often miss a key part of the analysis and the complexity of the decision-making process in the rising power. Most critically, how China's foreign policy decision makers view themselves and their position in the region and in the world needs to be taken into account. Such debates and discussion matter because they are deeply affected by and interact with the incentives and constraints from the outside.

In uncovering these internal debates and discussion on the future trajectory of China's rise, we notice the significance of external consensus as a legitimation strategy for China's policy elites and foreign policy decision makers. Put simply, how others view and perceive China's rise factors quite prominently into the Chinese leadership's foreign policy calculus, especially as it processes and debates the appropriate responses to the external normative influence and expectations of a legitimate power's behavior and conduct in global security. Such concerns regarding perception and legitimacy represent ideational variables that factor prominently in foreign policy analysis. Most important, they help us explain patterns of change and continuity in China's foreign and security policy. How?

That external recognition and validation matter and continue to weigh at the forefront of the country's foreign policy decision-making process provides a strong motivation and rationale for restraint as a crucial part of China's statecraft. In fact, China's foreign and security policy is neither hardwired for power politics with its neighbors and peers nor destined for an outright balancing or head-on collision with the United States, the global hegemon. Theories of international politics that put a premium on the material facets of power often come down to such dire predictions of great power rivalry and contestation. What has been less well theorized is the importance of relational power, and in particular how such nonmaterial aspects of power as legitimacy and authority can also underpin the foreign policy strategies of a large, powerful state. Opening up China's foreign policy black box, a key part of this chapter's analytical observations, indicates that cooperative diplomacy remains an important foreign policy paradigm, with the expectation that China would conform to international norms that command widespread support and strong consensus to achieve its long-sought identity and desire for recognition as a legitimate power.

This pursuit of a new identity as a recognized, legitimate power is reflected in China's shifting position on peacekeeping, sovereignty, and intervention. In fact, we see from the plausibility probe case study in the second part of this chapter the remarkable transformation in China's views on these pertinent security issues. Where there is a clear and cohesive consensus on managing or addressing a particular security conflict through UN peacekeeping operations, the likelihood for China to participate in and contribute to the multilateral security initiative increases, in spite of the relative costs and constraints to its material power. In the cases of the recent and ongoing conflicts in the DRC, Liberia, and Darfur, for instance, there is strong regional and international support for more robust and effective peacekeeping forces. Where chapter 7 of the UN Charter is invoked and applied to the mandate, peacekeeping troops are authorized to use all necessary and available military and nonmilitary means to carry out peace enforcement. By extension, these peacekeeping forces are no longer innocent or passive bystanders. Instead, there are legitimate humanitarian and legal grounds for the peacekeeping troops to protect innocent civilians and disarm militias that may be undermining the peace process or national reconciliation efforts.

That China would vote for and contribute troops to such expansive PKOs points to the gradual moderation in its traditional and narrow interpretation of positive international law and the inviolability of state sovereignty. PKOs with more robust mandates can be construed as external interventions. China's support in this regard reflects a cautious and delicate balancing act, but it nonetheless aligns with the majority and consensus view on peacekeeping norms. It is also responsive to growing international expectations of a large, powerful state's tangible contributions to such multilateral security initiatives and global public goods. Rather than pursuing unilateral interventions, China's peacekeeping commitments demonstrate that it is willing to constrain its material capabilities and conform to international consensus regarding UN peacekeeping mandates and security norms.

Even as China's material power increases at unprecedented rates, the growing gap and power differential do not automatically incentivize it to act on parochial, material interests or to pursue unilateral approaches to achieving security. Consistent with the empirical analyses in the South China Sea, the preliminary findings of cooperative diplomacy and support for multilateral peacekeeping force in this chapter's plausibility probe challenge the prevailing assumptions about the disruptive and unpredictable behavior of large, powerful states in an anarchic security environment.

Beyond the crucial tests in the South China Sea dispute and the plausibility probe in China's approach to peacekeeping, sovereignty, and intervention discussed thus far, the hypothesized mechanism for strong-state restraint as a legitimation strategy can also be applied to other issue areas. For instance, the extent to which strong levels of group consensus matter in inducing change in China's foreign policy behavior in the Six Party Talks on North Korea's nuclear program between 2003 and 2007 can be further set up and examined as a plausibility probe. Where there is near unanimity or where a majority of the stakeholders are on board with a proposal regarding diplomatic détente, the peaceful use of nuclear energy, trade resumption, or nuclear disarmament, we could engage in further in-depth process tracing of China's statements, positions, and policy outcomes to draw additional inferences on consensus-based conformity. Similarly, the Arms Trade Treaty of 2013, which seeks to regulate the global trade of conventional arms, could also be a consequential security topic for further probing. How have the emerging global norms on reducing the illicit trade of small arms and light weapons affected China's policy position and induced it to introduce and implement strategic trade controls on conventional arms? Other topical issues like the Paris Agreement of 2015 and China's evolving position on climate change and the environment can also benefit from further plausibility probes using the hypothesized mechanism for strong-state restraint. In short, the supplementary evidence for strong-state restraint as a legitimation strategy from these additional exercises can extend and substantiate the broader analysis on the nonmaterial considerations behind China's rise and identity as a legitimate power.

Chapter Six

CONCLUSIONS ON POWER AND RESTRAINT IN CHINA'S RISE

The empirical findings of this book lead to fairly clear conclusions: even with their accumulation of material capabilities, large, powerful states do not exert coercion as often as expected. In particular, strong-state restraint is more likely to occur when small states collectively articulate their security norms and develop a strong consensus as a key incentive. Why? Adherence to the strong group consensus enables the dominant state to demonstrate its cooperative intentions and to institutionalize defensive military postures that mitigate the negative effects of a security dilemma, all of which provide the concomitant benefits of gaining recognition and acceptance from its peers as a legitimate leader. Because external perception and validation matter in identity formation, it follows that conforming to the group's strong consensus is a key determinant for strong-state restraint as a legitimation strategy.

The probative argument for restraint is evident in a crucial test: China's security dynamics and interactions with its ASEAN neighbors in the South China Sea dispute. That the smaller, weaker states within ASEAN are able to develop security norms aimed at defusing tension shows that they are not as vulnerable to a large, dominant neighbor like China as many believe in the conventional narrative. Authority relations between large and small states are not simply driven by or a reflection of material power alone. In fact, there are institutions in place and mechanisms at the region's disposal that are far more effective in regulating security dynamics than simply resorting to military balancing or confrontation in the South China Sea conflict.

More specifically, the findings regarding strong-state restraint as a legitimation strategy provide three overarching theoretical and empirical findings, as well as policy implications, specifically with regard to strong-state restraint as a dynamic foreign policy behavior in international relations theory; the agency of small states in authority relations; the role of the United States and its preponderance of power in regional security; and how power and restraint factor into China's rise in global affairs. In this concluding chapter, we review each of these three key findings and their implications in turn.

STRONG-STATE RESTRAINT: A NEW CONCEPTUAL UNDERSTANDING

The first key finding provides a new theoretical basis to explain strong-state restraint as a legitimation strategy. The conventional wisdom in international security assumes restraint as an anomaly in state behavior, not least for the statecraft of a large, dominant state with rising ambitions. Accruing material power yields immense payoffs that allow states to exert political pressure through the credible use of force, threats, or coercion on others, all the while advancing their own parochial interests without being subjugated to the whims of their peers. Even if large, powerful states do not exert their material advantages, the credibility of military threat and the logic of deterrence are sufficient for arm-twisting smaller, weaker peers into submission. The pursuit and accumulation of material power is thus a key driving motivation and strategy for survival. For better or worse, this elegant and simple narrative has become the default explanation for state behavior in an anarchic security environment.

But this zero-sum competition between states is not the end-all of international politics. It is simply a theoretical claim premised on the primacy of material power. Drawing inspiration from the Melian dialogue that "the strong do what they can and the weak suffer what they must," this simplistic (and historically inaccurate) assumption has somehow become a near-truism in the study of international relations.[1] There are at least two major shortcomings embedded in the application of this historical analogy to contemporary world politics.

While the strong might be able to do what they can, it comes at a hefty price. Exerting material power is politically expedient, but an overreliance on doing so undercuts the ability to wield a stable form of influence, one that is enduring over time and that projects and commands authority. A global superpower that possesses the world's most advanced military firepower would still face stiff opposition and resistance from its peers if the former chooses coercion, unilateralism, and the use of force over multilateralism, cooperative diplomacy, and consensus-building dialogue to solve complex, nettlesome problems in international security. The Iraq War in 2003 is a case in point. The preemptive nature of the U.S.-led military invasion lies at the heart of the controversial war. A majority of U.S. peers, including long-standing allies in NATO, resisted and refused to sanction the use of force in such a manner against another sovereign state. In carrying out the military campaign, the United States doubled down to assert its dominance. But its ability to persuade others to support the endeavor in the lead-up to and at the height of the intervention was far more restricted, delimiting the notion that "might makes right." Power, in short, is not simply a by-product of material capacity. In fact, the preemptive invasion of Iraq has generated so many debilitating ripple effects that observers have called into question how much longer the United States can maintain its leadership in global affairs.[2]

Likewise, whereas the weak suffer what they must, it is neither endured in vain nor without any end in sight. The smaller and weak states in international politics actually have more agency than we are led to believe. Every action that a large, powerful state takes is carefully monitored, scrutinized, and assessed by its smaller peers, and like the laws of Newtonian mechanics, there is an equal and opposite reaction. The perception of how the dominant state pursues its material advantages is something that can neither be controlled nor determined unilaterally. If the dominant state values relational over material power, contributes to international public goods, and upholds the existing norms accepted by its peers and the majority of states in international society, then a sense of rightful leadership and authority—legitimacy—emerges with the support and recognition of the smaller states. Influence that draws on such deference and validation from one's peers is far more enduring, stable, and impactful than influence that derives purely from military clout.

It is fair to probe why a large, powerful state might even care about legitimacy in the first place. In other words, why does external perception or validation by others matter if the state can simply turn to coercion, threats, and intimidation to induce change in the behavior of others as a first resort? After all, it has the material wherewithal to do so. Paradoxically, flexing military muscle is not a portrayal of strength. What makes a state strong and confident is the ability to constrain itself to attain the kind of influence that is voluntarily recognized and validated by its peers. Forgoing legitimacy and resorting to coercive tactics and military force may yield compliance from smaller states, but this submission arises from fear and reluctance. The constant exertion of material power may be politically expedient, but the benefits gained—measured in an ability to prevail over time—are ephemeral and fleeting.

A large, powerful state that exercises its material advantages judiciously and with prudence is thus more readily acceptable and perceived to be rightful by its neighbors. The rights conferred on a legitimate power by its peers come with an understanding that the former is expected to serve as a force of moderation and that it would not radically overturn the established and accepted norms, values, and institutional arrangements at the expense of small states. In such a "restraining-to-thrive" foreign policy approach, refraining from coercion as a first resort produces the concomitant effect of achieving more legitimate power and influence, not less, for the dominant state.

As discussed earlier, strong-state restraint represents a qualitatively different kind of foreign policy outcome than tactical adjustments. As a legitimation strategy, restraint's emphasis is on relational (not material) power. Using coercion or veiled threats based on material capabilities is antithetical to the end-goal of attaining the validation and acceptance of peers as a leader and legitimate power. While the bargaining model may see a large, powerful state's reliance on the credibility of its military threat as a strategy to "play nice" (while implicitly or subtly coercing its smaller peers into submission), such actions do not fit the theoretical model for strong-state restraint as a legitimation strategy.

Put simply, the probative argument here on strong-state restraint goes beyond cheap talk. The foreign policy paradigm is based on *idealpolitik* considerations, whereby the large, powerful state has a clear and distinct assessment of the efficacy of the use of force, be it veiled or explicit. External security threats do not necessarily warrant reciprocal retaliation or preemptive, coercive actions. Instead, such threats are often seen as situational and mutable, through which continuous dialogue can help attenuate the negative effects of a security dilemma. If the source of the external threat is due less to the fixed nature of its rivals, then increasing levels of interactions can eventually lead to cooperative outcomes. The motivation behind strong-state restraint is thus orthogonal to power politics, let alone the logic of consequences.

The oft-emphasized Melian dialogue is thus imbued with a confrontational premise that paints an overly simplistic analogy of contemporary politics and power dynamics in authority relations between large states and their smaller, weaker peers. That the strong do what they can does not mean that they can get away with doing so scot-free. There are repercussions and consequences for exploiting their material advantages. If the goal is to expand and broaden their influence by inducing voluntary change in the behavior of others, or to get its smaller neighbors to do what they otherwise might not do without putting up a fight, then coercion, no matter how subtle, is all but counterproductive.

Similarly, the weak are not as helpless or incapable of standing up for themselves. Given that self-legitimation is an oxymoron, whether one's actions are deemed rightful depends on the perception and approval of others. Small states are thus empowered to confer such legitimacy, providing the large, powerful state with the right to rule. The unique political arrangement is akin to a social compact, resting on the premise that the large, powerful state must first and foremost lead by example and exercise restraint. In return, the smaller states give deference. This mutually reinforcing obligation underpins a form of power dynamics and authority relations that is fundamentally more stable and pertinent for state survival and security in an anarchic environment.

If legitimacy motivates a dominant state to take on self-constraining security commitments, what precisely is the mechanism for restraint? Any discussion of restraint in the foreign policy statecraft of a large, powerful state as a legitimation strategy needs to further account for when such behavior is more (or less) likely to occur.

As discussed throughout the book, a key determining factor for strong-state restraint is the presence of strong group consensus. In particular, when small states band together and work to develop a strong consensus on their preferred security norms, the clarity in their collective position provides a credible incentive for their large neighbor to consider and adopt foreign policy changes that reflect the shared preferences of the smaller states. Hence, the presence of strong group consensus is particularly important to observe empirically for restraint to take place. Why?

Authority relations are fundamentally interactional, dynamic, and relational. For instance, states engage with each other to coordinate on a host of issues, ranging from trade negotiations via security dialogues to educational and cultural exchanges, all of which reflect the importance and ubiquity of social interactions that occur bilaterally or multilaterally on a regularized basis. Such state-level engagements mirror the verbal and non-verbal communication that undergirds group dynamics in social settings.

In particular, the presence of in-group/out-group interactions provides a powerful expectation for conforming to strong group consensus. What members of the in-group say or do during the interactive process matters, and the stronger the consensus from within the group, the more compelling it becomes for recalcitrant members or those external to the group to consider the consensus agreement seriously.[3] How one's peers think and behave thus has consequential impact on one's own course of action, even in difficult or controversial situations. If everyone else is on board or supports a particular view, conformity to group consensus provides sufficient motivation to induce change in behavior—more so than rational information, economic incentives, or other material gains and benefits—because developing an identity based on the group to which one seeks to belong provides a sense of acceptance, place, and position in the community.[4] Put simply, an entity's identity, however aspirational, is conferred and confirmed by its peer group. As such, the incentivizing draw to be part of an "us" or the "in-group" is supported by key findings that continuous social interactions with the group and exposure to its preferences generate a strong sense of influence on one's behavior, beliefs, and identity.[5]

Similarly, a large, powerful state's motivation to take on self-constraining commitments reflects the social dynamics of validation and recognition from its peers. It is more likely to exercise restraint when there is a strong group consensus among its peers on a set of norms to manage a security conflict without material force and with cooperative diplomacy instead. Strong-state restraint would thus see a preference shift in foreign policy outcomes, whereby the dominant state's approach evolves toward supporting the group's preference to de-escalate and ratchet down tension. Such changes include moving away from unilateral militarization, coercion, and the use of force, and thus valuing the input and preferences of the group's consensus. In so doing, the large, powerful state is able to clarify its cooperative intentions and institutionalize defensive military postures to mitigate the negative effects of a security dilemma, all of which would yield the concomitant benefits of gaining support and acceptance from its peers as a recognized, legitimate leader and power.

If group consensus induces strong-state restraint, how then might this ideational factor account for coercive behavior as well? When there is visible discord and disunity in the group, the large, dominant state's consideration for material power capabilities becomes more prominent as a foreign policy option. For instance, a weakened consensus due to fragmentation within the external group means the source of persuasion and normative influence regarding the benefits of multilateral security initiatives would be missing. This would render the large, powerful state more likely to practice power politics, where the emphasis shifts toward its material sources of power and the zero-sum nature of international security. There would be a higher tolerance for conflict and a stronger preference for the display of material power through offensive, coercive, and unilateral approaches to maintain its security. Threats, implicit or explicit, would become more prevalent as a tool to coerce its smaller peers into submission. The odds of defiance and deflection of multilateral negotiations or agreements that lack strong group backing and endorsement become higher, unless such proposals minimize constraints on its material capabilities while maximizing constraints on others. Increasing levels of bellicose foreign policy actions for the large, powerful state would thus be the corollary of group discord and fragmentation.

As discussed previously, it is important for the hypothesized mechanism to be able to explain conflictual tendencies as well. For one, it expands the explanatory power of the probative argument, demonstrating that such ideational factors are not epiphenomenal to material or structural accounts of state behavior. In fact, by illustrating how ideational variables can explain both deviant and nondeviant cases—noncooperative and cooperative behavior, respectively—it further delimits and impugns the all-too-simplistic premise of power politics and the material basis of power as the default assumption of state behavior in international relations theory. There is compelling theoretical basis to consider idealpolitik and realpolitik behaviors as functions of the social and interactive process that is group consensus.

In short, foreign policy statecraft rarely follows a linear, unidirectional trajectory. Coercion is therefore by no means the preferred foreign policy option, as is often presumed in the conventional wisdom about state behavior, not least for a large, powerful state. In fact, there is no reason to expect that, just because a dominant state has the material capabilities, it would exploit those advantages and pursue its parochial, self-interests by default or as a first resort. This is especially pertinent for a rising power and where the stakes and implications of its foreign policy actions are significantly higher and more carefully scrutinized by its peers. The social and relational aspects of power, such as legitimacy, are not mere afterthoughts for foreign policy decision makers of a large, powerful state. Hence the implication of this major contribution is fairly evident: given that external validation matters in the identity formation of a dominant state, adhering and conforming to cooperative security norms is part and parcel of its legitimation strategy toward becoming a recognized power and leader by its peers.

Critics of this argument may be sympathetic to the observation that large, powerful states can and do practice restraint and may agree with the limitations of realist assumptions, but they nonetheless remain skeptical about the causal process and the empirics. A common retort might sound like this: "How do we know that the large, powerful state is not just 'playing nice' for now or simply making window-dressing, tactical adjustments at best? You may have shown that there is no explicit use of force, but the credibility of military threats is still there." The rationale behind such critique is problematic but understandable. It goes on to show how prevalent and deeply entrenched the material constructs of power politics are in the extant literature as the standard-bearer for foreign policy statecraft. If we accept the probative argument for strong-state restraint as a legitimation strategy, we cannot at the same time move the goalpost and regress to a material-based logic as the default metric for adjudicating change in behavior, and thus relegating restraint to nothing more than a bargaining tactic or cheap talk. As clarified earlier, the emphasis and motivation of strong-state restraint are drawn from ideational factors and relational considerations of power. Moreover, restraint as an outcome rests on a foreign policy paradigm that sees the efficacy of the use of force in a fundamentally different way from the assumptions embedded in power politics.

SMALL-STATE AGENCY IN AUTHORITY RELATIONS

The second key finding is that small states have an important role to play in inducing strong-state restraint. Their agency, in other words, should not be underestimated. In particular, when they band together and articulate their preferences through a regional platform or institution, small states' consensus becomes a formidable source of influence with which large, powerful states have to contend.

How do small states retain their agency and project their influence? Empirically, in Southeast Asia, the claimant and nonclaimant states to the South China Sea engage with each other through ASEAN to propose and develop regional norms and security initiatives aimed at defusing and ratcheting down tension while collectively pushing back on the material power superiority of a large, powerful state like China. ASEAN as a regional organization does not rely on coercion or the use of sanctions to rectify behaviors of nonconformity. But its ability to incentivize change in foreign policy behavior of its member states and strategic partners in the region for over half a century lies in its ability to wield collective influence. In particular, when all ten member states' policies are aligned, it allows ASEAN to develop a strong regional consensus based on a set of norms and shared preferences to manage security conflicts in the absence of material force and with cooperative diplomacy instead.

Even though ASEAN member states are not formally allied, the consensus derived from their policy alignment shows they are not as vulnerable to China as many believe. Recall the hypothesized mechanism for restraint in chapter 2: the stronger and more cohesive the consensus to ameliorate the security dilemma through cooperative security, the more likely it is for China's foreign policy to reflect the group's consensus and support the regional, multilateral security agreement. Put simply, strong

ASEAN consensus yields China's restraint; weak ASEAN consensus leaves the way clear for China's aggression.

A common ASEAN security outlook aimed at ameliorating the security dilemma thus raises the stakes for a rising power like China to continue its militarization policies without considering the consequences of ignoring or side-stepping the collective preferences of its neighbors. The incentives for acceptance and recognition from smaller peers remain important considerations for China, especially for its narrative as a large, powerful state with growing regional and global ambitions. In heeding regional consensus, there are broader, longer-term considerations for the dominant state's security approach to shift toward supporting and accepting ASEAN's collective security preference, rather than deflecting it. Such changes would entail moving away from unilateral militarization. In so doing, China would be able to demonstrate its cooperative intentions to mitigate the negative effects of a security dilemma, all the while gaining the necessary support and acceptance from its peers in the region as a legitimate leader, a recognition that can be bestowed by smaller states only without material force or coercion.

As discussed in the empirical findings of chapter 3, when ASEAN acts as a collective bloc, its consensus becomes particularly effective in inducing restraint in China's behavior. Between 2012 and 2018 we observed at least six quarters in which strong ASEAN consensus and its collective influence induced restraint in China's foreign policy actions in the maritime dispute. In particular, strong levels of regional consensus were grounded on substantive measures, such as proposing new diplomatic actions to delimit China's coercive activities, elevating the region's concerns over specific threats like the unilateral deployment of military assets, and calling for new agreement and initiatives to regulate the conduct of behavior in the maritime dispute. As a result, we observed China's behavior conforming to regional concerns and adhering to ASEAN-proposed diplomatic approaches to diffuse tensions, as articulated and reflected in the strong regional consensus. With China seeking regional leadership and with acceptance from its peers as a legitimate power at stake, ignoring the collective view of its peers in ASEAN would significantly undermine its quest to prevail and augment its overall influence come at a great social cost. Exercising restraint in the face of strong regional consensus thus becomes an appropriate and desirable course of action for a large, powerful state like China.

To be sure, strong regional consensus can be difficult to achieve, given the disparate and sometimes irreconcilable interests across the ten ASEAN member states, especially between the claimant and nonclaimant states to the maritime dispute. This is exacerbated by ASEAN's limited institutional mechanisms for conflict management, all of which would incentivize China to act unilaterally and pursue power politics. In fact, in the instances when ASEAN consensus was weak, we saw a clear pattern of behavior: China's fundamental evaluation of the strategic environment in the maritime dispute hardened toward a more realpolitik outlook. Its power play in the South China Sea became more prominent and increased in frequency as a result. Based on the empirical data gathered in 2012–2018, we saw a clear and positive association between periods of weak ASEAN consensus and China's aggressive approach in the maritime dispute, notably through foreign policy actions that rely on coercive intimidation as well as the deployment of its military, paramilitary, and other material assets to target and minimize its rivals' capabilities in the South China Sea.

Individually, ASEAN member states recognize that they are not in a position to match or confront China's material capabilities head-on. Instead, the region's advantage lies in its ability to pool the group's weight and influence. ASEAN members acknowledge the regional balance of power has been tipping in China's favor, and the challenge is to play to their collective strength to address and manage the ongoing maritime dispute.

At the Munich Security Conference in February 2019, for instance, Singaporean minister of defense Ng Eng Hen highlighted and affirmed ASEAN's collective position as its most significant asset and advantage in dealing with a large, powerful neighbor like China. Ng observed that the empirical reality and the facts on the ground in the South China Sea have changed quite significantly, citing China's rapid militarization of a number of land features in the maritime dispute. But he also noted that a tit-for-tat response would be disastrous, with regional contestation spiraling into a security dilemma and an eventual arms race. Ng added, "If any side chooses to be more assertive or underestimates the resolve of the other party, more trouble and uncertainty may ensue."[6] That is perhaps why, in coping with a rapidly changing regional security environment, ASEAN's approach is not to respond with threats but to consistently push through a rules-based outlook instead to defuse tension in the maritime conflict. The regional Code of Conduct that is in the works, in particular, is meant to enmesh and bind China ever more closely to a set of rules that can help mitigate conflict, return to diplomacy, and reassert the centrality of ASEAN in regional security.

The broader policy implications of small-state agency are significant on at least two levels. First, it demonstrates that Southeast Asian claimant states are not rushing to strike bilateral deals with China on the maritime dispute. Even though a game-theoretic logic would expect the junior and weaker parties in any authority relations to succumb to the stronger power's demands—given its material advantages and the credibility of its military threats—this is not the case in the South China Sea. It is clear that the small claimant states in Southeast Asia are not breaking ranks. In fact, no claimant state to date has capitulated to China's unilateral demands. Instead, the resolve to work through ASEAN remains the main strategic preference and priority for Southeast Asian states.

Second, just because the claimant states are not settling with China on Beijing's terms for now does not mean that they are holding out and eagerly anticipating U.S. intervention to come to their defense either. They welcome U.S. presence in the region, recognizing that the United States is and will remain a Pacific power, but this understanding is qualitatively different from banking solely on U.S. security guarantees to improve their odds of survival and security.

In short, the effects of small states working collectively to develop a set of regional security norms cannot be understated. In fact, ASEAN consensus matters more than we think in providing the kind of legitimacy that China cares about as the latter seeks an expanded leadership role in the region and beyond. ASEAN norms—the organization's emphasis on diplomacy, deliberation, and decision making by consensus—have served as the building blocks for regional stability for over five decades, and Southeast Asia has managed its regional conflicts through these shared values and principles without having to resort to the use of force. When applied to the South China Sea context, the very same norms and principles that have served ASEAN well in the past continue to have salience in its security relations with an imposing, large power like China.

A MORE STRATEGIC U.S. SECURITY ROLE IN ASIA

Given the findings on strong-state restraint and on small-state agency in inducing such behavior, what are the implications for U.S. security strategy in the Asia-Pacific region? The third key finding is one of the most significant departures from the mainstream perspective in international relations theory: strong-state restraint as a foreign policy outcome has little to do with U.S. preponderance of power and its deep engagement or military involvement in the South China Sea.

There is considerable evidence in the empirical research presented to back the observation that U.S. deep engagement is neither necessary nor sufficient for deterring China's coercive behavior in the South China Sea. In fact, the security dilemma in the South China Sea intensified when regional fragmentation was exacerbated by increasing levels of U.S. military activities in the region, especially between 2017 and 2018. Ratcheting up the number of U.S. freedom of navigation operations—at least half a dozen of them in 2017 and 2018, when the region was divided and lacked a cohesive approach to China's provocations in the South China Sea— actually saw the unintended consequences of deep engagement: increasing belligerence and coercive activities in China's foreign policy behavior in the maritime dispute. In fact, the empirical findings and data showed that there was a tit-for-tat dynamic between China's behavior and increasing levels of U.S. FONOPs that ended up with more frequent displays of China's aggressiveness in the South China Sea.

Consistent with the book's argument that material capability is but one aspect of power, the assessment of U.S. security role in the South China Sea dispute reveals the limitations of military means alone in constraining or deterring China's coercion, especially when done so unilaterally. This is not to say that the United States has no role in the region or in the conflict. On the contrary, the United States is a pivotal power in Asia, but it can do more with less. As discussed earlier, this means less reliance on a strategy of deep engagement that fundamentally rests on the logic of military deterrence or expending material assets to address every security conflict in the region. Instead, a recalibration of U.S. security strategy as a force multiplier requires a more effective display of power and influence, one that would strengthen (and to a broader extent restore) its legitimacy and leadership in the region. This can be achieved by being more attuned to

ASEAN's security preferences, priorities, and threat perceptions of China, as well as by supporting the region's institutional capabilities to forge strong consensus when confronted with continued uncertainties in the South China Sea. As a senior Singaporean official puts it to his U.S. counterparts, "The choice is a very stark one—do you want to be part of the region, or do you want to be out of the region? And if you are out of the region . . . your only lever to shape the architecture, to influence events, is the U.S. Seventh Fleet and that's not the lever you want to use."[7]

The empirical analysis in this book shows that strong regional consensus can curb China's increasing material power capabilities in the South China Sea. That ASEAN may not always be successful in restraining China does not mean it is ineffective or that it should be written off. The likelihood for China's coercion, belligerence, and militarization increases when there is regional fragmentation. But when there is strong regional consensus, the effects of regional norm setting and identity building have been shown to moderate China's narrow and material self-interests in the maritime dispute.

In supporting ASEAN's diplomatic preference for a rules-based approach to managing the South China Sea conflict, the United States would be in a stronger position to enhance its resolve and influence. The U.S.–ASEAN Sunnylands Summit in 2016, for instance, provided the ideal forum to forge a closer alignment of security interests and was a demonstration of U.S. leadership and attention to regional priorities. In the early days of the Joe Biden administration, there are indicative signs of the United States working more intently with security partners and allies in Asia to respond to China's rise. Emphasizing the significance of U.S. coordination with regional partners, Secretary of State Antony Blinken explains the Biden administration's approach in foreign policy: "The more China hears, not just our opprobrium, but a chorus of opprobrium from around the world, the better the chance that we'll get some changes."[8]

Getting toward a convergence of interests between the United States and ASEAN member states would require sustained diplomatic coordination, communication, and transparency. No matter how painstakingly frustrating such an approach may be, making the diplomatic investment up front would yield important dividends in rebuilding U.S. legitimacy in Asia. Future policy and scholarship that continue to assert U.S. primacy without consideration for Southeast Asian preferences would undermine the U.S. position in relation to large, powerful competitors like China and lead to a deterioration in an increasingly important partnership with ASEAN in the years ahead.

POWER AND RESTRAINT: IMPLICATIONS OF CHINA'S RISE FOR REGIONAL SECURITY

The key attributes of China's rise—its rapidly modernizing armed forces, opaque and nondemocratic system of governance, technological leapfrogging capabilities, and ascending economic wealth—make it a hard and least likely case for strong-state restraint. Why? According to the logic of power politics, the conventional narrative sees and expects that in a security environment dominated by the United States, China's surge will put it in a contending position to balance against and challenge the hegemon. Any constraints on China's relative power capabilities would be eschewed in favor of policies that promote the efficacy of the use of force to expand its influence and to defend its security and sovereignty. Likewise, multilateral security arrangements are often treated with skepticism and seen as entrapments constraining China's ability to assert its material interests. Undergirding all this is a fairly deeply ingrained realpolitik worldview among China's foreign policy decision makers, "reinforced by an account of modern history where China has been a victim at the hands of militarily and economically more powerful states in a highly competitive and dangerous international system."[9]

The overarching message in this book, however, makes a fairly clear case that a large, powerful state like China can just as easily exercise restraint, not least in consequential security issues that affect its power projection capabilities or that touch on its core interests like sovereignty and territorial integrity. China's restraint in the South China Sea, in particular, is not an episodic, one-off change in its foreign policy behavior. The pattern of behavior gives heavy causal weight to the impact of strong ASEAN consensus in inducing such behavior. Beyond identifying and testing the hypothesized mechanism for strong-state restraint, replicating its scope condition would increase the likelihood for the end-result of restraint to become the pattern, rather than an anomaly.

In other words, if we know and are able to identify when China would yield, then repeating those conditions can help ensure that China would continue to practice restraint and refrain from imposing or exerting its material advantages—explicitly or implicitly—on its smaller, weaker peers in the maritime dispute. As Steve Chan observes:

> If Beijing refrains from using its stronger capabilities to impose a settlement of its maritime disputes and instead accommodates other claimant states in reaching compromises with them, this behavior communicates a peaceful disposition in conducting its foreign relations in general. The reverse also holds. To the extent that Beijing applies its increasing power for self-aggrandizement, this behavior signals aggressive intentions. . . . How Beijing intends to use its increasing power presents a more demanding and important question than the prognosis that it is likely to further improve its relative power.[10]

The challenge, as pointed out here, is that change in either direction in foreign policy statecraft is reversible. Just as a large, powerful state like China can be induced to take on self-constraining commitments, its behavior can also regress toward more coercive practices, especially when the condition for strong-state restraint is absent or missing. ASEAN's division and inability to coalesce around a common set of security norms or threat perceptions in the ongoing maritime dispute would weaken the group's consensus. Such regional fragmentation provides a strategic opportunity for China to carry out its divide-and-rule approach, pick off individual claimant states, and exert its material superiority in the maritime dispute.

ASEAN's ability to maintain a consistently strong and cohesive consensus is not a fait accompli, but nor are the challenges to achieving such unity and collective diplomatic approach insurmountable. It requires an assiduous effort to increase and deepen the level of regional coordination to ensure that there is strong regional consensus first and foremost among ASEAN members and that this key condition for inducing restraint is readily at hand to minimize the odds for a large, powerful state like China to reverse from its policy of restraint and slide back toward the direction of coercion and belligerence. ASEAN members increasingly recognize the urgency and importance of regional consensus, unity, and the institution's centrality to regional security. As articulated in the 2019 "ASEAN Outlook on the Indo-Pacific," it is clear that the Southeast Asian leaders are concerned with the rise of competing "material powers ... [that] requires avoiding the deepening of mistrust, miscalculation, and patterns of behavior based on a zero-sum game." ASEAN members further underscore the significance of maintaining an "inclusive regional architecture" and the need to "continue being an honest broker within the strategic environment of competing interests."[11]

It is important to reiterate here that the conclusion is not that China's foreign policy will always reflect restraint. Instead, the argument is that as long as the condition for strong-state restraint is present, there is a valid rationale and powerful incentive for a rising, dominant power like China to hold up its end of the bargain and to demonstrate its self-constraining commitments, not least in the South China Sea dispute or in other contentious and highly consequential issues in international security. Why?

Simply looking at the rapid developments of China's material capabilities is not enough and is often misleading. As astounding or alarming as they seem, narratives that rely on the material manifestations of power often miss a key part of the analysis and the complexity of the decision-making process in the rising power. Explaining and predicting the implications of China's rise require that analysts and observers do not study this political phenomenon in isolation from regional developments and influence. Instead, it is important to analyze change in China's behavior as a function of its increasing interactions with its peers in the region and beyond. Put simply, what is equally—if not more—pertinent to understanding the future trajectory of China's foreign and security policy strategy is assessing how China's foreign policy decision makers view themselves and their position in the region and in the world. Such internal debates and discussion matter because they are deeply affected by and interact with the incentives and constraints from the outside.

Being accepted and recognized as a legitimate power is arguably the most important consideration behind taking on self-constraining commitments in international security, even if it comes at a significant cost to material capabilities. In surveying some of the relevant foreign policy discussion, the research discussed in this book uncovers the significance of external consensus as a legitimation strategy for China's policy elites and foreign policy decision makers. In short, how others in the international community view and perceive China's rise continues to factor prominently in the leadership's foreign policy calculus, especially as it processes and debates the appropriate responses to the external normative influence and expectations of a legitimate power's behavior and conduct in global security.

That external recognition and validation matter and continue to weigh at the forefront of the country's foreign policy decision-making process provides a strong motivation and rationale for strong-state restraint as a crucial part of China's statecraft. In fact, China's foreign and security policy is neither hardwired for power politics with its neighbors and peers nor destined for an outright balancing or head-on collision with the United States. Theories of international politics that put a premium on the material facets of power often come down to such dire predictions of great power rivalry and contestation. What has been less well theorized is the importance of relational power, and in particular how such nonmaterial aspects of power as legitimacy and authority can also underpin the foreign policy strategies of a large, powerful state.

As discussed in the book, opening up China's foreign policy black box through identifying the nexus between strong ASEAN consensus, for instance, and change in China's internal foreign policy decision-making process provides important insights into the country's resolve and intentions. The different responses, discussion, and articulation of views by China's leaders, senior officials, scholars, and policy elites provide a more comprehensive assessment of how the country is striking a delicate balance between pursuing the different aspects of hard, material power and the relational, social forms of power like legitimacy that factor into the construction of the narrative behind China's rise. In so doing, we can better differentiate whether China is bluffing, talking tough, or truly geared toward exerting its newfound material power capabilities in aggressive ways.[12] This is especially relevant in understanding and explaining change in China's foreign policy behavior in the South China Sea conflict, in other consequential security issues that touch on sovereignty and intervention, and beyond.

Even as China's material power increases at unprecedented rates, the growing gap and power differential do not automatically incentivize it to act on parochial, material interests or to pursue unilateral approaches to achieving security. The probative argument for strong-state restraint as a legitimation strategy suggests that cooperative diplomacy remains an important foreign policy paradigm, with the expectation that China would continue to conform to regional and international security norms as long as they command widespread support and strong consensus among its peers. With this condition and incentive in place, the reversal from coercion to restraint offers a cautiously optimistic outlook for the implications of China's rise for regional and global security, as well as for U.S.-China relations. Restraint as a foreign policy outcome would thus occur irrespective of material capabilities. Put simply, the variation in a large, powerful state's foreign policy behavior rests on the presence of a nonmaterial, ideational factor: strong regional consensus. This is especially important at a time when China seeks to expand its influence and achieve its long-sought identity and desire for international recognition, validation, and acceptance. Understanding why and when China's foreign policy can change in the direction of restraint provides the theoretical foundation on which relevant policy recommendations can be made to reflect what has worked in the recent past, what has not, and what is likely to work in the future in further incentivizing China to assume the role of a legitimate power.

FINAL OBSERVATIONS

It remains to be seen how U.S.-China relations will unfold in the years ahead. In the early days of the Biden administration, bilateral ties set off on a fiery start.[13] While it may be tempting for the juggernauts in an impending power contestation to demonstrate their resolve through tough rhetoric, coercive actions, or even the use of force, it is worth bearing in mind that such overreliance on material capabilities by either side would end up undercutting the broader agenda for regional leadership and global influence.

Instead, a legitimate power of the twenty-first century requires cultivating the kind of authority relations with its smaller (but no less important) peers that are built on respect, mutual understanding, and an ironclad commitment not to exploit its material advantages. That legitimacy can be neither achieved nor demanded in isolation means small states in the region are not peripheral but central to international politics.

The dangers of sensationalizing the power struggle between the United States and China are manifold. For instance, it may become a self-fulfilling prophecy, to the detriment of Southeast Asia, where the spillover effects of any hard power rivalry would be most salient. Moreover, it trivializes and obfuscates the agency of small states in the region, along with the tangible benefits and contributions their consensus and perspectives bring to the table for a more durable peace. Sitting at the forefront of China's rise, and having been the beneficiaries of U.S. largesse for over five decades, Southeast Asian states understand firsthand the intricacies and pragmatic necessity of working with rather than against formidable powers to seek common ground and to reduce tension and rivalry.

Looking ahead, any power that seeks to take on the mantle of regional leadership—whether that be the United States, China, or both in a shared role—would need to recognize the centrality of ASEAN and adhere to the group's security norms and consensus that have shown to contribute to regional security and stability. The imperative of paying closer attention to the concerns and priorities of the region from the inside out will only grow as the strategic center of gravity in the Indo-Pacific shifts toward Southeast Asia in the years ahead.

DISCOURSE ANALYSIS OF ASEAN SUMMIT STATEMENTS, 2012-2018

TABLE A.1
20th ASEAN Summit, April 3-4, 2012

Terms related to South China Sea repeatedly used in summit declaration	References (#)	Lexical density (%)
Declaration on Conduct of Parties in the South China Sea	5	5
China	4	3
ASEAN	4	4
United Nations	2	2
implementation	2	2
joint	2	2

SENSE OF URGENCY

• Word choice in the summit statement reaffirmed general ASEAN and UN principles for security and stability.

SPECIFICITY OF THE THREAT

• Avoided any specific, recent incidents in the South China Sea dispute.

PROPOSAL FOR DIPLOMATIC ACTION

• Referred to the long-standing calls for the region to implement the Declaration on the Conduct of Parties in the South China Sea.

LEVEL OF CONSENSUS

• Weak ASEAN consensus.
• Summit statement did not provide a clear message or sentiment of urgency or threat.
• Instead, references were made to ASEAN's long-standing principle of implementation of the DOC, without stipulating a time frame or mechanism that would engage and commit China and the region to the implementation of the DOC.
• No strong push for any form of concrete action in the South China Sea.

TABLE A.2
21st ASEAN Summit, November 17–20, 2012

Terms related to South China Sea repeatedly used in summit declaration	References (#)	Lexical density (%)
Declaration on Conduct of Parties in the South China Sea	4	3
concerned	4	3
disputes	3	2
commitment	3	2
importance	3	2
United Nations	2	1
underscored	2	1
reaffirmed	2	1
agreed	2	1
peace and stability	2	1

SENSE OF URGENCY

• The text and word choice included repeated references to issues that are of concern to member states, with such words as "reaffirmed," "underscored," "agreed," and "commitment" used repeatedly.

SPECIFICITY OF THE THREAT

- Made direct reference to the South China Sea dispute and increasing tension and mentioned the need for self-restraint and negotiation "without resorting to threat or use of force" for the first time in summit statement.
- Unprecedented use of such phrases, which set the new norm in subsequent ASEAN summit statements.

PROPOSAL FOR DIPLOMATIC ACTION

- Emphasized the need to implement the DOC and to follow the United Nations Convention on the Law of the Sea and other recognized principles of international law.

LEVEL OF CONSENSUS

- Strong ASEAN consensus.
- Repeated use of action verbs in the summit statement to emphasize priorities and ASEAN's collective commitments.
- First reference to self-restraint and the need for all parties to negotiate "without resorting to threat or use of force" reflect banding together of member states—claimant and nonclaimant alike.

TABLE A.3
22nd ASEAN Summit, April 24–25, 2013

Terms related to South China Sea repeatedly used in summit declaration	References (#)	Lexical density (%)
Declaration on Conduct of Parties in the South China Sea	4	4
China	4	4
ASEAN	3	3
importance	3	3
reaffirmed	2	2

SENSE OF URGENCY

- Word choice in the summit statement pointed to ASEAN's continued discussion and observation of the latest situation in the South China Sea.

SPECIFICITY OF THE THREAT

- Avoided any specific, recent incidents in the South China Sea dispute.

PROPOSAL FOR DIPLOMATIC ACTION

- Identified broad regional desire to work with China, "including through mutually agreed joint cooperative activities and projects."
- Tasked ASEAN foreign ministers to engage further with their Chinese counterpart to work on the details for regional cooperative projects.

LEVEL OF CONSENSUS

- Weak ASEAN consensus.
- Summit statement noted the evolving situation in the South China Sea but did not spell out specific incidents that may be upending the status quo.
- The diplomatic proposal to focus on regional, joint projects was new but devoid of details. Instead, the statement tasked foreign ministers to work with China on the next steps in this regard.

TABLE A.4
23rd ASEAN Summit, October 9–10, 2013

Terms related to South China Sea repeatedly used in summit declaration	References (#)	Lexical density (%)
Declaration on Conduct of Parties in the South China Sea	7	4
China	7	4
ASEAN	6	3
Code of Conduct	4	2
consultation	3	2
accordance	3	2
implementation	3	2

SENSE OF URGENCY

- No strong deviation from previous summit statement.
- Continued emphasis on regional discussion of the latest situation in the South China Sea.

APPENDIX

SPECIFICITY OF THE THREAT

- Avoided any specific, recent incidents in the South China Sea dispute.

PROPOSAL FOR DIPLOMATIC ACTION

- No new developments, but the statement welcomed the commencement of ASEAN–China consultations with regard to a regional Code of Conduct on the South China Sea.

LEVEL OF CONSENSUS

- Weak ASEAN consensus.
- Like the previous statement, reiterated that the region was observing and discussing the latest situation in the South China Sea without spelling out any details about the nature or urgency of the discussion.
- General in-principle agreement among ASEAN member states to continue to work in "consultation" with China for the eventual "implementation" of the COC.

TABLE A.5
24th ASEAN Summit, May 10–11, 2014

Terms related to South China Sea repeatedly used in summit declaration	References (#)	Lexical density (%)
Declaration on Conduct of Parties in the South China Sea	2	2
ASEAN	2	2
importance	2	2
foreign ministers	2	2
developments	2	2

SENSE OF URGENCY

- Unprecedented structure of the statement on the maritime dispute and regional security started with: "We expressed serious concerns over ongoing developments" in the South China Sea.

- Introduced for the first time in an ASEAN summit statement the importance of respecting "freedom of navigation" and "over-flight" above the South China Sea.

SPECIFICITY OF THE THREAT

- Strong levels of regional concerns over the latest ongoing developments in the South China Sea.
- Reminded claimant states to observe and implement fully the DOC to "create an environment of trust and confidence."

PROPOSAL FOR DIPLOMATIC ACTION

- Utilized action verbs that "called on all parties" and "emphasized the need for expeditiously working" toward easing of tension, starting with the work toward the early conclusion of the COC.
- Referred to the ASEAN foreign ministers' statement released prior to the summit statement as a reference for the next diplomatic steps.
- Noted ASEAN's establishment of direct, confidential communication links between regional defense ministers in handling crises or emergency situations, in particular related to maritime security.

LEVEL OF CONSENSUS

- Very strong ASEAN consensus.
- Unlike the previous two summit statements, this statement rallied regional support, strong consensus, and endorsement over China's provocations in the South China Sea, specifically on the latter's oil rig activities in the contested area of Vietnam's exclusive economic zone.
- The introduction of language urging all claimant and nonclaimant states in the region to respect "freedom of navigation" as well as "over-flight" in the South China Sea was unprecedented and hitherto missing from summit statements.
- Stipulated proposals to address the challenges and ongoing tension in the South China Sea, including direct references to ASEAN foreign ministers' agreement and the regional defense ministers' communication link to handle contingencies and maritime security emergencies.

TABLE A.6
25th ASEAN Summit, November 10–12, 2014

Terms related to South China Sea repeatedly used in summit declaration	References (#)	Lexical density (%)
ASEAN	5	3
Declaration on Conduct of Parties in the South China Sea	4	2
region	3	2
early	3	2
peace and stability	2	1
collective commitments	2	1
trust	2	1

SENSE OF URGENCY

- Reaffirmed general ASEAN and UN principles of adhering to international law.
- Less palpable sense of urgency in the statement, with references to building "trust" that reflect the "collective commitments" of the region.

SPECIFICITY OF THE THREAT

- Reaffirmed similar observations in the previous summit statement, noting that the region "remained concerned" over the situation in the South China Sea.

PROPOSAL FOR DIPLOMATIC ACTION

- Welcomed progress in the COC negotiations and statements, including the agreement to "intensify consultations."

LEVEL OF CONSENSUS

- Weak ASEAN consensus.
- The strong consensus in the previous summit statement resulted in progress on ASEAN–China negotiations on the COC. The current statement did not increase the collective approach to press for further adjustments or concessions from China.

TABLE A.7
26th ASEAN Summit, April 26–27, 2015

Terms related to South China Sea repeatedly used in summit declaration	References (#)	Lexical density (%)
Code of Conduct in the South China Sea	2	2
peace and stability	2	2
effective	2	2
trust	2	2
confidence	2	2
consultations	2	2

SENSE OF URGENCY

• Repeated emphasis in the summit statement on activities that have "eroded trust" and "confidence" in the region and "may undermine peace and stability."

SPECIFICITY OF THE THREAT

• Summit statement on the South China Sea opened with regional leaders expressing "serious concerns" on "land reclamation," an unprecedented and direct reference to the kind of activity that ASEAN regards as eroding regional peace and security.

PROPOSAL FOR DIPLOMATIC ACTION

• Urged that consultations be intensified and for expeditious establishment of the COC.
• Tasked regional foreign ministers to urgently address the COC issue with China.

LEVEL OF CONSENSUS

• Very strong ASEAN consensus.
• Regional leaders expressed strong concerns and dissatisfaction over recent land reclamation undertaken in the South China Sea, linking such unilateral provocation to increasing tensions.
• A sense of urgency on speeding up the progress on the COC is palpable in this summit statement.

TABLE A.8
27th ASEAN Summit, November 18–22, 2015

Terms related to South China Sea repeatedly used in summit declaration	References (#)	Lexical density (%)
ensure	3	3
urged	3	3
Code of Conduct in the South China Sea	2	2
peace and stability	2	2
security	2	2
effective	2	2

SENSE OF URGENCY

- Similar to the previous summit statement, regional leaders "urged" self-restraint.

SPECIFICITY OF THE THREAT

- Unprecedented and direct reference by regional leaders to the "increased presence of military assets" deployed in the maritime dispute.

PROPOSAL FOR DIPLOMATIC ACTION

- No new diplomatic initiatives mentioned, except for calls to continue progress on the COC negotiations and to implement the DOC.

LEVEL OF CONSENSUS

- Strong ASEAN consensus.
- Fewer substantive issues mentioned compared to the previous statement, but regional concerns over the "presence of military assets" publicly acknowledged for the first time.

APPENDIX

TABLE A.9
28th and 29th ASEAN Summits (Combined Summit), September 6–8, 2016

Terms related to South China Sea repeatedly used in summit declaration	References (#)	Lexical density (%)
implementation	6	3
China	5	2
Code of Conduct in the South China Sea	4	2
Declaration on Conduct of Parties in the South China Sea	4	2
confidence	4	2
trust	3	1
further complicate the situation	2	1

SENSE OF URGENCY

- Summit statement began with an acknowledgement that the region "remains seriously concerned" over tensions in the South China Sea, especially how activities that "further complicate the situation" affect regional security.

SPECIFICITY OF THE THREAT

- Regional leaders pointed to land reclamation as a specific source of concern.
- Added extra emphasis on ASEAN preferences for "non-militarization" in the South China Sea dispute.

PROPOSAL FOR DIPLOMATIC ACTION

- Underscored the importance of "achieving further substantive progress" on the implementation of the COC and called for further "confidence building and preventive measures."

LEVEL OF CONSENSUS

- Strong ASEAN consensus.
- Member states were in strong agreement over what the challenges in the South China Sea entailed and their collective intent to send a clear and strong message about the region's preference for "non-militarization."

TABLE A.10
30th ASEAN Summit, April 28-29, 2017

Terms related to South China Sea repeatedly used in summit declaration	References (#)	Lexical density (%)
Code of Conduct in the South China Sea	3	2
peace and stability	3	2
reaffirmed	2	1
welcomed	2	1
operationalization	2	1
took note	2	1

SENSE OF URGENCY

- Reaffirmed general ASEAN principles of adhering to international law.
- Less palpable sense of urgency in the statement, with word choices such as "welcomed" and "took note" in the key clauses recognizing the ongoing progress made with China.

SPECIFICITY OF THE THREAT

- No specific mention of security issues undermining regional security in the South China Sea.

PROPOSAL FOR DIPLOMATIC ACTION

- No new initiatives; instead, the statement laid out some of the progress made with the different meetings related to COC negotiations.
- Reference to a timeline of the COC, with indication of a framework in place by mid-2017.

LEVEL OF CONSENSUS

- Weak ASEAN consensus.
- Notable consensus over a timeline for the COC framework, but other than that, the statement seemed passive and lacked any specific call to action.

TABLE A.11
31st ASEAN Summit, November 10-14, 2017

Terms related to South China Sea repeatedly used in summit declaration	References (#)	Lexical density (%)
China	4	3
Code of Conduct in the South China Sea	3	2
Declaration on Conduct of Parties in the South China Sea	3	2
reaffirmed	3	2
confidence	3	2
effective	2	1
substantive	2	1

SENSE OF URGENCY

• Reaffirmed general ASEAN principles of adhering to international law.

SPECIFICITY OF THE THREAT

• No specific mention of any ongoing developments undermining regional security in the South China Sea.

PROPOSAL FOR DIPLOMATIC ACTION

• Summit statement took note of the adoption of a "substantive" regional framework for COC negotiations with China.
• Regional leaders acknowledged the positive diplomatic momentum and "reaffirmed" the importance of continued dialogue on the substantive output of the COC negotiations.

LEVEL OF CONSENSUS

• Weak ASEAN consensus.
• Notable consensus over the COC framework adoption, but beyond that diplomatic development the summit statement did not indicate a sense of urgency and fell short of identifying specific actions that may be destabilizing regional security in the South China Sea.

TABLE A.12
32nd ASEAN Summit, April 27-28, 2017

Terms related to South China Sea repeatedly used in summit declaration	References (#)	Lexical density (%)
peace, stability, and security	3	2
tensions	3	2
activities	3	2
trust	3	2
reaffirmed	2	1
confidence	2	1
welcomed	2	1
further complicate	2	1

SENSE OF URGENCY

- Reaffirmed general ASEAN principles of adhering to international law.
- Regional leaders took note of "tensions" and "activities" that may "further complicate" the cooperative relationship between ASEAN and China.

SPECIFICITY OF THE THREAT

- Summit statement expressed general concerns over recent land reclamation in the South China Sea.

PROPOSAL FOR DIPLOMATIC ACTION

- Member states underscored ongoing progress on COC negotiations and the importance of a "mutually agreed timeline" for the early conclusion of the COC.

LEVEL OF CONSENSUS

- Weak ASEAN consensus.
- To the extent that concerns over regional security were expressed, regional leaders referred to them in general terms with frequently used terms and stock phrases common in previous summit statements.

TABLE A.13
33rd ASEAN Summit, November 11–15, 2018

Terms related to South China Sea repeatedly used in summit declaration	References (#)	Lexical density (%)
Code of Conduct in the South China Sea	4	2
confidence	4	2
importance	4	2
peace and stability	3	1
tensions	3	1
activities	3	1
trust	3	1
self-restraint	2	1
reaffirmed	2	1

SENSE OF URGENCY

- Reaffirmed long-standing ASEAN principles of adhering to international law.
- General stock phrases used to reiterate ASEAN's call for "peace and stability" and "self-restraint" in the South China Sea.

SPECIFICITY OF THE THREAT

- Similar to the previous summit statement, there was a general discussion on land reclamation, with member states calling on the region to "avoid actions" that "erode trust and confidence."

PROPOSAL FOR DIPLOMATIC ACTION

- Summit statement "emphasized the need to maintain an environment conducive to the COC negotiations."

LEVEL OF CONSENSUS

- Weak ASEAN consensus.
- Summit statement reiterated long-standing ASEAN principles for regional peace, dialogue, and security. No new concerns were aired, and diplomatic initiatives remained focused on making continued progress with China on the COC negotiations.

NOTES

1. THE PUZZLE AND ARGUMENT

1. John Mearsheimer, "Back to the Future: Instability in Europe After the Cold War," *International Security* 15, no. 1 (1990): 12.
2. Evelyn Goh, "The Modes of China's Influence: Cases from Southeast Asia," *Asian Survey* 54, no. 5 (2014): 825–48; Stacie E. Goddard, "When Right Makes Might: How Prussia Overturned the European Balance of Power," *International Security* 33, no. 3 (2008): 110–42; and Deborah Larson and Alexei Shevchenko, "Status Seekers: Chinese and Russian Responses to U.S. Primacy," *International Security* 34, no. 4 (2010): 63–95.
3. David A. Lake, "International Legitimacy Lost? Rule and Resistance When America Is First," *Perspectives on Politics* 16, no. 1 (2018): 6–21.
4. Christian Reus-Smit, "Power, Legitimacy, and Order," *Chinese Journal of International Politics* 7, no. 3 (2014): 341–59.
5. G. John Ikenberry and Daniel H. Nexon, "Hegemony Studies 3.0: The Dynamics of Hegemonic Orders," *Security Studies* 28, no. 3 (2019): 395–421, along with the research articles in that special issue.
6. See M. Taylor Fravel, "All Quiet in the South China Sea: Why China Is Playing Nice (for Now)," *Foreign Affairs*, March 22, 2012; Robert Kaplan, "The South China Sea Is the Future of Conflict," *Foreign Policy*, August 15, 2011; and Chris Rahman and Martin M. Tsamenyi, "A Strategic Perspective on Security and Naval Issues in the South China Sea," *Ocean Development and International Law* 41, no. 4 (2010): 315–33.
7. Steve Chan, *China's Troubled Waters: Maritime Disputes in Theoretical Perspective* (Cambridge: Cambridge University Press, 2016), 187–88.
8. Aaron Friedberg, "Ripe for Rivalry: Prospects for Peace in a Multipolar Asia," *International Security* 18, no. 3 (1993): 5–33. Also see Joshua Shifrinson and Stephan

Haggard, "Power Shifts: Connecting IR Theory with the Chinese Case," *Journal of East Asian Studies* 20 (2020): 131–86; Adam P. Liff and G. John Ikenberry, "Racing Toward Tragedy? China's Rise, Military Competition in the Asia Pacific, and the Security Dilemma," *International Security* 39, no. 2 (2014): 52–91; Avery Goldstein, "First Things First: The Present (If Not Clear) Danger of Crisis Instability in U.S.-China Relations," *International Security* 37, no. 4 (2013): 49–89; and Andrew S. Erickson, "America's Security Role in the South China Sea," *Naval War College Review* 69, no. 1 (2016): 1–14.

9. William C. Wohlforth et al., "Testing Balance-of-Power Theory in World History," *European Journal of International Relations* 13, no. 2 (2007): 155–85; John A. Vasquez, "The Realist Paradigm and Degenerative Versus Progressive Research Programs: An Appraisal of Neotraditional Research on Waltz's Balancing Proposition," *American Political Science Review* 91, no. 4 (1997): 899–912; and Paul Schroeder, "Historical Reality vs. Neo-Realist Theory," *International Security* 19, no. 1 (1994): 108–48.

10. James D. Morrow, *Order Within Anarchy: The Laws of War as an International Institution* (Cambridge: Cambridge University Press, 2014); and R. Harrison Wagner, *War and the State: The Theory of International Politics* (Ann Arbor: University of Michigan Press, 2007).

11. William C. Wohlforth et al., "A Comedy of Errors? A Reply to Mette Eilstrup-Sangiovanni," *European Journal of International Relations* 13, no. 2 (2009): 382.

12. For a thorough critique of the material basis of power, see Michael Barnett and Raymond Duvall, "Power in International Politics," *International Organization* 59, no. 1 (2005): 39–75; and for a thorough analysis of the different forms of power in international relations theory, see David A. Baldwin, *Power and International Relations: A Conceptual Approach* (Princeton, N.J.: Princeton University Press, 2016).

13. Stacie E. Goddard and Ronald R. Krebs, "Rhetoric, Legitimation, and Grand Strategy," *Security Studies* 24, no. 5 (2015): 5–36. Goddard and Krebs present a novel and important argument about legitimation approaches in the formation of grand strategy, but their argument is confined to modern democracies. For countries where political accountability to their domestic constituents is not achieved through openly contested elections, they acknowledge on page 24 that "legitimation of grand strategy plays little role in totalitarian or concentrated authoritarian regimes because governments can extract the needed resources via repression and can secure the support of a small circle of elites through the distribution of rents. In other regime types, which require mobilizing the support of more of the population, repression and cooptation are too expensive."

14. See, for example, G. John Ikenberry, *After Victory: Institutions, Strategic Restraint, and the Rebuilding of Order After Major Wars* (Princeton, N.J.: Princeton University Press, 2000).

15. Alastair Iain Johnston, "What (If Anything) Does East Asia Tell Us About International Relations Theory?," *Annual Review of Political Science* 15 (2012): 65.

16. See, for example, Frank Schimmelfennig, "NATO Enlargement: A Constructivist Explanation," *Security Studies* 8, no. 2–3 (1999): 198–234; Peter Haas, "Compliance with EU Directives: Insights from International Relations and Comparative

Politics," *Journal of European Public Policy* 5 (1998): 17–37; John Ruggie, *Constructing the World Polity: Essays on International Institutionalization* (New York: Routledge, 1998); Andrew Moravcsik, "The Origins of Human Rights Regimes: Democratic Delegation in Postwar Europe," *International Organization* 54, no. 2 (2000): 217–52; and Jeffrey Checkel, "Why Comply? Social Learning and European Identity Change," *International Organization* 55, no. 3 (2001): 553–88.

17. Some notable scholarship in this vein of research includes Evelyn Goh, "Great Powers and Hierarchical Order in Southeast Asia: Analyzing Regional Security Strategies," *International Security* 32, no. 3 (2008): 113–57; Amitav Acharya, "How Ideas Spread: Whose Norms Matter? Norm Localization and Institutional Change in Asian Regionalism," *International Organization* 58, no. 2 (2004): 239–75; and Yuen Foong Khong, "Coping with Strategic Uncertainty: Institutions and Soft Balancing in ASEAN's Post-Cold War Strategy," in *Rethinking Security in East Asia*, ed. Peter Katzenstein, Allen Carlson, and J. J. Suh (Stanford, Calif.: Stanford University Press, 2004), 172–208.

18. Alastair Iain Johnston, *Social States: China in International Institutions, 1980–2000* (Princeton, N.J.: Princeton University Press, 2008).

19. Barbara Geddes, "How the Cases You Choose Affect the Answers You Get: Selection Bias in Comparative Politics," *Political Analysis* 2 (1990): 131–50.

20. M. Taylor Fravel, *Strong Borders, Secure Nation: Cooperation and Conflict in China's Territorial Disputes* (Princeton, N.J.: Princeton University Press, 2008).

21. M. Taylor Fravel, "China's Strategy in the South China Sea," *Contemporary Southeast Asia* 33, no. 3 (2011): 292–319.

22. David C. Kang, *East Asia Before the West: Five Centuries of Trade and Tribute* (New York: Columbia University Press, 2010).

23. Goh, "The Modes of China's Influence," 834. Also see Evelyn Goh, *Rising China's Influence in Developing Asia* (Oxford: Oxford University Press, 2016).

24. Allen Carlson, *Unifying China, Integrating with the World: Securing Chinese Sovereignty in the Reform Era* (Stanford, Calif.: Stanford University Press, 2008).

25. See, for example, Samuel Kim, *China, the United Nations and World Order* (Princeton, N.J.: Princeton University Press, 1979); Samuel Kim, *China and the World: New Directions in Chinese Foreign Relations* (Boulder, Colo.: Westview Press, 1984); and Samuel Kim, *The International Relations of Northeast Asia* (Lanham, Md.: Rowman and Littlefield, 2003).

26. Harold Jacobson and Michel Oksenberg, *China's Participation in the IMF, the World Bank, and GATT* (Ann Arbor: University of Michigan Press, 1990); and Margaret Pearson, "China's WTO Implementation in Comparative Perspective," *Review of International Affairs* 3, no. 4 (2004): 567–83.

27. See, for example, Steve Chan, *Looking for Balance: China, the United States, and Power Balancing in East Asia* (Stanford, Calif.: Stanford University Press, 2012); Thomas Christensen, *The China Challenge: Shaping the Choices of a Rising Power* (New York: Norton, 2015); Rosemary Foot, *The Practice of Power: U.S. Relations with China Since 1949* (Oxford: Oxford University Press, 1995); Bates Gill, *Rising Star: China's New Security Diplomacy* (Washington, D.C.: Brookings Institution Press, 2007); Avery Goldstein, *Rising to the Challenge: China's Grand Strategy and International Security* (Stanford, Calif.: Stanford University Press, 2005);

David Shambaugh, *China Goes Global: The Partial Power* (New York: Oxford University Press, 2013); Susan Shirk, *China: Fragile Superpower* (New York: Oxford University Press, 2007); and Robert Sutter, *Foreign Relations of the PRC: The Legacies and Constraints of China's International Politics since 1949* (Lanham, Md.: Rowman and Littlefield, 2018).

28. See, for example, Amitav Acharya, *The Making of Southeast Asia: International Relations of a Region* (Ithaca, N.Y.: Cornell University Press, 2013); Alice Ba, *(Re) Negotiating East and Southeast Asia: Regions, Regionalisms, and the Association of Southeast Asian Nations* (Stanford, Calif.: Stanford University Press, 2009); Mely Caballero-Anthony, *Regional Security in Southeast Asia: Beyond the ASEAN Way* (Singapore: Institute of Southeast Asian Studies, 2005); Donald Emmerson, "Challenging ASEAN: A 'Topological' View," *Contemporary Southeast Asia* 29, no. 3 (2007): 424–46; Goh, "Great Powers and Hierarchical Order in Southeast Asia"; Jurgen Haacke, *ASEAN's Diplomatic and Security Culture: Origins, Development and Prospects* (London: Routledge, 2003); Natasha Hamilton-Hart, *Hard Interests, Soft Illusions: Southeast Asia and American Power* (Ithaca, N.Y.: Cornell University Press, 2012); and Ann Marie Murphy, "Great Power Rivalries, Domestic Politics, and Southeast Asian Foreign Policy: Exploring the Linkages," *Asian Security* 13, no. 3 (2017): 165–82.

29. Remarks by Amitav Acharya at a keynote lecture on "ASEAN at 50: Reflections on its Past, Present, and Future," ASEAN Studies Center, Institute of Southeast Asian Studies, Singapore, February 1, 2017.

2. THEORIZING ABOUT POWER, LEGITIMACY, AND RESTRAINT

1. Stephen Walt, "The Renaissance of Security Studies," *International Studies Quarterly* 35, no. 2 (1991).

2. See, for example, Jack S. Levy, *War in the Modern Great Power System* (Lexington: University Press of Kentucky, 1983); Robert Art and Kenneth Waltz, *The Use of Force: Military Power and International Politics* (New York: Rowman and Littlefield, 1971); Harold Sprout and Margaret Sprout, *Foundations of National Power* (Princeton, N.J.: Princeton University Press, 1945); and Robert Osgood and Robert Tucker, *Force, Order, and Justice* (Baltimore, Md.: Johns Hopkins University Press, 1967).

3. Ray Cline, *World Power Assessment: A Calculus of Strategic Drift* (Boulder, Colo: Westview Press, 1975); Robert Gilpin, *U.S. Power and Multinational Corporation* (New York: Basic Books, 1975); and Robert Art, "American Foreign Policy and the Fungibility of Force," *Security Studies* 5, no. 4 (1996): 7–42.

4. Stacie E. Goddard, "When Right Makes Might: How Prussia Overturned the European Balance of Power," *International Security* 33, no. 3 (2008): 110–42; Evelyn Goh, "The Modes of China's Influence Cases from Southeast Asia," *Asian Survey* 54, no. 5 (2014): 825–48; and Brantly Womack, "China and Southeast Asia: Asymmetry, Leadership and Normalcy," *Pacific Affairs* 76, no. 4 (2003): 529–48.

5. Stefano Guzzini, "Structural Power: The Limits of Neorealist Power Analysis," *International Organization* 47, no. 3 (1993): 446.

6. Harold Laswell and Abraham Kaplan, *Power and Society: A Framework for Political Inquiry* (New Haven, Conn.: Yale University Press, 1950), 92.

7. Christian Reus-Smit, "Power, Legitimacy, and Order," *Chinese Journal of International Politics* 7, no. 3 (2014): 342.

8. For a more thorough analysis on the emerging debates of legitimacy and the U.S. war in Iraq, see Barry Posen, *Restraint: A New Foundation for U.S. Grand Strategy* (Ithaca, N.Y.: Cornell University Press, 2014); Richard Betts, "Striking First: A History of Thankfully Lost Opportunities," *Ethics and International Affairs* 17, no. 1 (2003): 17–24; and Ian Clark, *Legitimacy in International Society* (Oxford: Oxford University Press, 2007).

9. David Bell, *Power, Influence, and Authority* (Oxford: Oxford University Press, 1975).

10. Reus-Smit, "Power, Legitimacy, and Order," 344.

11. John Dowling and Jeffrey Pfeffer, "Organizational Legitimacy: Social Values and Organizational Behavior," *Pacific Sociological Review* 18, no. 1 (1975): 122.

12. Mark C. Suchman, "Managing Legitimacy: Strategic and Institutional Approaches," *Academy of Management Review* 20, no. 3 (1995): 574.

13. See, for example, Ian Hurd, "Legitimacy and Authority in International Politics," *International Organization* 53, no. 2 (1999): 379–408; Ian Hurd, *After Anarchy: Legitimacy and Power in the United Nations Security Council* (Princeton, N.J.: Princeton University Press 2008); David Lake, *Hierarchy in International Relations* (Ithaca, N.Y.: Cornell University Press, 2009); Michael Barnett and Raymond Duvall, "Power in International Politics," *International Organization* 59, no. 1 (2005): 39–75; and David Baldwin, *Power and International Relations: A Conceptual Approach* (Princeton, N.J.: Princeton University Press, 2016).

14. David A. Lake, "The New Sovereignty in International Relations," *International Studies Review* 5, no. 3 (2003): 304.

15. David A. Lake, "International Legitimacy Lost? Rule and Resistance When America Is First," *Perspectives on Politics* 16, no. 1 (2018): 10.

16. Reus-Smit, "Power, Legitimacy, and Order."

17. E. J. Payne, *Burke: Select Works* (Clark, N.J.: Lawbook Exchange, 2005), 177.

18. Laswell and Kaplan, *Power and Society*; and Robert Dahl, *Modern Political Analysis* (Englewood Cliffs, N.J.: Prentice Hall, 1963).

19. John French and Bertram Raven, "The Bases of Social Power," in *Studies of Social Power*, ed. Dorwin Cartwright (Ann Arbor: University of Michigan, 1959), 150–67.

20. Morris Zelditch, "Processes of Legitimation: Recent Developments and New Direction," *Social Psychology Quarterly* 64, no. 1 (2001): 4–17.

21. Peter Blau, "Critical Remarks on Weber's Theory of Authority," *American Political Science Review* 57, no. 2 (1963): 307.

22. Hedley Bull, *The Anarchical Society: A Study of Order in World Politics* (Basingstoke, UK: Macmillan, 1995), 196.

23. For a more thorough analysis on how social compacts for legitimacy are underpinned by a set of shared norms and values, see, for example, Evelyn Goh, *The Struggle for Order: Hegemony, Hierarchy, and Transition in Post-Cold War East Asia* (Oxford: Oxford University Press, 2013); and Ian Clark, "Towards an English School Theory of Hegemony," *European Journal of International Relations* 15, no. 2 (2009): 203–28.

24. Gerry Simpson, *Great Powers and Outlaw States: Unequal Sovereigns in the International Legal Order* (Cambridge: Cambridge University Press, 2004), 68.

25. Erik Ringmar, *Identity, Interest and Action: A Cultural Explanation of Sweden's Intervention in the Thirty Years War* (Cambridge: Cambridge University Press, 1996), 13.

26. See, for example, Martha Finnemore, *National Interests in International Society* (Ithaca, N.Y.: Cornell University Press, 1996); Thomas Risse-Kappen, "Democratic Peace–Warlike Democracies? A Social Constructivist Interpretation of the Liberal Argument," *European Journal of International Relations* 1, no. 4 (1995): 491–517; Jonathan Mercer, "Anarchy and Identity," *International Organization* 49, no. 2 (1995): 229–52; Arthur Lupia and Mathew D. McCubbins, *The Democratic Dilemma: Can Citizens Learn What They Need to Know?* (Cambridge: Cambridge University Press, 1998); and Philip G. Zimbardo and Michael R. Leippe, *The Psychology of Attitude Change and Social Influence* (New York: McGraw Hill, 1991).

27. Ringmar, *Identity, Interest and Action.*

28. John M. Orbell, Robyn M. Dawes, and Alphons J.C. Van de Kragt, "Explaining Discussion-Induced Cooperation," *Journal of Personality and Social Psychology* 54, no. 5 (1998): 811–19. More on social identity theory can be found in Henri Tajfel, "Social Psychology of Intergroup Relations," *Annual Review of Psychology* 33 (1982): 1–39; Henri Tajfel and Henry C. Turner, "The Social Identity Theory of Intergroup Behavior," in *Key Readings in Social Psychology*, ed. John T. Jost and Jim Sidanius (New York: Psychology Press, 2004), 276–293; and Marilynn B. Brewer and Rupert Brown, "Intergroup Relations," in *The Handbook of Social Psychology*, ed. Daniel T. Gilbert and Sustan T. Flake (Boston: McGraw Hill, 1998), 554–94.

29. Martha Finnemore, "Norms, Culture, and World Politics: Insights from Sociology's Institutionalism," *International Organization* 50, no. 2 (1996): 325–27.

30. Andrew Betz, John Skowronski, and Thomas Ostrom, "Shared Realities: Social Influence and Stimulus Memory," *Social Cognition* 14, no. 2 (1996): 116.

31. Oran Young, "The Effectiveness of International Institutions: Hard Cases and Critical Variables," in *Governance Without Government: Order and Change in World Politics*, ed. James Rosenau and Ernst-Otto Czempiel (Cambridge: Cambridge University Press, 1992), 177.

32. Richard Perloff, *The Dynamics of Persuasion* (Hillsdale, N.J.: Lawrence Erlbaum Associates, 1993), 14.

33. Alastair Iain Johnston, *Social States: China in International Institutions, 1980–2000* (Princeton, N.J.: Princeton University Press, 2008).

34. See, for example, Jeffrey T. Checkel, "Why Comply? Social Learning and European Identity Change," *International Organization* 55, no. 3 (2001): 553–88; Thomas Risse and Kathryn Sikkink, "The Socialization of International Human Rights Norms Into Domestic Practices: Introduction," in *The Power of Human Rights: International Norms and Domestic Change*, ed. Thomas Risse, Steve C. Ropp, and Kathryn Sikkink (Cambridge: Cambridge University Press, 1999), 1–38; Jeffrey T. Checkel, "Going Native in Europe? Theorizing Social Interaction in European Institutions," *Comparative Political Studies* 36 (2003): 209–31; Jeffrey Lewis, "The Janus Face of Brussels: Socialization and Everyday Decision Making in the European Union," in *International Institutions and Socialization in Europe*, ed. Jeffrey Checkel (New York: Cambridge University Press, 2007), 137–70; and Alexandra Gheciu, "Security

Institutions as Agents of Socialization? NATO and the 'New Europe,'" in *International Institutions and Socialization in Europe*, ed. Jeffrey T. Checkel (New York: Cambridge University Press, 2007), 171–210.

35. Ronald Jepperson, Alexander Wendt, and Peter Katzenstein, "Norms, Identity and Culture in National Security," in *The Culture of National Security*, ed. Peter Katzenstein (New York: Columbia University Press, 1996), 33–75.

36. Yong Deng, *China's Struggle for Status: The Realignment of International Relations* (Cambridge: Cambridge University Press, 2008), 53.

37. On why intentions and resolve matter for a rising power with increasing material capabilities, see Andrew Kydd, "Sheep in Sheep's Clothing: Why Security Seekers Do Not Fight Each Other," *Security Studies* 7, no. 1 (1997): 114–54; Robert Powell, "Bargaining Theory and International Conflict," *Annual Review of Political Science* 5 (2002): 1–30; James Fearon, "Rationalist Explanations for War," *International Organization* 49, no. 3 (1995): 379–414; Clayton Thyne, "Cheap Signals with Costly Consequences: The Effect of Interstate Relations on Civil War," *Journal of Conflict Resolution* 50, no. 6 (2006): 937–61; Brandon Yoder, "Uncertainty, Shifting Power and Credible Signals in US–China Relations: Why the 'Thucydides Trap' Is Real, but Limited," *Journal of Chinese Political Science* 24 (2019): 87–104; and David Kang, *American Grand Strategy and East Asian Security in the Twenty-First Century* (New York: Cambridge University Press, 2017).

38. Jennifer Gandhi and Adam Przeworski, "Authoritarian Institutions and the Survival of Autocrats," *Comparative Political Studies* 40, no. 11 (2007): 1279–1301; and Joseph Wright, "Do Authoritarian Institutions Constrain? How Legislatures Affect Economic Growth and Investment," *American Journal of Political Science* 52, no. 2 (April 2008): 322–43.

39. Joe Hagan et al., "Foreign Policy by Coalition: Deadlock, Compromise, and Anarchy," *International Studies Review* 3, no. 2 (2001): 169–216.

40. Andrew Nathan, "A Factionalism Model for CCP Politics," *China Quarterly* 53 (1973): 34–66; and Victor Shih, *Factions and Finance in China* (Cambridge: Cambridge University Press, 2008).

41. See, for example, Kenneth Lieberthal and Michael Oksenberg, *Policy Making in China* (Princeton, N.J.: Princeton University Press, 1988); and Andrew Mertha, "Fragmented Authoritarianism 2.0," *China Quarterly* 200 (2009): 995–1012.

42. Amy King and M. V. Ramana, "The China Syndrome? Nuclear Power Growth and Safety After Fukushima," *Asian Perspective* 39, no. 4 (2015): 607–36.

43. Mertha, "Fragmented Authoritarianism 2.0."

44. Benjamin van Rooij, Rachel Stern, and Kathinka Furst, "The Authoritarian Logic of Regulatory Pluralism: Understanding China's New Environmental Actors," *Regulation & Governance* 10, no. 1 (2016): 3–13.

45. Jessica Teets, "Let Many Civil Societies Bloom: The Rise of Consultative Authoritarianism in China," *China Quarterly* 213 (March 2013): 19–38.

46. Shih, *Factions and Finance in China.*

47. Lieberthal and Oksenberg, *Policy Making in China.*

48. David M. Lampton, "A Plum for a Peach," in *Bureaucracy, Politics, and Decision Making in Post-Mao China*, ed. Kenneth Lieberthal and David M. Lampton (Berkeley: University of California Press, 2002), 33–58.

49. Alastair Iain Johnston, "Learning Versus Adaptation: Explaining Change in Chinese Arms Control Policy in the 1980s and 1990s," *China Journal* 35 (January 1996): 27–61.
50. Alice Miller, "The Politburo Standing Committee Under Hu Jintao," *China Leadership Monitor* 35 (2011): 2–4.
51. See, for example, Hongyi Lai, *The Domestic Sources of China's Foreign Policy: Regimes, Leadership, Priorities, and Process* (New York: Routledge, 2010); Linda Jakobson and Dean Knox, *New Foreign Policy Actors in China*, SIPRI Policy Paper 26 (Stockholm: Stockholm International Peace Research Institute, 2010); and James Reilly, "A Wave to Worry About? The Role of Public Opinion in Chinese Foreign Policy," *Journal of Contemporary China* 23, no. 86 (2014): 197–215.
52. Robert Ross, "China's Naval Nationalism: Sources, Prospects, and the U.S. Response," *International Security* 34, no. 2 (2009): 46–81.
53. Samuel P. Huntington, *The Soldier and the State* (Cambridge, Mass.: Harvard University Press, 1957); and Bengt Abrahamsson, "Military Professionalization and Estimates on the Probability of War," in *Military Profession and Military Regimes*, ed. Jacques van Doorn (The Hague: Mouton, 1969), 35–51.
54. Jack Snyder, *The Ideology of the Offensive* (Ithaca, N.Y.: Cornell University Press, 1984); and Barry Posen, *The Sources of Military Doctrine* (Ithaca, N.Y.: Cornell University Press, 1984).
55. Zhang Qingming, "Bureaucratic Politics and Chinese Foreign Policy-Making," *Chinese Journal of International Politics* 9, no. 4 (2016): 454.

3. ASEAN CONSENSUS IN THE SOUTH
CHINA SEA CONFLICT, 2012-2018

1. Robert Kaplan, "The South China Sea Is the Future of Conflict," *Foreign Policy*, August 15, 2011.
2. Ralph Emmers, *Geopolitics and Maritime Territorial Disputes in East Asia* (London: Routledge, 2010), 4, 122.
3. Alastair Iain Johnston, "How New and Assertive Is China's New Assertiveness?," *International Security* 37, no. 4 (spring 2013): 19.
4. Amitav Acharya, "ASEAN at 50: Reflections on its Past, Present, and Future," keynote remarks presented to ASEAN Studies Center, Institute of Southeast Asian Studies, Singapore, February 1, 2017.
5. Eugene Tan, "The ASEAN Charter as 'Legs to Go Places': Ideational Norms and Pragmatic Legalism in Community Building in Southeast Asia," *Singapore Year Book of International Law* 12 (2008): 173.
6. Ong Keng Yong, ASEAN secretary-general, "Forty Years of ASEAN: Can the European Union Be a Model for Asia?," remarks presented to Konrad Adenauer Foundation, Berlin, Germany, July 16, 2007.
7. Tan, "The ASEAN Charter as 'Legs to Go Places,'" 174.
8. Mark Beeson, "ASEAN's Ways: Still Fit for Purpose?," *Cambridge Review of International Affairs* 22, no. 3 (2009): 333.
9. Amitav Acharya, "The Myth of ASEAN Centrality?," *Contemporary Southeast Asia* 39, no. 2 (2017): 273.

10. See, for example, Yuen Foong Khong, "Coping with Strategic Uncertainty: The Role of Institutions and Soft Balancing in Southeast Asia's Post–Cold War Strategy," in *Rethinking Security in East Asia: Identity, Power, and Efficiency*, ed. J. J. Suh, Peter Katzenstein, and Allen Carlson (Stanford, Calif.: Stanford University Press, 2004), 172–208; and Amitav Acharya, "Power Shift or Paradigm Shift? China's Rise and Asia's Emerging Security Order," *International Studies Quarterly* 58, no. 1 (2014): 158–73.

11. For analytical examples of China's reliance on coercion, see Xiaoyu Pu, *Rebranding China: Contested Status Signaling in the Changing Global Order* (Stanford, Calif.: Stanford University Press, 2019), especially chap. 4; and Ketian Zhang, "Cautious Bully: Reputation, Resolve, and Beijing's Use of Coercion in the South China Sea," *International Security* 44, no. 1 (2019): 117–59. The analysis in M. Taylor Fravel's *Strong Borders, Secure Nation: Cooperation and Conflict in China's Territorial Disputes* (Princeton, N.J.: Princeton University Press, 2008) provides a more nuanced understanding of changes in China's negotiation strategy in historical border conflicts. As discussed in chapter 1, the present argument builds on Fravel's work in several ways. Here, we provide a regional analysis of ASEAN–China interactions and look beyond the material considerations in China's bargaining strategy. The findings also demonstrate how variation in China's restraint has occurred even as it has grown far more powerful, materially speaking, than when Fravel was writing over a decade ago.

12. Allen Carlson, *Unifying China, Integrating with the World: Securing Chinese Sovereignty in the Reform Era* (Stanford, Calif.: Stanford University Press, 2008).

13. This logic of inquiry builds on a similar vein of research in Alastair Iain Johnston's work on strategic culture and on China's evolving role in international institutions. See, for example, Alastair Iain Johnston, *Cultural Realism: Strategic Culture and Grand Strategy in Chinese History* (Princeton, N.J.: Princeton University Press, 1995); and Johnston, *Social States: China in International Institutions, 1980–2000* (Princeton, N.J.: Princeton University Press, 2008).

14. Interviews with senior colonels at PLA National Defense University and scholar-practitioners at the China Institutes for Contemporary International Relations, April 2017.

15. Luo Yuan, *Yingdan gehun: Luo Yuan jiangjun lun guofang* [Eagle's courage and dove's spirit: General Luo Yuan on national defense] (Beijing: Zhongguo youyi chubangongsi, 2015).

16. Interviews with scholar-practitioners at the PLA Academy of Military Science and the China Institute for International Strategic Studies, January 2018.

17. Feng Zhang, "Chinese Thinking on the South China Sea and the Future of Regional Security," *Political Science Quarterly* 132, no. 3 (2017): 449–50.

18. "Chinese Fishing Vessels Block Vietnamese Boats," *BBC Monitoring Asia Pacific*, June 18, 2014.

19. Linda Jakobson, *China's Unpredictable Maritime Security Actors* (Sydney: Lowy Institute for International Policy, 2014).

20. Anh Huyen, "24th ASEAN Summit Shows Spirit of Unity," *Voice of Vietnam*, May 2014, http://vovworld.vn/en-us/Current-Affairs/24th-ASEAN-summit-shows-spirit-of-unity/236637.vov.

21. ASEAN, "ASEAN Foreign Ministers' Statement on the Current Developments in the South China Sea," May 10, 2014, http://www.asean.org/storage/images /documents/24thASEANSummit/ASEAN Foreign Ministers Statement on the current developments in the south china sea.pdf.

22. Interviews with Vietnamese foreign affairs officials and ASEAN Secretariat officials, May 2016 and March 2018.

23. Myanmar Ministry of International Trade and Industry, "Chairman's Statement of the 24th ASEAN Summit," May 2014, http://www.miti.gov.my/miti/resources /Chairman_Statement_of_24th_ASEAN_Summit.pdf?mid=410.

24. ASEAN, "Joint Communiqué of the 47th ASEAN Foreign Ministers' Meeting," August 8, 2014, http://www.asean.org/storage/images/documents/47thAMMandR elatedMeetings/Joint Communique of 47th AMM as of 9-8-14 P.M. pm.pdf.

25. Zhang, "Chinese Thinking on the South China Sea," 457.

26. Shi Yinhong, "Guanyu zhongguo de yazhou xitaipingyang zhanlue he nanhai wenti" [On China's Asia–Western Pacific strategy and the South China Sea issue], *Dongnanya yanjiu* [Southeast Asian studies] 5 (2016): 33–38; and Ju Hailong, "Zhongfei haishang guanxi de tubian jiqi yuanyin yu yingxiang" [The sudden change in China–Philippines maritime security relations and its causes and influences], *Guoji anquan yanjiu* [Journal of international security studies] 6 (2013): 79–82.

27. Yan Xuetong, "Zhengzhi lingdao yu daguo jueqi anquan" [Moral realism and the security strategy for rising China], *Guoji anquan yanjiu* [Journal of international security studies] 34 (2016): 3–19.

28. "China Deploys HQ-9 Surface-to-Air Missiles to Woody Island," *Jane's Defence Weekly*, February 2016.

29. ASEAN, "Chairman's Statement of the 10th East Asia Summit," November 25, 2015, http://www.asean.org/wp-content/uploads/2015/12/Chairmans-Statement-of-the -10th-East-Asia-Summit-Final-25-Nov.pdf.

30. Tan Hui Yee, "ASEAN 'Resets Ties with China,'" *Straits Times*, July 2016.

31. Prashanth Parameswaran, "What Really Happened at the ASEAN–China Special Kunming Meeting," *Diplomat*, June 2016.

32. Simon Roughneen, "ASEAN Takes a Firmer Stance on the South China Sea," *Nikkei Asian Review*, June 2016.

33. "Singapore Caught in the Middle as China–ASEAN Country Coordinator," *Straits Times*, June 2016.

34. "China–South China Sea White Paper," *China Central Television*, July 2016, http:// newscontent.cctv.com/NewJsp/news.jsp?fileId=365288; https://www.fmprc.gov.cn /nanhai/eng/wjbxw_1/t1381980.htm.

35. Tan, "ASEAN 'Resets Ties with China.'"

36. Ben Westcott, "Duterte Will 'Go to War' Over South China Sea Resources, Minister Says," *CNN*, May 29, 2018, https://www.cnn.com/2018/05/29/asia/duterte -cayetano-south-china-sea-intl/index.html.

37. Greg Torode and Simon Scarr, "Concrete and Coral: Beijing's South China Sea Building Boom Fuels Concerns," *Reuters*, May 2018, https://www.reuters.com /article/us-china-southchinasea-insight/concrete-and-coral-beijings-south-china -sea-building-boom-fuels-concerns-idUSKCN1IO3GA.

38. Robert Haddick, "Salami Slicing in the South China Sea," *Foreign Policy*, August 3, 2012.

39. Steve Chan, *China's Troubled Waters: Maritime Disputes in Theoretical Perspective* (Cambridge: Cambridge University Press, 2016), 34.
40. Nicole Smolinske and Lance Jackson, "Duterte Bets Beijing Visit Will Reset the Philippines' Difficult China Relations," *CSIS cogitASIA*, October 17, 2016, https://www.cogitasia.com/duterte-bets-beijing-visit-will-reset-the-philippines-difficult-china-relations/; and Ben Blanchard, "Duterte Aligns Philippines with China, Says U.S. Has Lost," *Reuters*, October 20, 2016, https://www.reuters.com/article/us-china-philippines-idUSKCN12K0AS.
41. Krissy Aguilar, "Palace: Duterte Won't Give 'An Inch' of PH Territory to Other States," *Inquirer.net*, August 24, 2020, https://globalnation.inquirer.net/190386/palace-duterte-wont-give-an-inch-of-ph-territory-to-other-states.
42. Karen Lema, "Unified ASEAN Can Avert South China Sea Conflict: Philippine Minister," *Reuters*, November 25, 2020, https://www.reuters.com/article/uk-south-chinasea-philippines/unified-asean-can-avert-south-china-sea-conflict-philippine-minister-idUKKBN2851IQ; and Jim Gomez, "China, Philippine Defense Chiefs Discuss Territorial Dispute," *Associated Press*, September 11, 2020, https://apnews.com/article/beijing-south-china-sea-territorial-disputes-philippines-china-626f161d b42af40758bc9f7912dfb450.
43. Bill Hayton, *Vietnam and the United States: An Emerging Security Partnership* (Sydney: United States Studies Centre, University of Sydney, 2015), 5.
44. Richard Heydarian, "ASEAN Finally Pushes Back on China's Sea Claims," *Asia Times*, June 30, 2020; and Drake Long, "Three ASEAN States Push Back on Beijing in the South China Sea," *Benar News*, April 15, 2020, https://www.benarnews.org/english/news/malaysian/ship-concern-04152020155155.html.
45. Catherine Wong, "'Divide and Conquer ASEAN': China Tries to Go One on One with Malaysia to Settle South China Sea Disputes," *South China Morning Post*, May 18, 2019, https://www.scmp.com/news/china/diplomacy/article/3010790/divide-and-conquer-asean-china-tries-go-one-one-malaysia.
46. Bhavan Jaipragas, "Malaysia Won't Back Down on Sensitive Issues Even as It Bolsters Economic Ties with China," *South China Morning Post*, April 23, 2019, https://www.scmp.com/week-asia/politics/article/3007221/malaysia-wont-back-down-sensitive-issues-even-it-bolsters.
47. Johnston, *Social States*, xix.
48. Remarks by Ng Eng Hen, Singaporean minister for defense, at the Munich Security Conference and NATO Centre of Excellence for Operations in Confined and Shallow Waters Maritime Security Roundtable in Berlin, Germany, February 16, 2019, https://www.mindef.gov.sg/web/portal/mindef/news-and-events/latest-releases/article-detail/2019/February/16feb19_speech.

4. A CAUTIONARY ASSESSMENT OF U.S. DEEP ENGAGEMENT IN THE SOUTH CHINA SEA

1. See, for example, Michael Green, *By More Than Providence: Grand Strategy and American Power in the Asia Pacific Since 1783* (New York: Columbia University Press, 2017); Robert Art, *A Grand Strategy for America* (Ithaca, N.Y.: Cornell University Press, 2003); Brett Benson, *Constructing International Security: Alliances,*

Deterrence, and Moral Hazard (Cambridge: Cambridge University Press, 2012); Stephen G. Brooks, G. John Ikenberry, and William C. Wohlforth, "Don't Come Home, America: The Case against Retrenchment," *International Security* 37, no. 2 (2012): 7–51; Jesse Johnson and Brett Ashley Leeds, "Defense Pacts: A Prescription for Peace?," *Foreign Policy Analysis* 7, no. 1 (2011): 45–65; Jeremy Pressman, *Warring Friends: Alliance Restraint in International Politics* (Ithaca, N.Y.: Cornell University Press, 2008); Victor Cha, "Powerplay: Origins of the U.S. Alliance System in Asia," *International Security* 34, no. 3 (2009): 158–96; and Stephen Walt, "Alliances in a Unipolar World," *World Politics* 61, no. 1 (2009): 86–120.

2. Tim Huxley and Benjamin Schreer, "Standing Up to China," *Survival* 57, no. 6 (2016): 127–44.

3. Yuen Foong Khong, "Power as Prestige in World Politics," *International Affairs* 95, no. 1 (2019): 119–42; Bruce Jentleson, "Refocusing U.S. Grand Strategy on Pandemic and Environment Mass Destruction," *Washington Quarterly* 43, no. 3 (2020): 7–29; and Aaron Friedberg, "The Debate Over U.S. China Strategy," *Survival* 57, no. 3 (2015): 89–110.

4. For more on the logic of chain-ganging and buck-passing in alliances and security partnerships, see Thomas Christensen and Jack Snyder, "Chained Gangs and Passed Bucks: Predicting Alliance Patterns in Multipolarity," *International Organization* 44, no. 2 (1990): 137–68; Dominic Tierney, "Does Chain-Ganging Cause the Outbreak of War?," *International Studies Quarterly* 55, no. 2 (2011): 285–304; Michael Beckley, "The Myth of Entangling Alliances," *International Security* 39, no. 4 (2015): 7–48; and Mason Richey, "Buck-passing, Chain-ganging and Alliances in the Multipolar Indo-Asia-Pacific," *International Spectator* 55, no. 1 (2020): 1–17.

5. Barry Posen, *Restraint: A New Foundation for U.S. Grand Strategy* (Ithaca, N.Y.: Cornell University Press, 2014); Eugene Gholz, Daryl G. Press, and Harvey M. Sapolsky, "Come Home, America: The Strategy of Restraint in the Face of Temptation," *International Security* 21, no. 4 (1997): 5–48; Christopher Layne, "From Preponderance to Off-shore Balancing: America's Future Grand Strategy," *International Security* 22, no. 1 (1997): 86–124; Douglas Gibler, "The Costs of Reneging: Reputation and Alliance Formation," *Journal of Conflict Resolution* 52, no. 3 (2008): 426–54; and Brooks, Ikenberry, and Wohlforth, "Don't Come Home, America," 10.

6. Richard Betts, "The Political Support for American Primacy," *International Affairs* 81, no. 1 (2005): 1–14; and Christopher Layne, *The Peace of Illusions: American Grand Strategy from 1940 to the Present* (Ithaca, N.Y.: Cornell University Press, 2006).

7. Stephen G. Brooks and William C. Wohlforth, "Assessing the Balance," *Cambridge Review of International Affairs* 24, no. 2 (2011): 201–19.

8. Brooks, Ikenberry, and Wohlforth, "Don't Come Home, America," 11.

9. G. John Ikenberry, "Between the Eagle and the Dragon: America, China, and Middle State Strategies in East Asia," *Political Science Quarterly* 131, no. 1 (2016): 9–43. It is important to acknowledge that there are indeed many "issue-specific orders" governing the international system. At face value, the current U.S.-led order in the security sphere is dominated by the logic of deep engagement. In Asia, this means a robust U.S. force posture, sustaining and increasing military deployments, and security involvement and commitments through a hub-and-spokes alliance system. On this important distinction between "issue-specific orders" and a singular,

overarching "U.S.-led liberal world order," see Alastair Iain Johnston, "The Failure of the 'Failure of Engagement' with China," *Washington Quarterly* 42, no. 2 (2019): 99–114.

10. Alexander George and Richard Smoke, *Deterrence in American Foreign Policy: Theory and Practice* (New York: Columbia University Press, 1974); and Robert Jervis, "Deterrence Theory Revisited," *World Politics* 31, no. 2 (1979): 289–324.

11. Stephen Walt, "More or Less: The Debate on U.S. Grand Strategy," *Foreign Policy*, January 2, 2013, http://foreignpolicy.com/2013/01/02/more-or-less-the-debate-on-u-s-grand-strategy/.

12. "U.S. Defense Guidance," *National Security Archive*, 1992.

13. "The National Security Strategy of the United States of America," *White House*, 2002.

14. "Assessing the January 2012 Defense Strategic Guidance," *Congressional Research Service*, 2013.

15. U.S. Department of Defense, *Indo-Pacific Strategy Report* (Washington, D.C.: U.S. Government Printing Office, 2019), https://media.defense.gov/2019/Jul/01/2002152311/-1/-1/1/Department-of-Defense-Indo-Pacific-Strategy-Report-2019.pdf.

16. Hoover Institution, *Chinese Influence and American Interests: Promoting Constructive Vigilance* (Stanford, CA: Hoover Institution Press, 2018).

17. Hoover Institution, *Chinese Influence and American Interests*, 193.

18. Stein Tønnesson, *Explaining the East Asian Peace: A Research Story* (Copenhagen: Nordic Institute of Asian Studies Press, 2017); Lanxin Xiang, "Xi's Dream and China's Future," *Survival* 58, no. 3 (2016): 53–62; Johnston, "What (If Anything) Does East Asia Tell Us About International Relations Theory?"; David Kang, *China Rising: Peace, Power, and Order in East Asia* (New York: Columbia University Press, 2007); and Feng Zhang, "China's Curious Nonchalance Towards the Indo-Pacific," *Survival* 61, no. 3 (2019): 187–212.

19. Jervis, "Deterrence Theory Revisited," 296.

20. David Kang, "Getting Asia Wrong: The Need for New Analytical Frameworks," *International Security* 27, no. 4 (2003): 57.

21. Erik Gartzke and Jon Lindsay, *Cross-Domain Deterrence: Strategy in an Era of Complexity* (Oxford: Oxford University Press, 2019).

22. Transcript of a public discussion on U.S.–China relations hosted by the Woodrow Wilson Center for International Scholars in Washington, D.C., October 17, 2019, https://www.wilsoncenter.org/event/live-webcast-the-nixon-forum-us-china-relations.

23. Evelyn Goh, *The Struggle for Order: Hegemony, Hierarchy, and Transition in Post-Cold War East Asia* (Oxford: Oxford University Press, 2013).

24. Tom Allard, "Exclusive: Indonesia Rejected U.S. Request to Host Spy Planes—Officials," *Reuters*, October 20, 2020, https://www.reuters.com/article/indonesia-usa-idUSKBN2750M7.

25. Jeffrey Bader, "Changing China Policy: Are We in Search of Enemies?," Brookings China Strategy Paper no. 1, June 2015, https://www.brookings.edu/wp-content/uploads/2016/06/Changing-China-policy-Are-we-in-search-of-enemies.pdf, 5.

26. Tom Allard and Stanley Widianto, "Indonesia to U.S., China: Don't Trap Us in Your Rivalry," *Reuters*, September 8, 2020, https://www.reuters.com/article/us-indonesia-politics-foreign-minister-idUSKBN25Z1ZD.

27. "Malaysia Calls for ASEAN Support Against Beijing Over South China Sea," *Today Online*, December 19, 2016, https://www.todayonline.com/world/asia/malaysia-calls-asean-support-against-beijing-over-s-china-sea.

28. Alexander George and Andrew Bennett, *Case Studies and Theory Development in the Social Sciences* (Cambridge, Mass.: MIT Press, 2005), 80–81.

29. Author interviews with officials at the Philippine Department of National Defense, March 2018, and at the U.S. Indo-Pacific Command, June 2019.

30. Philippine Department of Foreign Affairs, "U.S. Reiterates It Will Honor Obligations Under MDT Amid Standoff," *Official Gazette of the Republic of the Philippines*, May 3, 2012, https://www.officialgazette.gov.ph/2012/05/03/u-s-reiterates-it-will-honor-obligations-under-mutual-defense-treat-amid-standoff-in-bajo-de-masinloc-scarborough-shoal/.

31. Carlyle Thayer, "ASEAN's Code of Conduct in the South China Sea: A Litmus Test for Community Building?," *Asia-Pacific Journal* 10, no. 34 (2012): 13.

32. Thayer, "ASEAN's Code of Conduct in the South China Sea," 13.

33. Thayer, "ASEAN's Code of Conduct in the South China Sea," 13.

34. Thayer, "ASEAN's Code of Conduct in the South China Sea," 13–14.

35. Carlyle Thayer, "Is the Philippines an Orphan?," *Diplomat*, May 2, 2012, http://thediplomat.com/2012/05/is-the-philippines-an-orphan/.

36. Bill Hayton, *Vietnam and the United States: An Emerging Security Partnership* (Sydney: United States Studies Center at the University of Sydney, 2015).

37. Anh Huyen, "24th ASEAN Summit Shows Spirit of Unity," *Voice of Vietnam*, May 9, 2014, http://vovworld.vn/en-us/Current-Affairs/24th-ASEAN-summit-shows-spirit-of-unity/236637.vov.

38. ASEAN, "ASEAN Foreign Ministers' Statement on the Current Developments in the South China Sea," May 10, 2014, http://www.asean.org/storage/images/documents/24thASEANSummit/ASEAN Foreign Ministers Statement on the current developments in the south china sea.pdf.

39. Interviews with scholar-practitioners at the Diplomatic Academy of Vietnam, April 2017.

40. Interviews with scholar-practitioners at the Diplomatic Academy of Vietnam, April 2017.

41. Demetri Sevastopulo, "South China Seas: Troubled Waters," *Financial Times*, June 20, 2014, https://www.ft.com/content/313432b0-f78f-11e3-b2cf-00144feabdc0.

42. Ben Westcott, "Duterte Will 'Go to War' Over South China Sea Resources, Minister Says," *CNN*, May 29, 2018, https://www.cnn.com/2018/05/29/asia/duterte-cayetano-south-china-sea-intl/index.html.

43. Interviews with senior officials at the Philippine Department of National Defense, March 2018.

44. Rachel Odell, "How Strategic Norm-Shaping Undergirds America's Command of the Commons," MIT Political Science Department Research Paper No. 2019–23, August 31, 2019, http://dx.doi.org/10.2139/ssrn.3451412.

45. Nick Bisley, "We Should Think Carefully About an Australian FONOP in the South China Sea," Lowy Institute, February 2016, https://www.lowyinstitute.org/the-interpreter/we-should-think-carefully-about-australian-fonop-south-china-sea.

46. Greg Torode and Simon Scarr, "Concrete and Coral: Beijing's South China Sea Building Boom Fuels Concerns," *Reuters*, May 2018, https://www.reuters.com

/article/us-china-southchinasea-insight/concrete-and-coral-beijings-south-china-sea-building-boom-fuels-concerns-idUSKCN1IO3GA.

47. Torode and Scarr, "Concrete and Coral."

48. Hal Brands, "The Unexceptional Superpower: American Grand Strategy in the Age of Trump," *Survival* 59, no. 6 (2017): 32.

5. CHINA'S IDENTITY AS A LEGITIMATE POWER

1. See, for example, Øystein Tunsjø, *The Return of Bipolarity in World Politics: China, the United States, and Geostructural Realism* (New York: Columbia University Press, 2018); Denny Roy, *Return of the Dragon* (New York: Columbia University Press, 2013); and Aaron Friedberg and Robert Ross, "Here Be Dragons: Is China a Military Threat?," *National Interest* 103 (September/October 2009): 19–34.

2. Jinghan Zheng, "Constructing a 'New Type of Great Power Relations': The State of Debate in China (1998–2014)," *British Journal of Politics and International Relations* 18, no. 2 (2016): 422–42; and David M. Lampton, "A New Type of Major-Power Relationship: Seeking a Durable Foundation for U.S.–China Ties," *Asia Policy* 16 (2013): 51–68.

3. See, for example, Feng Zhang, *Chinese Hegemony: Grand Strategy and International Institutions in East Asian History* (Stanford, Calif.: Stanford University Press, 2015); Thomas Christensen, *The China Challenge: Shaping the Choices of a Rising Power* (New York: Norton, 2015); and Evelyn Goh, *Rising China's Influence in Developing Asia* (Oxford: Oxford University Press, 2016).

4. All figures are calculated on constant 2010 U.S. dollars. "World Development Indicators Online," *World Bank*, http://data.worldbank.org/data-catalog/world-development-indicators.

5. Data drawn from the Stockholm International Peace Research Institute (SIPRI) Military Expenditure Database, https://www.sipri.org/databases/milex.

6. Qin Yaqing, "Continuity Through Change: Background Knowledge and China's International Strategy," *Chinese Journal of International Politics* 7, no. 3 (2014): 285.

7. Zheng Bijian, "China's 'Peaceful Rise' to Great-Power Status," *Foreign Affairs* 84, no. 5 (September/October 2005), https://www.foreignaffairs.com/articles/asia/2005-09-01/chinas-peaceful-rise-great-power-status.

8. "PRC's New Diplomacy Stress on More Active International Role," *Liaowang* (Beijing), July 11, 2005, trans. World News Connection.

9. Bates Gill, *Rising Star: China's New Security Diplomacy* (Washington, D.C.: Brookings Institution Press, 2007), 8.

10. Xi Jinping elaborated on the full details of the Chinese Dream in his address to the first session of the 12th National People's Congress on March 17, 2013.

11. Yang Jiechi, "Innovations in China's Diplomatic Theory and Practice Under New Circumstances," *Qiushi Journal* 6, no. 1 (2014), http://english.qstheory.cn/magazine/201401/201401/t20140121_315115.htm.

12. Christopher Johnson, *Decoding China's Emerging "Great Power" Strategy in Asia* (Washington, D.C.: Center for Strategic and International Studies, 2014), 16–17.

13. "Xi Jinping: China to Further Friendly Relations with Neighboring Countries," *Xinhua*, October 26, 2013, http://news.xinhuanet.com/english/china/2013-10/26/c_125601680.htm.

14. Ministry of Foreign Affairs of the People's Republic of China, "The Central Conference on Work Relating to Foreign Affairs Was Held in Beijing," November 29, 2014, http://www.fmprc.gov.cn/mfa_eng/zxxx_662805/t1215680.shtml.

15. Johnson, *Decoding China's Emerging "Great Power" Strategy in Asia*, 19.

16. Michael Swaine, "China's Assertive Behavior, Part One: On Core Interests," *China Leadership Monitor*, no. 34 (2010), https://www.hoover.org/sites/default/files/uploads/documents/CLM34MS.pdf.

17. Adam P. Liff and G. John Ikenberry, "Racing Toward Tragedy? China's Rise, Military Competition in the Asia Pacific, and the Security Dilemma," *International Security* 39, no. 2 (2014): 52–91.

18. Yong Deng, *China's Struggle for Status: The Realignment of International Relations* (Cambridge: Cambridge University Press, 2008), 39.

19. Liu Mingfu, *Zhongguo meng: hou Meiguo shidai de daguo siwei yu zhanlue dingwei* [The Chinese Dream: Great-power thinking and strategic posture in the post-U.S. era] (Beijing: Zhongguo youyi chubangongsi, 2010); and Yan Xuetong, "From Keeping a Low Profile to Striving for Achievement," *Chinese Journal of International Politics* 7, no. 2 (2014): 153–84.

20. Wang Jisi, "Zhongguo de guoji dingwei yu taoguangyanghui youshuozuowei de zhanlue sixiang" [The international positioning of China and the strategic principle of keeping a low profile while getting something accomplished], *Guoji wenti yanjiu* [International studies], no. 5 (2011): 29–30.

21. Wang Huning, "Zuowei guojia shili de wenhua: ruanquanli" [Soft power: Culture as the strength of the country], *Fudan xuebao shehui kexue ban* [Fudan University journal: Social science edition] 3 (1993): 91–96.

22. Qin Yaqing, "Guojia shenfen zhanlue wenhua he anquan liyi" [National identity, strategic culture, and security interests], *Shiji jingji yu zhengzhi* [World economics and politics], no. 1 (2003): 12.

23. Liu Feitao, "Quanli zeren yu daguo renting: jianlun zhongguo yingdui guojishehui zeren de yingyou taidu" [Power, responsibility, and great power identity: On the should-be attitude of China toward its international responsibility], *Taipingyang xuebao* [Pacific journal], no. 12 (2004): 25.

24. Zhang Ruizhuang, "Guoji geju bianhua yu zhongguo dingwei" [Change of international system and China's positioning], *Xiandai guoji guanxi* [Contemporary international relations], no. 4 (2013): 21.

25. Pu Xiaoyu, "Controversial Identity of a Rising China," *Chinese Journal of International Politics* 10, no. 2 (2017): 137.

26. Michael Martina and Benjamin Kang Lim, "China's Xi Anointed 'Core Leader,' on Par with Mao, Deng," *Reuters*, October 27, 2016, http://www.reuters.com/article/us-china-politics/chinas-xi-anointed-core-leader-on-par-with-mao-deng-idUSKCN12R1CK.

27. Alice Miller, "The 19th Central Committee Politburo," *China Leadership Monitor*, no. 55, January 23, 2018, https://www.hoover.org/sites/default/files/research/docs/clm55-am-final.pdf.

28. Yan Xuetong, "Political Leadership and Power Redistribution," *Chinese Journal of International Politics* 9, no. 1 (2016): 8.

29. Cheng Li, "The New Bipartisanship Within the Chinese Communist Party," *Orbis* 49 (2005): 388.

30. Kenneth Lieberthal and Michael Oksenberg, *Policy Making in China* (Princeton, N.J.: Princeton University Press, 1988).

31. For more on the role of plausibility probes and the use of "illustrative" case studies, see, for example, Jack Levy, "Case Studies: Types, Designs, and Logics of Inference," *Conflict Management and Peace Science* 25 (2008): 1–18; Harry Eckstein, "Case Studies and Theory in Political Science," in *Handbook of Political Science*, ed. Fred Greenstein and Nelson Polsby (Reading, Mass.: Addison-Wesley, 1975), 79–138; and Alexander George and Andrew Bennett, *Case Studies and Theory Development in the Social Sciences* (Cambridge, Mass.: MIT Press, 2005), 75.

32. UN Department of Peacekeeping Operations, "UN Missions Summary Detailed by Country," February 2020, https://peacekeeping.un.org/en/troop-and-police -contributors.

33. See, for example, Laura Neak, "UN Peacekeeping: In the Interest of Community or Self?," *Journal of Peace Research* 32, no. 2 (1995): 181–96; and Trevor Findlay, *Challenges for the New Peacekeepers* (Oxford: Oxford University Press, 1996), 8.

34. Nicholas J. Wheeler, *Saving Strangers: Humanitarian Intervention in International Society* (Oxford: Oxford University Press, 2000), 299–310.

35. See, for example, Robert Keohane and Lisa Martin, "The Promise of Institutionalist Theory," *International Security* 20, no. 1 (1995): 39–51; Edward Mansfield and Jon Pevehouse, "Democratization and International Organizations," *International Organization* 60, no. 1 (2006): 137–67; and James Lebovic, "United for Peace? Democracies and United Nations Peace Operations After the Cold War," *Journal of Conflict Resolution* 48, no. 6 (2004): 910–36.

36. Alex Bellamy and Paul Williams, *Providing Peacekeepers: The Politics, Challenges, and Future of United Nations Peacekeeping Contributions* (Oxford: Oxford University Press, 2013), 9.

37. See, for example, Courtney Fung, *China and Intervention at the UN Security Council: Reconciling Status* (New York: Oxford University Press, 2019); Samuel Kim, "China's International Organization Behavior," *Chinese Foreign Policy: Theory and Practice*, ed. Thomas Robinson and David Shambaugh (Oxford: Clarendon Press, 1995), 401–34; and Yin He, *China's Changing Policy on UN Peacekeeping Operations* (Stockholm: Institute for Security and Development Policy, 2007). Parts of the analysis in this section are adapted from Chin-Hao Huang, "Principles and Praxis of China's Peacekeeping," *International Peacekeeping* 18, no. 3 (2011): 257–70.

38. Kim, "China's International Organization Behavior."

39. Sophie Richardson, *China, Cambodia, and the Five Principles of Peaceful Coexistence* (New York: Columbia University Press, 2009).

40. Michael Martina and David Brunnstrom, "China's Xi Says to Commit 8,000 Troops for U.N. Peacekeeping Force," *Reuters*, September 29, 2015, http://www .reuters.com/article/us-un-assembly-china-idUSKCN0RS1Z120150929.

41. "New U.N. Chief in China, Calls for Human Rights Respect," *Reuters*, November 28, 2016, http://www.reuters.com/article/us-china-un-idUSKBN13N0TV.

42. "'Brahimi Report': Report of the Panel on United Nations Peace Operations," *United Nations Conferences, Meetings, and Events*, November 13, 2000, http://www .un.org/en/events/pastevents/brahimi_report.shtml.

43. "Security Council, Responding to 'Brahimi Report,' Adopts Wide-Ranging Resolution on Peacekeeping Resolutions," *United Nations Meetings Coverage and Press Releases*, https://www.un.org/press/en/2000/20001113.sc6948.doc.html.

44. For a comprehensive analysis on the Brahimi report, see, for example, Alex Bellamy and Paul Williams, "Conclusion: What Future for Peace Operations? Brahimi and Beyond," *International Peacekeeping* 11, no. 1 (2004): 183–212; Christine Gray, "Peacekeeping After the Brahimi Report: Is There a Crisis of Credibility for the UN?," *Journal of Conflict and Security Law* 6, no. 2 (2001): 267–88; Sorpong Peou, "The UN, Peacekeeping, and Collective Human Security: From an Agenda for Peace to the Brahimi Report," *International Peacekeeping* 9, no. 2 (2002): 51–68; and Nigel White, "Commentary on the Report of the Panel on United Nations Peace Operations (The Brahimi Report)," *Journal of Conflict and Security Law* 6, no. 1 (2001): 127–46.

45. United Nations Security Council, "S/PV.4220: Overview of Security Council Meeting Records," November 13, 2000, https://undocs.org/S/PV.4220.

46. "Security Council Moves to Enhance Protection of Civilians in Conflict," *United Nations Meetings Coverage and Press Releases*, April 19, 2000, https://www.un.org/press/en/2000/20000419.sc6847.doc.html.

47. UN Department of Peacekeeping Operations and Department of Field Support, "A New Partnership Agenda: Chartering a New Horizon for UN Peacekeeping," July 2009, https://peacekeeping.un.org/sites/default/files/newhorizon_0.pdf.

48. Taylor Seybolt, *Humanitarian Military Intervention: The Conditions for Success and Failure* (Oxford: Oxford University Press, 2007); and Gareth Evans, "Responding to Atrocities: The New Geopolitics of Intervention," *SIPRI Yearbook 2012* (Oxford: Oxford University Press, 2012).

49. United Nations Security Council, "S/PV.6153: Official Records of the Security Council," June 29, 2009, https://undocs.org/S/PV.6153.

50. United Nations Security Council, "S/PV.6178: Official Records of the Security Council," August 5, 2009, https://undocs.org/S/PV.6178.

51. On China's pragmatic interpretation of and increasing malleability with sovereignty in foreign affairs, see Allen Carlson, *Unifying China, Integrating with the World: Securing Chinese Sovereignty in the Reform Era* (Stanford, Calif.: Stanford University Press, 2008).

52. United Nations Security Council, "S/PV.6928: Overview of Security Council Meeting Records," March 5, 2013, https://undocs.org/S/PV.6928.

53. Interviews with senior UN officials in Kinshasa and New York and with AU officials in Addis Ababa, June 2014.

54. For a similar trend line in other conflict areas and interventions, see Courtney Fung, *China and Intervention at the UN Security Council: Reconciling Status* (New York: Oxford University Press, 2019). Fung argues that seeking recognition from both its intervention peer groups of great powers and developing states helps explain China's changing position on interventions.

55. "Security Council Extends Mandate of United Nations Mission in Liberia, Adopting Resolution 2333 (2016) by 12 Votes in Favor, 3 Abstentions," *United Nations Meetings Coverage and Press Releases*, December 23, 2016, https://www.un.org/press/en/2016/sc12654.doc.htm.

56. The Addis Agreement of November 2006, also known as the Annan Plan, called for a three-step expansion of a hybrid AU–UN peacekeeping force in Darfur and for Khartoum to commit to a ceasefire in the region.

57. Dan Large, "China's Sudan Engagement: Changing Northern and Southern Political Trajectories in Peace and War," *China Quarterly* 199 (September 2009): 610–26; and Chin-Hao Huang, "U.S.–China Relations and Darfur," *Fordham International Law Journal* 31, no. 4 (2008): 827–42.

58. Edward Cody, "China Given Credit for Darfur Role," *Washington Post*, January 13, 2007, https://www.washingtonpost.com/archive/politics/2007/01/13/china-given -credit-for-darfur-role-span-classbankheadus-official-cites-new-willingness-to -wield-influence-in-sudanspan/6b815084-4ad6-427c-ab94-0a4d642cf0c9/.

59. Cody, "China Given Credit for Darfur Role."

60. "Diplomat Views China's Role on Darfur Issue, Stresses 'Even-Handedness,'" *BBC News*, June 2, 2007.

61. Interviews with senior AU diplomats and Chinese specialists and scholars on African affairs, January 2010.

62. Richard McGregor, "Iran, Nigeria, Sudan Off China Incentive List," *Financial Times*, March 2, 2007.

63. Ministry of Foreign Affairs of the People's Republic of China, "Statement by Ambassador Zhang Yishan at the Special Committee on Peacekeeping Operations," February 1, 2005, https://www.fmprc.gov.cn/ce/ceun/eng/zghlhg/hphaq /whxd/t182269.htm.

64. Forum on China and Africa Cooperation, "FOCAC Sharm-el-Sheikh Action Plan 2010–2012," November 8, 2009, http://www.fmprc.gov.cn/zflt/eng/dsjbzjhy/hywj /t626387.htm.

65. Forum on China–Africa Cooperation, "The Fifth Ministerial Conference of the Forum on China–Africa Cooperation Beijing Action Plan 2013–2015," July 23, 2012, http://www.focac.org/eng/ltda/dwjbzjjhys/hywj/t954620.htm.

66. Forum on China and Africa Cooperation, "FOCAC Beijing Action Plan 2019– 2021," September 12, 2018, https://focacsummit.mfa.gov.cn/eng/hyqk_1/t1594297 .htm.

67. Forum on China and Africa Cooperation, "FOCAC Beijing Action Plan 2019–2021."

68. "Qian Qichen Urges Further Promotion of International Human Rights," *Xinhua*, October 20, 2008.

69. Allen Carlson, "China's Approach to Sovereignty and Intervention," in *New Directions in the Study of China's Foreign Policy*, ed. Alastair Iain Johnston and Robert Ross (Stanford, Calif.: Stanford University Press, 2006), 217–41.

70. Lei Jiang and Wang Haijun, "Xianxing duiwai yuanzhu zhong fujia zhengzhi tiaojian chayi fenxi: jiyu zhongguo yu xifang waiyuan shijian de bijiao yanjiu" [An analysis on the variance-attached political condition in current foreign aid: Based on a comparative study on the practice of foreign aid of China and Western countries], *Taipingyang xuebao* [Pacific journal] 19, no. 7 (2011): 53–62.

71. See, for example, Yan Haiyan, "Baohu de zheren jisei" [An analysis of the responsibility to protect], *Xibu faxue Pinglun* [Western law review], no. 1 (2010): 125–29; Xu Guojin, "Guojia lüxing guoji renquan yiwu de xiandu" [The limits on state

performance of human rights obligations], *Zhongguo faxue* [Chinese legal science], no. 2 (1992): 13–20; and Zeng Lingliang, "Lun lengzhan hou shidai de guojia zhuquan" [A discussion of state sovereignty in the post–Cold War era], *Zhongguo faxue* [Chinese legal science], no. 1 (1998): 109–20.

72. Carlson, "China's Approach to Sovereignty and Intervention." See also Liu Jie, *Renquan yu guojia zhuquan* [Human rights and state sovereignty] (Shanghai: Shanghai renmin chubanshe, 2004); Cheng Shuaihua, "Guojia zhuquan yu guoji renquan de ruogan wenti" [Issues involving international human rights and state sovereignty], *Ouzhou* [*Europe*], no. 1 (2000): 32–35; and Shi Yinhong, "Lun ershi shiji guoji guifan tixi" [A discussion of the system of international norms in the twentieth century], *Guoji luntan* [International forum], no. 6 (2000): 8–10.

73. Carlson, *Unifying China, Integrating with the World.*

74. United Nations Security Council, "S/PV.5261: Overview of Security Council Meeting Records," September 14, 2005, https://undocs.org/S/PV.5261.

75. Ministry of Foreign Affairs of the People's Republic of China, "Statement by Ambassador Zhang Yishan at the Security Council's Open Debate on 'The Role of the Security Council in Humanitarian Crises,'" July 12, 2005, https://www.fmprc.gov.cn/ce/ceun/eng/chinaandun/securitycouncil/thematicissues/other_thematicissues/t203694.htm.

6. CONCLUSIONS ON POWER AND RESTRAINT IN CHINA'S RISE

1. Historians and observers have noted the oft-erroneous application of Thucydides's account of the Peloponnesian War to the emerging global rivalry in contemporary international politics. See, for example, Donald Kagan, *Thucydides: The Reinvention of History* (London: Penguin, 2010); Arthur Waldron, "There Is No Thucydides Trap," *SupChina*, June 12, 2017, https://supchina.com/2017/06/12/no-thucydides-trap/; Steve Chan, "More Than One Trap: Problematic Interpretations and Overlooked Lessons from Thucydides," *Journal of Chinese Political Science* 24, no. 1 (2019): 11–24; Eric Robinson, "Thucydides on the Causes and Outbreak of the Peloponnesian War," in *The Oxford Handbook of Thucydides*, ed. Sara Forsdyke, Edith Foster, and Ryan Balot, March 2017, https://www.oxfordhandbooks.com/view/10.1093/oxfordhb/97801 99340385.001.0001/oxfordhb-9780199340385-e-23; and Matthew Klein, "For the Love of Zeus, Stop Misusing Thucydides," *Financial Times*, June 27, 2017, https://ftalphaville.ft.com/2017/06/27/2190601/for-the-love-of-zeus-stop-misusing-thucydides/.

2. See, for example, David A. Lake, "Relational Authority and Legitimacy in International Relations," *American Behavioral Scientist* 53, no. 3 (2009): 331–53; Kishore Mahbubani, *Beyond the Age of Innocence: Rebuilding Trust Between American and the World* (New York: Public Affairs, 2005); and Francis Fukuyama, *America at the Crossroads: Democracy, Power, and the Neoconservative Legacy* (New Haven, Conn.: Yale University Press, 2007).

3. Martha Finnemore, *National Interests in International Society* (Ithaca, N.Y.: Cornell University Press, 1996); Thomas Risse-Kappen, "Democratic Peace–Warlike

Democracies? A Social Constructivist Interpretation of the Liberal Argument," *European Journal of International Relations* 1, no. 4 (1995): 491–517; Jonathan Mercer, "Anarchy and Identity," *International Organization* 49, no. 2 (1995): 229–52; and Philip Zimbardo and Michael Leippe, *The Psychology of Attitude Change and Social Influence* (New York: McGraw Hill, 1991).

4. Erik Ringmar, *Identity, Interest and Action: A Cultural Explanation of Sweden's Intervention in the Thirty Years War* (Cambridge: Cambridge University Press, 1996).

5. John Orbell, Robyn Dawes, and Alphonus J. C. Van de Kragt, "Explaining Discussion-Induced Cooperation," *Journal of Personality and Social Psychology* 54, no. 5 (1998): 811–19; Tajfel, "Social Psychology of Intergroup Relations;" Tajfel and Turner, "The Social Identity Theory of Intergroup Behavior," in *Key Readings in Social Psychology*, ed. John T. Jost and Jim Sidanius (New York: Psychology Press, 2004), 276–93; and Marilynn B. Brewer and Rupert Brown, "Intergroup Relations," in *The Handbook of Social Psychology*, ed. Daniel T. Gilbert and Sustan T. Flake (Boston: McGraw Hill, 1998), 554–94.

6. Defense Minister Ng Eng Hen, remarks made at the Munich Security Conference and NATO Centre of Excellence for Operations in Confined and Shallow Waters Maritime Security Roundtable, Berlin, February 2019.

7. "Singapore Says TPP Vital for U.S. to Be Taken Seriously in Asia," *Reuters*, June 16, 2015, https://www.reuters.com/article/us-usa-trade-singapore-idUSKBN0OV2NF 20150615.

8. Secretary of State Antony Blinken, "The Biden Administration's Priorities for U.S. Foreign Policy," remarks presented by to the United States House Committee on Foreign Affairs, Washington, D.C., March 10, 2021.

9. Alastair Iain Johnston, *Social States: China in International Institutions, 1980–2000* (Princeton, N.J.: Princeton University Press, 2008), 37. For additional analysis of≈China's realpolitik worldviews, see Thomas Christensen, "Chinese Realpolitik," *Foreign Affairs* 75, no. 5 (September/October 1998): 37–52; and William Callahan, "National Insecurities: Humiliation, Salvation, and Chinese Nationalism," *Alternatives* 29, no. 2 (2004): 199–218.

10. Steve Chan, *China's Troubled Waters: Maritime Disputes in Theoretical Perspective* (Cambridge: Cambridge University Press, 2016), 36.

11. ASEAN, "ASEAN Outlook on the Indo-Pacific," June 22, 2019, https://asean.org /wp-content/uploads/2019/06/ASEAN-Outlook-on-the-Indo-Pacific_FINAL _22062019.pdf.

12. See, for example, James Fearon, "Rationalist Explanations for War," *International Organization* 49, no. 3 (1995): 379–414; Robert Powell, "Bargaining Theory and International Conflict," *Annual Review of Political Science* 5 (2002): 1–30; and Kang, *American Grand Strategy and East Asian Security in the Twenty-First Century* (New York: Cambridge University Press, 2017).

13. "U.S. and China Trade Angry Words at High-Level Alaska Talks," *BBC News*, March 19, 2021.

REFERENCES

Abrahamsson, Bengt. 1969. "Military Professionalization and Estimates on the Probability of War." In *Military Profession and Military Regimes*, ed. Jacques van Doorn, 35–51. The Hague: Mouton.

Acharya, Amitav. 2004. "How Ideas Spread: Whose Norms Matter? Norm Localization and Institutional Change in Asian Regionalism." *International Organization* 58, no. 2: 239–75.

——. 2013. *The Making of Southeast Asia: International Relations of a Region*. Ithaca, N.Y.: Cornell University Press.

——. 2014. "Power Shift or Paradigm Shift? China's Rise and Asia's Emerging Security Order." *International Studies Quarterly* 58, no. 1: 158–73.

——. 2017. "ASEAN at 50: Reflections on Its Past, Present, and Future," keynote remarks to ASEAN Studies Center, Institute of Southeast Asian Studies, Singapore, February 1.

——. 2017. "The Myth of ASEAN Centrality?" *Contemporary Southeast Asia* 39, no. 2: 273–79.

Aguilar, Krissy. 2020. "Palace: Duterte Won't Give 'an Inch' of PH Territory to Other States." *Inquirer.net*, August 24. https://globalnation.inquirer.net/190386/palace -duterte-wont-give-an-inch-of-ph-territory-to-other-states.

Allard, Tom. 2020. "Exclusive: Indonesia Rejected U.S. Request to Host Spy Planes—Officials." *Reuters*, October 20. https://www.reuters.com/article/indonesia-usa -idUSKBN2750M7.

Allard, Tom, and Stanley Widianto. 2020. "Indonesia to U.S., China: Don't Trap Us in Your Rivalry." *Reuters*, September 8. https://www.reuters.com/article/us-indonesia -politics-foreign-minister-idUSKBN25Z1ZD.

Art, Robert. 1996. "American Foreign Policy and the Fungibility of Force." *Security Studies* 5, no. 4: 7–42.

——. 2003. *A Grand Strategy for America*. Ithaca, N.Y.: Cornell University Press.

Art, Robert, and Kenneth Waltz. 1971. *The Use of Force: Military Power and International Politics*. New York: Rowman and Littlefield.

Association of Southeast Asian Nations. 2014. "ASEAN Foreign Ministers' Statement on the Current Developments in the South China Sea." May 10. http://www.asean.org/storage/images/documents/24thASEANSummit/ASEAN Foreign Ministers Statement on the current developments in the south china sea.pdf.

——. 2014. "Joint Communiqué of the 47th ASEAN Foreign Ministers' Meeting." August 8. https://asean.org/wp-content/uploads/2012/05/Joint-Communique-of-47th-AMM.pdf.

——. 2015. "Chairman's Statement of the 10th East Asia Summit." November 25. http://www.asean.org/wp-content/uploads/2015/12/Chairmans-Statement-of-the-10th-East-Asia-Summit-Final-25-Nov.pdf.

——. 2019. "ASEAN Outlook on the Indo-Pacific." June 22. https://asean.org/wp-content/uploads/2019/06/ASEAN-Outlook-on-the-Indo-Pacific_FINAL_22062019.pdf.

Ba, Alice. 2009. *(Re)Negotiating East and Southeast Asia: Regions, Regionalisms, and the Association of Southeast Asian Nations*. Stanford, Calif.: Stanford University Press.

Bader, Jeffrey. 2015. "Changing China Policy: Are We in Search of Enemies?" Brookings China Strategy Paper no. 1.

Baldwin, David A. 2016. *Power and International Relations: A Conceptual Approach*. Princeton, N.J.: Princeton University Press.

Barnett, Michael, and Raymond Duvall. 2005. "Power in International Politics." *International Organization* 59, no. 1: 39–75.

BBC Monitoring Asia Pacific. 2014. "Chinese Fishing Vessels Block Vietnamese Boats," June 18.

BBC News. 2007. "Diplomat Views China's Role on Darfur Issue, Stresses 'Even-Handedness," June.

——. 2021. "U.S. and China Trade Angry Words at High-Level Alaska Talks," March 19.

Beckley, Michael. 2015. "The Myth of Entangling Alliances." *International Security* 39, no. 4: 7–48.

Beeson, Mark. 2009. "ASEAN's Ways: Still Fit for Purpose?" *Cambridge Review of International Affairs* 22, no. 3: 333–43.

Bell, David. 1975. *Power, Influence, and Authority*. Oxford: Oxford University Press.

Bellamy, Alex, and Paul Williams. 2004. "Conclusion: What Future for Peace Operations? Brahimi and Beyond." *International Peacekeeping* 11, no. 1: 183–212.

——. 2013. *Providing Peacekeepers: The Politics, Challenges, and Future of United Nations Peacekeeping Contributions*. Oxford: Oxford University Press.

Benson, Brett. 2012. *Constructing International Security: Alliances, Deterrence, and Moral Hazard*. Cambridge: Cambridge University Press.

Betts, Richard. 2003. "Striking First: A History of Thankfully Lost Opportunities." *Ethics and International Affairs* 17, no. 1: 17–24.

——. 2005. "The Political Support for American Primacy." *International Affairs* 81, no. 1: 1–14.

Betz, Andrew, John Skowronski, and Thomas Ostrom. 1996. "Shared Realities: Social Influence and Stimulus Memory." *Social Cognition* 14, no. 2: 113–40.

Bisley, Nick. 2016. "We Should Think Carefully About an Australian FONOP in the South China Sea." Lowy Institute. https://www.lowyinstitute.org/the-interpreter /we-should-think-carefully-about-australian-fonop-south-china-sea.

Blau, Peter. 1963. "Critical Remarks on Weber's Theory of Authority." *American Political Science Review* 57, no. 2: 305–16.

Blanchard, Ben. 2016. "Duterte Aligns Philippines with China, Says U.S. Has Lost." *Reuters*, October 20. https://www.reuters.com/article/us-china-philippines -idUSKCN12K0AS.

Blinken, Antony. 2021. "The Biden Administration's Priorities for U.S. Foreign Policy." Remarks presented to United States House Committee on Foreign Affairs, Washington, D.C., March 10.

Brands, Hal. 2017. "The Unexceptional Superpower: American Grand Strategy in the Age of Trump." *Survival* 59, no. 6: 7–40.

Brewer, Marilynn B., and Rupert Brown. 1998. "Intergroup Relations." In *The Handbook of Social Psychology*, ed. Daniel T. Gilbert and Sustan T. Flake, 554–94. Boston: McGraw Hill.

Brooks, Stephen G., and William C. Wohlforth. 2011. "Assessing the Balance." *Cambridge Review of International Affairs* 24, no. 2: 201–19.

Brooks, Stephen, G. John Ikenberry, and William Wohlforth. 2012. "Don't Come Home, America: The Case Against Retrenchment." *International Security* 37, no. 2: 7–51.

Bull, Hedley. 1995. *The Anarchical Society: A Study of Order in World Politics.* Basingstoke, UK: Macmillan.

Caballero-Anthony, Mely. 2005. *Regional Security in Southeast Asia: Beyond the ASEAN Way.* Singapore: Institute of Southeast Asian Studies.

Callahan, William. 2004. "National Insecurities: Humiliation, Salvation, and Chinese Nationalism." *Alternatives* 29, no. 2: 199–218.

Carlson, Allen. 2006. "China's Approach to Sovereignty and Intervention." In *New Directions in the Study of China's Foreign Policy*, ed. Alastair Iain Johnston and Robert Ross, 217–41. Stanford, Calif.: Stanford University Press.

——. 2008. *Unifying China, Integrating with the World: Securing Chinese Sovereignty in the Reform Era.* Stanford, Calif.: Stanford University Press.

Cha, Victor. 2010. "Powerplay: Origins of the US Alliance System in Asia." *International Security* 34, no. 3: 158–96.

Chan, Steve. 2012. *Looking for Balance: China, the United States, and Power Balancing in East Asia.* Stanford, Calif.: Stanford University Press.

——. 2016. *China's Troubled Waters: Maritime Disputes in Theoretical Perspective.* Cambridge: Cambridge University Press.

——. 2019. "More than One Trap: Problematic Interpretations and Overlooked Lessons from Thucydides." *Journal of Chinese Political Science* 24, no. 1: 11–24.

Checkel, Jeffrey T. 2001. "Why Comply? Social Learning and European Identity Change." *International Organization* 55, no. 3: 553–88.

——. 2003. "Going Native in Europe? Theorizing Social Interaction in European Institutions." *Comparative Political Studies* 36: 209–31.

Cheng Shuaihua. 2000. "Guojia zhuquan yu guoji renquan de ruogan wenti" [Issues involving international human rights and state sovereignty]. *Ouzhou* [Europe] 1: 32–35.

China Central Television. 2016. "China–South China Sea White Paper," July. http://newscontent.cctv.com/NewJsp/news.jsp?fileId=365288.

Christensen, Thomas. 1998. "Chinese Realpolitik." *Foreign Affairs* 75, no. 5: 37–52.

——. 2015. *The China Challenge: Shaping the Choices of a Rising Power*. New York: Norton.

Christensen, Thomas, and Jack Snyder. 1990. "Chained Gangs and Passed Bucks: Predicting Alliance Patterns in Multipolarity." *International Organization* 44, no. 2: 137–68.

Clark, Ian. 2007. *Legitimacy in International Society*. Oxford: Oxford University Press.

——. 2009. "Towards an English School Theory of Hegemony." *European Journal of International Relations* 15, no. 2: 203–28.

Cline, Ray. 1975. *World Power Assessment: A Calculus of Strategic Drift*. Boulder, Colo.: Westview Press.

Cody, Edward. 2007. "China Given Credit for Darfur Role." *Washington Post*, January 13.

Congressional Research Service. 2013. "Assessing the January 2012 Defense Strategic Guidance."

Dahl, Robert. 1963. *Modern Political Analysis*. Englewood Cliffs, N.J.: Prentice Hall.

Deng, Yong. 2008. *China's Struggle for Status: The Realignment of International Relations*. Cambridge: Cambridge University Press.

Dowling, John, and Jeffrey Pfeffer. 1975. "Organizational Legitimacy: Social Values and Organizational Behavior." *Pacific Sociological Review* 18, no. 1: 122–36.

Eckstein, Harry. 1975. "Case Studies and Theory in Political Science." In *Handbook of Political Science*, ed. Fred Greenstein and Nelson Polsby, 79–138. Reading, Mass.: Addison-Wesley.

Emmers, Ralph. 2010. *Geopolitics and Maritime Territorial Disputes in East Asia*. London: Routledge.

Emmerson, Donald. 2007. "Challenging ASEAN: A 'Topological' View." *Contemporary Southeast Asia* 29, no. 3: 424–46.

Erickson, Andrew S. 2016. "America's Security Role in the South China Sea." *Naval War College Review* 69, no. 1: 1–14.

Evans, Gareth. 2012. "Responding to Atrocities: The New Geopolitics of Intervention." *SIPRI Yearbook 2012*. Oxford: Oxford University Press.

Fearon, James. 1995. "Rationalist Explanations for War." *International Organization* 49, no. 3: 379–414.

Findlay, Trevor. 1996. *Challenges for the New Peacekeepers*. Oxford: Oxford University Press.

Finnemore, Martha. 1996. *National Interests in International Society*. Ithaca, N.Y.: Cornell University Press.

——. 1996. "Norms, Culture, and World Politics: Insights from Sociology's Institutionalism." *International Organization* 50, no. 2: 325–27.

Foot, Rosemary. 1995. *The Practice of Power: U.S. Relations with China Since 1949*. Oxford: Oxford University Press.

Forum on China–Africa Cooperation. 2009. "FOCAC Sharm-el-Sheikh Action Plan 2010-2012." November. http://www.fmprc.gov.cn/zflt/eng/dsjbzjhy/hywj/t626387.htm.

———. 2012. "The Fifth Ministerial Conference of the Forum on China–Africa Coopera-tion Beijing Action Plan 2013–2015." July. http://www.focac.org/eng/ltda/dwjbzjjhys/hywj/t954620.htm.

———. 2012. "FOCAC Beijing Action Plan 2019–2021." September. https://focacsummit.mfa.gov.cn/eng/hyqk_1/t1594297.htm.

Fravel, M. Taylor. 2008. *Strong Borders, Secure Nation: Cooperation and Conflict in China's Territorial Disputes*. Princeton, N.J.: Princeton University Press.

———. 2011. "China's Strategy in the South China Sea." *Contemporary Southeast Asia* 33, no. 3: 292–319.

———. 2012. "All Quiet in the South China Sea: Why China Is Playing Nice (for Now)," *Foreign Affairs*, March 22.

French, John, and Bertram Raven. 1959. "The Bases of Social Power." In *Studies of Social Power*, ed. Dorwin Cartwright, 150–67. Ann Arbor: University of Michigan Press.

Friedberg, Aaron. 1993. "Ripe for Rivalry: Prospects for Peace in a Multipolar Asia." *International Security* 18, no. 3: 5–33.

———. 2015. "The Debate Over U.S. China Strategy." *Survival* 57, no. 3: 89–110.

Friedberg, Aaron, and Robert Ross. 2009. "Here Be Dragons: Is China a Military Threat?" *National Interest* 103 (September/October): 19–34.

Fukuyama, Francis. 2007. *America at the Crossroads: Democracy, Power, and the Neo-conservative Legacy*. New Haven, Conn.: Yale University Press.

Fung, Courtney. 2019. *China and Intervention at the UN Security Council: Reconciling Status*. New York: Oxford University Press.

Gandhi, Jennifer, and Adam Przeworski. 2007. "Authoritarian Institutions and the Survival of Autocrats." *Comparative Political Studies* 40, no. 11: 1279–1301.

Gartzke, Erik, and Jon Lindsay. 2019. *Cross-Domain Deterrence: Strategy in an Era of Complexity*. Oxford: Oxford University Press.

Geddes, Barbara. 1990. "How the Cases You Choose Affect the Answers You Get: Selection Bias in Comparative Politics." *Political Analysis* 2: 131–50.

George, Alexander, and Andrew Bennett. 2005. *Case Studies and Theory Development in the Social Sciences*. Cambridge, Mass.: MIT Press.

George, Alexander, and Richard Smoke. 1974. *Deterrence in American Foreign Policy: Theory and Practice*. New York: Columbia University Press.

Gheciu, Alexandra. 2007. "Security Institutions as Agents of Socialization? NATO and the 'New Europe.'" In *International Institutions and Socialization in Europe*, ed. Jeffrey T. Checkel, 171–210. New York: Cambridge University Press.

Gholz, Eugene, Daryl G. Press, and Harvey M. Sapolsky. 1997. "Come Home, America: The Strategy of Restraint in the Face of Temptation." *International Security* 21, no. 4: 5–48.

Gibler, Douglas. 2008. "The Costs of Reneging: Reputation and Alliance Formation." *Journal of Conflict Resolution* 52, no. 3: 426–54.

Gill, Bates. 2007. *Rising Star: China's New Security Diplomacy*. Washington, D.C.: Brookings Institution Press.

Gilpin, Robert. 1975. *U.S. Power and Multinational Corporation*. New York: Basic Books.

Goddard, Stacie E. 2008. "When Right Makes Might: How Prussia Overturned the European Balance of Power." *International Security* 33, no. 3: 110–42.

Goddard, Stacie E., and Ronald R. Krebs. 2015. "Rhetoric, Legitimation, and Grand Strategy." *Security Studies* 24, no. 5: 5–36.

Goh, Evelyn. 2008. "Great Powers and Hierarchical Order in Southeast Asia: Analyzing Regional Security Strategies." *International Security* 32, no. 3: 113–57.

——. 2013. *The Struggle for Order: Hegemony, Hierarchy, and Transition in Post-Cold War East Asia*. Oxford: Oxford University Press.

——. 2014. "The Modes of China's Influence Cases from Southeast Asia." *Asian Survey* 54, no. 5: 825–48.

——. 2016. *Rising China's Influence in Developing Asia*. Oxford: Oxford University Press.

Goldstein, Avery. 2005. *Rising to the Challenge: China's Grand Strategy and International Security*. Stanford, Calif.: Stanford University Press.

——. 2013. "First Things First: The Present (If Not Clear) Danger of Crisis Instability in U.S.–China Relations." *International Security* 37, no. 4: 49–89.

Gomez, Jim. 2020. "China, Philippine Defense Chiefs Discuss Territorial Dispute." *Associated Press*. September 11. https://apnews.com/article/beijing-south-china -sea-territorial-disputes-philippines-china-626f161db42af40758bc9f7912dfb450.

Gray, Christine. 2001. "Peacekeeping After the Brahimi Report: Is There a Crisis of Credibility for the UN?" *Journal of Conflict and Security Law* 6, no. 2: 267–88.

Green, Michael. 2017. *By More than Providence: Grand Strategy and American Power in the Asia Pacific Since 1783*. New York: Columbia University Press.

Guzzini, Stefano. 1993. "Structural Power: The Limits of Neorealist Power Analysis." *International Organization* 47, no. 3: 443–78.

Haacke, Jurgen. 2003. *ASEAN's Diplomatic and Security Culture: Origins, Development and Prospects*. London: Routledge.

Haas, Peter. 1998. "Compliance with EU Directives: Insights from International Relations and Comparative Politics." *Journal of European Public Policy* 5: 17–37.

Haddick, Robert. 2012. "Salami Slicing in the South China Sea." *Foreign Policy*, August.

Hagan, Joe, Philip P. Everts, Haruhiro Fukui, and John D. Stempel. 2001. "Foreign Policy by Coalition: Deadlock, Compromise, and Anarchy." *International Studies Review* 3, no. 2: 169–216.

Hamilton-Hart, Natasha. 2012. *Hard Interests, Soft Illusions: Southeast Asia and American Power*. Ithaca, N.Y.: Cornell University Press.

Hayton, Bill. 2015. *Vietnam and the United States: An Emerging Security Partnership*. Sydney: United States Studies Centre, University of Sydney.

He, Yin. 2007. *China's Changing Policy on UN Peacekeeping Operations*. Stockholm: Institute for Security and Development Policy.

Heydarian, Richard. 2020. "ASEAN Finally Pushes Back on China's Sea Claims." *Asia Times*, June 30.

Hoover Institution. 2018. *Chinese Influence and American Interests: Promoting Constructive Vigilance*. Stanford, Calif.: Hoover Institution Press.

Huang, Chin-Hao. 2008. "U.S.–China Relations and Darfur." *Fordham International Law Journal* 31, no. 4: 827–42.

——. 2011. "Principles and Praxis of China's Peacekeeping." *International Peacekeeping* 18, no. 3: 257–70.

Huntington, Samuel P. 1957. *The Soldier and the State*. Cambridge, Mass.: Harvard University Press.

Hurd, Ian. 1999. "Legitimacy and Authority in International Politics." *International Organization* 53, no. 2: 379–408.

——. 2008. *After Anarchy: Legitimacy and Power in the United Nations Security Council*. Princeton, N.J.: Princeton University Press.

Huxley, Tim, and Benjamin Schreer. 2016. "Standing Up to China." *Survival* 57, no. 6: 127–44.

Huyen, Anh. 2014. "24th ASEAN Summit Shows Spirit of Unity." *Voice of Vietnam*, May 9. http://vovworld.vn/en-us/Current-Affairs/24th-ASEAN-summit-shows-spirit -of-unity/236637.vov.

Ikenberry, G. John. 2000. *After Victory: Institutions, Strategic Restraint, and the Rebuilding of Order After Major Wars*. Princeton, N.J.: Princeton University Press.

——. 2016. "Between the Eagle and the Dragon: America, China, and Middle State Strategies in East Asia." *Political Science Quarterly* 131, no. 1: 9–43.

Ikenberry, G. John, and Daniel H. Nexon. 2019. "Hegemony Studies 3.0: The Dynamics of Hegemonic Orders." *Security Studies* 28, no. 3: 395–421.

Jacobson, Harold, and Michel Oksenberg. 1990. *China's Participation in the IMF, the World Bank, and GATT*. Ann Arbor: University of Michigan Press.

Jaipragas, Bhavan. 2019. "Malaysia Won't Back Down on Sensitive Issues Even as It Bolsters Economic Ties with China." *South China Morning Post*, April 23. https:// www.scmp.com/week-asia/politics/article/3007221/malaysia-wont-back-down -sensitive-issues-even-it-bolsters.

Jakobson, Linda. 2014. *China's Unpredictable Maritime Security Actors*. Sydney: Lowy Institute for International Policy.

Jakobson, Linda, and Dean Knox. 2010. *New Foreign Policy Actors in China*, SIPRI Policy Paper 26. Stockholm: Stockholm International Peace Research Institute.

Jane's Defence Weekly. 2016. "China Deploys HQ-9 Surface-to-Air Missiles to Woody Island," February. http://www.janes.com/article/58071/china-deploys-hq-9-surface- to-air-missiles-to-woody-island.

Jentleson, Bruce. 2020. "Refocusing U.S. Grand Strategy on Pandemic and Environment Mass Destruction." *Washington Quarterly* 43, no. 3: 7–29.

Jepperson, Ronald, Alexander Wendt, and Peter Katzenstein. 1996. "Norms, Identity and Culture in National Security." In *The Culture of National Security*, ed. Peter Katzenstein, 33–75. New York: Columbia University Press.

Jervis, Robert. 1979. "Deterrence Theory Revisited." *World Politics* 31, no. 2: 289–324.

Johnson, Christopher. 2014. *Decoding China's Emerging "Great Power" Strategy in Asia*. Washington, D.C.: Center for Strategic and International Studies.

Johnson, Jesse, and Brett Ashley Leeds. 2011. "Defense Pacts: A Prescription for Peace?" *Foreign Policy Analysis* 7, no. 1: 45–65.

Johnston, Alastair Iain. 1995. *Cultural Realism: Strategic Culture and Grand Strategy in Chinese History*. Princeton, N.J.: Princeton University Press.

——. 1996. "Learning Versus Adaptation: Explaining Change in Chinese Arms Control Policy in the 1980s and 1990s." *China Journal* 35: 27–61.

——. 2008. *Social States: China in International Institutions, 1980-2000*. Princeton, N.J.: Princeton University Press.

——. 2012. "What (If Anything) Does East Asia Tell Us About International Relations Theory?" *Annual Review of Political Science* 15: 53–78.

——. 2013. "How New and Assertive Is China's New Assertiveness?" *International Security* 37, no. 4: 7–48.

——. 2019. "The Failure of the 'Failure of Engagement' with China." *Washington Quarterly* 42, no. 2: 99–114.

Ju Hailong. 2013. "Zhongfei haishang guanxi de tubian jiqi yuanyin yu yingxiang" (The sudden change in China–Philippines maritime security relations and its causes and influences]. *Guoji anquan yanjiu* [Journal of international security studies] 6: 79–82.

Kagan, Donald. 2010. *Thucydides: The Reinvention of History*. London: Penguin Books.

Kang, David. 2003. "Getting Asia Wrong: The Need for New Analytical Frameworks." *International Security* 27, no. 4: 57–85.

——. 2007. *China Rising: Peace, Power, and Order in East Asia*. New York: Columbia University Press.

——. 2010. *East Asia Before the West: Five Centuries of Trade and Tribute*. New York: Columbia University Press.

——. 2017. *American Grand Strategy and East Asian Security in the Twenty-First Century*. New York: Cambridge University Press.

Kaplan, Robert. 2011. "The South China Sea Is the Future of Conflict." *Foreign Policy*, August 15.

Keohane, Robert, and Lisa Martin. 1995. "The Promise of Institutionalist Theory." *International Security* 20, no. 1: 39–51.

Khong, Yuen Foong. 2004. "Coping with Strategic Uncertainty: The Role of Institutions and Soft Balancing in Southeast Asia's Post-Cold War Strategy." In *Rethinking Security in East Asia: Identity, Power, and Efficiency*, ed. J. J. Suh, Peter Katzenstein, and Allen Carlson, 172–208. Stanford, Calif.: Stanford University Press.

——. 2019. "Power as Prestige in World Politics." *International Affairs* 95, no. 1: 119–42.

Kim, Samuel. 1979. *China, the United Nations and World Order*. Princeton, N.J.: Princeton University Press.

——. 1984. *China and the World: New Directions in Chinese Foreign Relations*. Boulder, Colo.: Westview Press.

——. 1995. "China's International Organization Behavior." In *Chinese Foreign Policy: Theory and Practice*, ed. Thomas Robinson and David Shambaugh, 401–34. Oxford: Clarendon Press.

——. 2003. *The International Relations of Northeast Asia*. Lanham, Md.: Rowman and Littlefield.

King, Amy, and M. V. Ramana. 2015. "The China Syndrome? Nuclear Power Growth and Safety After Fukushima." *Asian Perspective* 39, no. 4: 607–36.

Klein, Matthew. 2017. "For the Love of Zeus, Stop Misusing Thucydides." *Financial Times*, June. https://ftalphaville.ft.com/2017/06/27/2190601/for-the-love-of-zeus-stop -misusing-thucydides/.

Kydd, Andrew. 1997. "Sheep in Sheep's Clothing: Why Security Seekers Do Not Fight Each Other." *Security Studies* 7, no. 1: 114–54.

Lai, Hongyi. 2010. *The Domestic Sources of China's Foreign Policy: Regimes, Leadership, Priorities, and Process*. New York: Routledge.

Lake, David A. 2003. "The New Sovereignty in International Relations." *International Studies Review* 5, no. 3: 303–23.

——. 2009. *Hierarchy in International Relations.* Ithaca, N.Y.: Cornell University Press.

——. 2009. "Relational Authority and Legitimacy in International Relations." *American Behavioral Scientist* 53, no. 3: 331–53.

——. 2018. "International Legitimacy Lost? Rule and Resistance When America Is First." *Perspectives on Politics* 16, no. 1: 6–21.

Lampton, David M. 2002. "A Plum for a Peach." In *Bureaucracy, Politics, and Decision Making in Post-Mao China,* ed. Kenneth Lieberthal and David M. Lampton, 33–58. Berkeley: University of California Press.

——. 2013. "A New Type of Major-Power Relationship: Seeking a Durable Foundation for U.S.–China Ties." *Asia Policy* 16: 51–68.

Large, Dan. 2009. "China's Sudan Engagement: Changing Northern and Southern Political Trajectories in Peace and War." *China Quarterly* 199: 610–26.

Larson, Deborah, and Alexei Shevchenko. 2010. "Status Seekers: Chinese and Russian Responses to U.S. Primacy." *International Security* 34, no. 4: 63–95.

Laswell, Harold, and Abraham Kaplan. 1950. *Power and Society: A Framework for Political Inquiry.* New Haven, Conn.: Yale University Press.

Layne, Christopher. 1997. "From Preponderance to Off-shore Balancing: America's Future Grand Strategy." *International Security* 22, no. 1: 86–124.

——. 2006. *The Peace of Illusions: American Grand Strategy from 1940 to the Present.* Ithaca, N.Y.: Cornell University Press.

Lebovic, James. 2004. "United for Peace? Democracies and United Nations Peace Operations After the Cold War." *Journal of Conflict Resolution* 48, no. 6: 910–36.

Lei Jiang and Wang Haijun. 2011. "Xianxing duiwai yuanzhu zhong fujia zhengzhi tiaojian chayi fenxi: jiyu zhongguo yu xifang waiyuan shijian de bijiao yanjiu" [An analysis on the variance attached political condition in current foreign aid: Based on a comparative study on the practice of foreign aid of China and Western countries]. *Taipingyang xuebao* [Pacific journal] 19, no. 7: 53–62.

Lema, Karen. 2020. "Unified ASEAN Can Avert South China Sea Conflict: Philippine Minister." *Reuters,* November 25. https://www.reuters.com/article/uk-southchinasea-philippines/unified-asean-can-avert-south-china-sea-conflict-philippine-minister-idUKKBN2851IQ.

Levy, Jack. 1983. *War in the Modern Great Power System.* Lexington: University Press of Kentucky.

——. 2008. "Case Studies: Types, Designs, and Logics of Inference." *Conflict Management and Peace Science* 25, no. 1: 1–18.

Lewis, Jeffrey. 2007. "The Janus Face of Brussels: Socialization and Everyday Decision Making in the European Union." In *International Institutions and Socialization in Europe,* ed. Jeffrey T. Checkel, 137–70. New York: Cambridge University Press.

Li, Cheng. 2005. "The New Bipartisanship Within the Chinese Communist Party." *Orbis* 49, no. 3: 387–400.

Liaowang. 2005. "PRC's New Diplomacy Stress on More Active International Role."

Lieberthal, Kenneth, and Michael Oksenberg. 1988. *Policy Making in China.* Princeton, N.J.: Princeton University Press.

Liff, Adam P., and G. John Ikenberry. 2014. "Racing Toward Tragedy? China's Rise, Military Competition in the Asia Pacific, and the Security Dilemma." *International Security* 39, no. 2: 52–91.

Liu Feitao. 2004. "Quanli zeren yu daguo renting: jianlun zhongguo yingdui guojishehui zeren de yingyou taidu" [Power, responsibility, and great power identity: On the should-be attitude of China toward its international responsibility]. *Taipingyang xuebao* [Pacific journal] 12: 25–32.

Liu Jie. 2004. *Renquan yu guojia zhuquan* [Human rights and state sovereignty]. Shanghai: Shanghai renmin chubanshe.

Liu Mingfu. 2010. Zhongguo meng: hou Meiguo shidai de daguo siwei yu zhanlue dingwei [The Chinese Dream: Great power thinking and strategic posture in the post-U.S. era]. Beijing: Zhongguo youyi chubangongsi.

Long, Drake. 2020. "Three ASEAN States Push Back on Beijing in the South China Sea." *Benar News*, April 15. https://www.benarnews.org/english/news/malaysian/ship-concern-04152020155155.html.

Luo Yuan. 2015. *Yingdan gehun: Luo Yuan jiangjun lun guofang* [Eagle's courage and dove's spirit: General Luo Yuan on national defense]. Beijing: Zhongguo youyi chubangongsi.

Lupia, Arthur, and Mathew McCubbins. 1998. *The Democratic Dilemma: Can Citizens Learn What They Need to Know?* Cambridge: Cambridge University Press.

Mahbubani, Kishore. 2005. *Beyond the Age of Innocence: Rebuilding Trust Between America and the World*. New York: Public Affairs.

Mansfield, Edward, and Jon Pevehouse. 2006. "Democratization and International Organizations." *International Organization* 60, no. 1: 137–67.

Martina, Michael, and David Brunnstrom. 2015. "China's Xi Says to Commit 8,000 Troops for U.N. Peacekeeping Force." *Reuters*, September. http://www.reuters.com/article/us-un-assembly-china-idUSKCN0RS1Z120150929.

Martina, Michael, and Benjamin Kang Lim. 2016. "China's Xi Anointed 'Core Leader,' On Par with Mao, Deng." *Reuters*, October. http://www.reuters.com/article/us-china-politics/chinas-xi-anointed-core-leader-on-par-with-mao-deng-idUSKCN12R1CK.

McGregor, Richard. "Iran, Nigeria, Sudan off China Incentive List." *Financial Times*, March.

Mearsheimer, John. 1990. "Back to the Future: Instability in Europe After the Cold War." *International Security* 15, no. 1: 5–56.

Mercer, Jonathan. 1995. "Anarchy and Identity." *International Organization* 49, no. 2: 229–52.

Mertha, Andrew. 2009. "Fragmented Authoritarianism 2.0." *China Quarterly* 200: 995–1012.

Miller, Alice. 2011. "The Politburo Standing Committee Under Hu Jintao." *China Leadership Monitor* 35: 2–4.

——. 2018. "The 19th Central Committee Politburo." *China Leadership Monitor* 55: 1–11.

Ministry of Foreign Affairs of the People's Republic of China. 2005. "Statement by Ambassador Zhang Yishan at the Security Council's Open Debate on 'The Role of the Security Council in Humanitarian Crises.'" July. https://www.fmprc.gov.cn/ce

/ceun/eng/chinaandun/securitycouncil/thematicissues/other_thematicissues
/t203694.htm.

———. 2005. "Statement by Ambassador Zhang Yishan at the Special Committee
on Peacekeeping Operations." February. https://www.fmprc.gov.cn/ce/ceun/eng
/zghlhg/hphaq/whxd/t182269.htm.

———. 2014. "The Central Conference on Work Relating to Foreign Affairs Was Held in
Beijing." November. http://www.fmprc.gov.cn/mfa_eng/zxxx_662805/t1215680.shtml.

Moravcsik, Andrew. 2000. "The Origins of Human Rights Regimes: Democratic
Delegation in Postwar Europe." *International Organization* 54, no. 2: 217–52.

Morrow, James D. 2014. *Order Within Anarchy: The Laws of War as an International
Institution.* Cambridge: Cambridge University Press.

Murphy, Ann Marie. 2017. "Great Power Rivalries, Domestic Politics, and Southeast
Asian Foreign Policy: Exploring the Linkages." *Asian Security* 13, no. 3: 165–82.

Myanmar Ministry of International Trade and Industry. 2014. "Chairman's Statement of
the 24th ASEAN Summit." May. http://www.miti.gov.my/miti/resources/Chairman
_Statement_of_24th_ASEAN_Summit.pdf?mid=410.

Nathan, Andrew. 1973. "A Factionalism Model for CCP Politics." *China Quarterly* 53:
34–66.

National Security Archive. 1992. "U.S. Defense Guidance."

Neak, Laura. 1995. "UN Peacekeeping: In the Interest of Community or Self?" *Journal
of Peace Research* 32, no. 2: 181–96.

Ng Eng Hen. 2019. Speech by Minister for Defense Dr. Ng Eng Hen at the Munich
Security Conference and NATO Centre of Excellence for Operations in Confined
and Shallow Waters Maritime Security Roundtable. February. https://www.mindef
.gov.sg/web/portal/mindef/news-and-events/latest-releases/article-detail/2019
/February/16feb19_speech.

Nixon Forum on U.S.–China Relations. 2019. Transcript of public discussion hosted
by Woodrow Wilson Center for International Scholars, Washington, D.C., October 17. https://www.wilsoncenter.org/event/live-webcast-the-nixon-forum-us-china
-relations.

Odell, Rachel. 2019. "How Strategic Norm-Shaping Undergirds America's Command
of the Commons." MIT Political Science Department Research Paper No. 2019–23,
August 31. http://dx.doi.org/10.2139/ssrn.3451412.

Ong Keng Yong. 2007. "Forty Years of ASEAN: Can the European Union Be a Model
for Asia?" Remarks delivered to Konrad Adenauer Foundation, Berlin, July 16.

Orbell, John, Robyn Dawes, and Alphonus J. C. Van de Kragt. 1998. "Explaining
Discussion-Induced Cooperation." *Journal of Personality and Social Psychology* 54,
no. 5: 811–19.

Osgood, Robert, and Robert Tucker. 1967. *Force, Order, and Justice.* Baltimore, Md.:
Johns Hopkins University Press.

Parameswaran, Prashanth. 2016. "What Really Happened at the ASEAN–China Special Kunming Meeting." *Diplomat,* June. http://thediplomat.com/2016/06/what
-really-happened-at-the-asean-china-special-kunming-meeting/.

Payne, E. J. 2005. *Burke: Select Works.* Clark, N.J.: Lawbook Exchange.

Pearson, Margaret. 2004. "China's WTO Implementation in Comparative Perspective." *Review of International Affairs* 3, no. 4: 567–83.

Peou, Sorpong. 2002. "The UN, Peacekeeping, and Collective Human Security: From an Agenda for Peace to the Brahimi Report." *International Peacekeeping* 9, no. 2: 51–68.

Perloff, Richard. 1993. *The Dynamics of Persuasion.* Hillsdale, N.J.: Erlbaum Associates.

Philippine Department of Foreign Affairs. 2012. "U.S. Reiterates It Will Honor Obligations Under MDT Amid Standoff." May 3. https://www.officialgazette.gov.ph /2012/05/03/u-s-reiterates-it-will-honor-obligations-under-mutual-defense-treat -amid-standoff-in-bajo-de-masinloc-scarborough-shoal/.

Posen, Barry. 1984. *The Sources of Military Doctrine.* Ithaca, N.Y.: Cornell University Press.

——. 2014. *Restraint: A New Foundation for U.S. Grand Strategy.* Ithaca, N.Y.: Cornell University Press.

Powell, Robert. 2002. "Bargaining Theory and International Conflict." *Annual Review of Political Science* 5: 1–30.

Pressman, Jeremy. 2008. *Warring Friends: Alliance Restraint in International Politics.* Ithaca, N.Y.: Cornell University Press.

Pu, Xiaoyu. 2017. "Controversial Identity of a Rising China." *Chinese Journal of International Politics* 10, no. 2: 131–49.

——. 2019. *Rebranding China: Contested Status Signaling in the Changing Global Order.* Stanford, Calif.: Stanford University Press.

Qin Yaqing. 2003. "Guojia shenfen zhanlue wenhua he anquan liyi" [National identity, strategic culture, and security interests]. *Shiji jingji yu zhengzhi* [World economics and politics] 1: 10–15.

——. 2014. "Continuity Through Change: Background Knowledge and China's International Strategy." *Chinese Journal of International Politics* 7, no. 3: 285–314.

Rahman, Chris, and Martin M. Tsamenyi. 2010. "A Strategic Perspective on Security and Naval Issues in the South China Sea." *Ocean Development and International Law* 41, no. 4: 315–33.

Reilly, James. 2014. "A Wave to Worry About? The Role of Public Opinion in Chinese Foreign Policy." *Journal of Contemporary China* 23, no. 86: 197–215.

Reus-Smit, Christian. 2014. "Power, Legitimacy, and Order." *Chinese Journal of International Politics* 7, no. 3: 341–59.

Reuters. 2015. "Singapore Says TPP vital for U.S. to Be Taken Seriously in Asia," June 16. https://www.reuters.com/article/us-usa-trade-singapore-idUSKBN0OV2 NF20150615.

——. 2016. "New U.N. Chief in China, Calls for Human Rights Respect," November. http://www.reuters.com/article/us-china-un-idUSKBN13N0TV.

Richardson, Sophie. *China, Cambodia, and the Five Principles of Peaceful Coexistence.* New York: Columbia University Press.

Richey, Mason. 2020. "Buck-Passing, Chain-Ganging and Alliances in the Multipolar Indo-Asia-Pacific." *International Spectator* 55, no. 1: 1–17.

Ringmar, Erik. 1996. *Identity, Interest and Action: A Cultural Explanation of Sweden's Intervention in the Thirty Years War.* Cambridge: Cambridge University Press.

Risse, Thomas, and Kathryn Sikkink. 1999. "The Socialization of International Human Rights Norms into Domestic Practices: Introduction." In *The Power of Human Rights: International Norms and Domestic Change,* ed. Thomas Risse,

Steve C. Ropp, and Kathryn Sikkink, 1–38. Cambridge: Cambridge University Press.

Risse-Kappen, Thomas. 1995. "Democratic Peace–Warlike Democracies? A Social Constructivist Interpretation of the Liberal Argument." *European Journal of International Relations* 1, no. 4: 491–517.

Robinson, Eric. 2017. "Thucydides on the Causes and Outbreak of the Peloponnesian War." In *The Oxford Handbook of Thucydides*, ed. Sara Forsdyke, Edith Foster, and Ryan Balot. https://www.oxfordhandbooks.com/view/10.1093/oxfordhb/978019934 0385.001.0001/oxfordhb-9780199340385-e-23.

Ross, Robert. 2009. "China's Naval Nationalism: Sources, Prospects, and the U.S. Response." *International Security* 34, no. 2: 46–81.

Roughneen, Simon. 2016. "ASEAN Takes a Firmer Stance on the South China Sea." *Nikkei Asian Review.* June. http://asia.nikkei.com/magazine/20160623-SHOWN -the-DOOR/Politics-Economy/ASEAN-takes-a-firmer-stance-on-the-South -China-Sea.

Roy, Denny. 2013. *Return of the Dragon.* New York: Columbia University Press.

Ruggie, John. 1998. *Constructing the World Polity: Essays on International Institutionalization.* New York: Routledge.

Schimmelfennig, Frank. 1999. "NATO Enlargement: A Constructivist Explanation." *Security Studies* 8, no. 2–3: 198–234.

Schroeder, Paul. 1994. "Historical Reality vs. Neo-Realist Theory." *International Security* 19, no. 1: 108–48.

Sevastopulo, Demetri. 2014. "South China Seas: Troubled Waters." *Financial Times,* June 20. https://www.ft.com/content/313432b0-f78f-11e3-b2cf-00144feabdco.

Severino, Rodolfo C. 2010. "ASEAN and the South China Sea." *Security Challenges* 6, no. 2: 37–47.

Seybolt, Taylor. 2007. *Humanitarian Military Intervention: The Conditions for Success and Failure.* Oxford: Oxford University Press.

Shambaugh, David. 2013. *China Goes Global: The Partial Power.* New York: Oxford University Press.

Shi Yinhong. 2000. "Lun ershi shiji guoji guifan tixi" [A discussion of the system of international norms in the twentieth century]. *Guoji luntan* [International forum] 6: 8–10.

——. 2016. "Guanyu zhongguo de yazhou xitaipingyang zhanlue he nanhai wenti" [On China's Asia-Western Pacific strategy and the South China Sea issue]. *Dongnanya yanjiu* [Southeast Asian studies] 5: 33–38.

Shifrinson, Joshua, and Stephan Haggard. 2020. "Power Shifts: Connecting IR Theory with the Chinese Case." *Journal of East Asian Studies* 20: 131–86.

Shih, Victor. 2008. *Factions and Finance in China.* Cambridge: Cambridge University Press.

Shirk, Susan. 2007. *China: Fragile Superpower.* New York: Oxford University Press.

Simpson, Gerry. 2004. *Great Powers and Outlaw States: Unequal Sovereigns in the International Legal Order.* Cambridge: Cambridge University Press.

Smolinske, Nicole, and Lance Jackson. 2016. "Duterte Bets Beijing Visit Will Reset the Philippines' Difficult China Relations." *CSIS cogitASIA*, October. https://www .cogitasia.com/duterte-bets-beijing-visit-will-reset-the-philippines-difficult-china -relations/.

Snyder, Jack. 1984. *The Ideology of the Offensive*. Ithaca, N.Y.: Cornell University Press.

Sprout, Harold, and Margaret Sprout. 1945. *Foundations of National Power*. Princeton, N.J.: Princeton University Press.

Stockholm International Peace Research Institute (SIPRI) Military Expenditure Database. https://www.sipri.org/databases/milex.

Suchman, Mark C. 1995. "Managing Legitimacy: Strategic and Institutional Approaches." *Academy of Management Review* 20, no. 3: 571–610.

Sutter, Robert. 2018. *Foreign Relations of the PRC: The Legacies and Constraints of China's International Politics Since 1949*. Lanham, Md.: Rowman and Littlefield.

Swaine, Michael. 2010. "China's Assertive Behavior, Part One: On Core Interests," *China Leadership Monitor* 34. https://www.hoover.org/sites/default/files/uploads /documents/CLM34MS.pdf.

Tajfel, Henri. 1982. "Social Psychology of Intergroup Relations." *Annual Review of Psychology* 33: 1–39.

Tajfel, Henri, and Henry C. Turner. 2004. "The Social Identity Theory of Intergroup Behavior." In *Key Readings in Social Psychology*, ed. John T. Jost and Jim Sidanius, 276–93. New York: Psychology Press.

Tan, Eugene. 2008. "The ASEAN Charter as 'Legs to Go Places': Ideational Norms and Pragmatic Legalism in Community Building in Southeast Asia." *Singapore Year Book of International Law* 12: 171–98.

Tan, Hui Yee. 2016. "ASEAN 'Resets Ties with China.'" *Straits Times*, July 26. http:// www.straitstimes.com/asia/se-asia/asean-resets-ties-with-china.

Teets, Jessica. 2013. "Let Many Civil Societies Bloom: The Rise of Consultative Authoritarianism in China." *China Quarterly* 213: 19–38.

Teo Cheng Wee. 2016. "Singapore Caught in the Middle as China–ASEAN Country Coordinator." *Straits Times*, June 24. http://www.straitstimes.com/opinion/singapore -caught-in-the-middle-as-china-asean-country-coordinator.

Thayer, Carlyle. 2012. "ASEAN's Code of Conduct in the South China Sea: A Litmus Test for Community Building?" *Asia Pacific Journal* 10, no. 34: 1–23.

——. 2012. "Is the Philippines an Orphan?" *Diplomat*, May. http://thediplomat.com /2012/05/is-the-philippines-an-orphan/.

Thyne, Clayton. 2006. "Cheap Signals with Costly Consequences: The Effect of Interstate Relations on Civil War." *Journal of Conflict Resolution* 50, no. 6: 937–61.

Tierney, Dominic. 2011. "Does Chain-Ganging Cause the Outbreak of War?" *International Studies Quarterly* 55, no. 2: 285–304.

Today Online. 2016. "Malaysia Calls for ASEAN Support Against Beijing Over South China Sea," December 19. https://www.todayonline.com/world/asia/malaysia-calls -asean-support-against-beijing-over-s-china-sea.

Tønnesson, Stein. 2017. *Explaining the East Asian Peace: A Research Story*. Copenhagen: Nordic Institute of Asian Studies Press.

Torode, Greg, and Simon Scarr. 2018. "Concrete and Coral: Beijing's South China Sea Building Boom Fuels Concerns." *Reuters*, May. https://www.reuters.com/article/us -china-southchinasea-insight/concrete-and-coral-beijings-south-china-sea -building-boom-fuels-concerns-idUSKCN1IO3GA.

Tunsjø, Øystein. 2018. *The Return of Bipolarity in World Politics: China, the United States, and Geostructural Realism*. New York: Columbia University Press.

United Nations Conferences, Meetings, and Events. 2000. "'Brahimi Report': Report of the Panel on United Nations Peace Operations." November. http://www.un.org /en/events/pastevents/brahimi_report.shtml.

——. 2000. "Security Council, Responding to 'Brahimi Report,' Adopts Wide-Ranging Resolution on Peacekeeping Resolutions." November. https://www.un.org/press /en/2000/20001113.sc6948.doc.html.

United Nations Department of Peacekeeping Operations. 2020. "UN Missions Summary Detailed by Country." February. https://peacekeeping.un.org/en/troop-and -police-contributors.

United Nations Department of Peacekeeping Operations and Department of Field Support. 2009. "A New Partnership Agenda: Chartering a New Horizon for UN Peacekeeping." July. https://peacekeeping.un.org/sites/default/files/newhorizon_0.pdf.

United Nations Meetings Coverage and Press Releases. 2000. "Security Council Moves to Enhance Protection of Civilians in Conflict." April. https://www.un.org /press/en/2000/20000419.sc6847.doc.html.

——. 2016. "Security Council Extends Mandate of United Nations Mission in Liberia, Adopting Resolution 2333 (2016) by 12 Votes in Favor, 3 Abstentions." December. https://www.un.org/press/en/2016/sc12654.doc.htm.

United Nations Security Council. 2000. "S/PV.4220: Overview of Security Council Meeting Records." November. https://undocs.org/S/PV.4220.

——. 2005. "S/PV.5261: Overview of Security Council Meeting Records." September 14. https://undocs.org/S/PV.5261.

——. 2009. "S/PV.6153: Official Records of the Security Council." June 29. https:// undocs.org/S/PV.6153.

——. 2009. "S/PV.6178: Official Records of the Security Council." August 5. https:// undocs.org/S/PV.6178.

——. 2013. "S/PV.6928: Overview of Security Council Meeting Records." March 5. https://undocs.org/S/PV.6928.

United States Department of Defense. 2019. *Indo-Pacific Strategy Report*. Washington, D.C.: U.S. Government Printing Office. https://media.defense.gov/2019/Jul/01 /2002152311/-1/-1/1/Department-Of-Defense-Indo-Pacific-Strategy-Report-2019.pdf.

van Rooij, Benjamin, Rachel Stern, and Kathinka Furst. 2016. "The Authoritarian Logic of Regulatory Pluralism: Understanding China's New Environmental Actors." *Regulation & Governance* 10, no. 1: 3–13.

Vasquez, John A. 1997. "The Realist Paradigm and Degenerative Versus Progressive Research Programs: An Appraisal of Neotraditional Research on Waltz's Balancing Proposition." *American Political Science Review* 91, no. 4: 899–912.

Wagner, R. Harrison. 2007. *War and the State: The Theory of International Politics*. Ann Arbor: University of Michigan Press.

Waldron, Arthur. 2017. "There is No Thucydides Trap." *SupChina*. June. https:// supchina.com/2017/06/12/no-thucydides-trap/.

Walt, Stephen. 1991. "The Renaissance of Security Studies." *International Studies Quarterly* 35, no. 2: 211–39.

——. 2009. "Alliances in a Unipolar World." *World Politics* 61, no. 1: 86–120.

——. 2013. "More or Less: The Debate on US Grand Strategy." *Foreign Policy*, January 2. http://foreignpolicy.com/2013/01/02/more-or-less-the-debate-on-u-s-grand -strategy/.

Wang Huning. 1993. "Zuowei guojia shili de wenhua: ruanquanli" [Soft power: Culture as the strength of the country]. *Fudan xuebao shehui kexue ban* [Fudan University journal: Social science edition] 3: 91–96.

Wang Jisi. 2011. "Zhongguo de guoji dingwei yu taoguangyanghui youshuozuowei de zhanlue sixiang" [The international positioning of China and the strategic principle of keeping a low profile while getting something accomplished]. *Guoji wenti yanjiu* [International studies] 5: 28–31.

Westcott, Ben. 2018. "Duterte Will 'Go to War' Over South China Sea Resources, Minister Says." *CNN*, May 29. https://www.cnn.com/2018/05/29/asia/duterte-cayetano -south-china-sea-intl/index.html.

Wheeler, Nicholas J. 2000. *Saving Strangers: Humanitarian Intervention in International Society.* Oxford: Oxford University Press.

White, Nigel. 2001. "Commentary on the Report of the Panel on United Nations Peace Operations (The Brahimi Report)." *Journal of Conflict and Security Law* 6, no. 1: 127–46.

White House. 2002. "The National Security Strategy of the United States of America."

Wohlforth, William C., Richard Little, Stuart J. Kaufman, David Kang, Charles A. Jones, Victoria Tin-Bor Hui, Arthur Eckstein, Daniel Deudney, and William L. Brenner. 2007. "Testing Balance-of-Power Theory in World History." *European Journal of International Relations* 13, no. 2: 155–85.

——. 2009. "A Comedy of Errors? A Reply to Mette Eilstrup-Sangiovanni." *European Journal of International Relations* 13, no. 2 (2009): 381–88.

Womack, Brantly. 2003. "China and Southeast Asia: Asymmetry, Leadership and Normalcy." *Pacific Affairs* 76, no. 4: 529–48.

Wong, Catherine. 2019. "'Divide and Conquer ASEAN': China Tries to Go One on One with Malaysia to Settle South China Sea Disputes." *South China Morning Post*, May 18. https://www.scmp.com/news/china/diplomacy/article/3010790/divide-and -conquer-asean-china-tries-go-one-one-malaysia.

Woodrow Wilson Center. 2019. Transcript of a Discussion on US–China Relations. Washington, D.C.: Woodrow Wilson Center for International Scholars.

World Bank. N.d. "World Development Indicators Online." http://data.worldbank.org /data-catalog/world-development-indicators.

Wright, Joseph. 2008. "Do Authoritarian Institutions Constrain? How Legislatures Affect Economic Growth and Investment." *American Journal of Political Science* 52, no. 2: 322–43.

Xiang, Lanxin. 2016. "Xi's Dream and China's Future." *Survival* 58, no. 3: 53–62.

Xinhua. 2008. "Qian Qichen Urges Further Promotion of International Human Rights." October.

——. 2013. "Xi Jinping: China to Further Friendly Relations with Neighboring Countries." October. http://news.xinhuanet.com/english/china/2013-10/26/c_125601680 .htm.

Xu Guojin. 1992. "Guojia lüxing guoji renquan yiwu de xiandu" [The limits on state performance of human rights obligation]. *Zhongguo faxue* [Chinese legal science] 2: 13–20.

Yan Haiyan. 2010. "Baohu de zheren jisei" [An analysis on the responsibility to protect]. *Xibu faxue pinglun* [Western law review] 1: 125–29.

Yan, Xuetong. 2014. "From Keeping a Low Profile to Striving for Achievement." *Chinese Journal of International Politics* 7, no. 2: 153–84.

——. 2016. "Political Leadership and Power Redistribution." *Chinese Journal of International Politics* 9, no. 1: 1–26.

——. 2016. "Zhengzhi lingdao yu daguo jueqi anquan" [Moral realism and the security strategy for rising China]. *Guoji anquan yanjiu* [Journal of international security studies] 34: 3–19.

Yang, Jiechi. 2014. "Innovations in China's Diplomatic Theory and Practice Under New Circumstances." *Qiushi Journal* 6, no. 1. http://english.qstheory.cn/magazine /201401/201401/t20140121_315115.htm.

Yang, Xiangfeng. 2020. "The Great Chinese Surprise: The Rupture with the United States Is Real and Is Happening." *International Affairs* 96, no. 2: 419–37.

Yoder, Brandon. 2019. "Uncertainty, Shifting Power and Credible Signals in US–China Relations: Why the 'Thucydides Trap' Is Real, but Limited." *Journal of Chinese Political Science* 24: 87–104.

Young, Oran. 1992. "The Effectiveness of International Institutions: Hard Cases and Critical Variables." In *Governance Without Government: Order and Change in World Politics*, ed. James Rosenau and Ernst-Otto Czempiel, 160–94. Cambridge: Cambridge University Press.

Zelditch, Morris. 2001. "Processes of Legitimation: Recent Developments and New Direction." *Social Psychology Quarterly* 64, no. 1: 4–17.

Zeng Lingliang. 1998. "Lun lengzhan hou shidai de guojia zhuquan" [A discussion of state sovereignty in the post–Cold War era." *Zhongguo faxue* [Chinese legal science] 1: 109–20.

Zeng, Yong. 2014. "China's South China Sea Policy Evolution from the Perspective of the 'Scarborough Shoal Model.'" *Forum on World Economics and Politics* 5: 127–44.

Zhang, Feng. 2015. *Chinese Hegemony: Grand Strategy and International Institutions in East Asian History*. Stanford, Calif.: Stanford University Press.

——. 2017. "Chinese Thinking on the South China Sea and the Future of Regional Security." *Political Science Quarterly* 132, no. 3: 435–66.

——. 2019. "China's Curious Nonchalance Towards the Indo-Pacific." *Survival* 61, no. 3: 187–212.

Zhang, Ketian. 2019. "Cautious Bully: Reputation, Resolve, and Beijing's Use of Coercion in the South China Sea." *International Security* 44, no. 1: 117–59.

Zhang, Qingming. 2016. "Bureaucratic Politics and Chinese Foreign Policy-Making." *Chinese Journal of International Politics* 9, no. 4: 435–58.

Zhang Ruizhuang. 2013. "Guoji geju bianhua yu zhongguo dingwei" [Change of international system and China's positioning]. *Xiandai guoji guanxi* [Contemporary international relations] 4: 20–22.

Zheng, Bijian. 2005. "China's 'Peaceful Rise' to Great-Power Status." *Foreign Affairs* 84, no. 5. https://www.foreignaffairs.com/articles/asia/2005-09-01/chinas-peaceful -rise-great-power-status.

Zheng, Jinghan. 2016. "Constructing a 'New Type of Great Power Relations': The State of Debate in China (1998–2014)." *British Journal of Politics and International Relations* 18, no. 2: 422–42.

Zimbardo, Philip, and Michael Leippe. 1991. *The Psychology of Attitude Change and Social Influence*. New York: McGraw Hill.

INDEX

CONTEMPORARY ASIA IN THE WORLD

David C. Kang and Victor D. Cha, Editors

CPSIA information can be obtained
at www.ICGtesting.com
Printed in the USA
JSHW011717301022
32340JS00001B/51